KERRIE DROBAN

FOREWORD BY DR. KATHERINE RAMSLAND

Surviving a Psychopath: In Court. In Life. In "Love."
Copyright © 2025 Kerrie Droban
Copyright © 2025 Foreword Dr. Katherine Ramsland
Published by Zhivago Press, an imprint of Zhivago Entertainment

www.ZhivagoEntertainment.com

All rights reserved. No part of this book may be reproduced, stored in a retrieval system, or transmitted in any form or by any means, electronic, mechanical, or otherwise, without the prior written permission of the publisher, except for brief quotations in articles and reviews.

Cover and Interior Design: Carol Waltz, www.BellaMediaManagement.com.

Printed in the United States of America for Worldwide Distribution

ISBNs: 978-9-69-729278-3 (trade paperbook), 978-9-69-729279-0 (ebook)

First Edition
10 9 8 7 6 5 4 3 2 1

FOR SARA

ALSO BY KERRIE DROBAN

RUNNING WITH THE DEVIL
THE ATF'S INFILTRATION OF THE ARIZONA HELLS ANGELS

PRODIGAL FATHER, PAGAN SON
GROWING UP INSIDE THE DANGEROUS WORLD
OF THE PAGAN'S MOTORCYCLE CLUB

VAGOS, MONGOLS AND OUTLAWS
MY INFILTRATION OF AMERICA'S DEADLIEST BIKER GANGS

A SOCIALITE SCORNED
THE MURDER OF A TUCSON HIGH ROLLER

THE LAST CHICAGO BOSS
MY LIFE WITH THE CHICAGO OUTLAWS MOTORCYCLE GANG

AURORA
THE PSYCHIATRIST WHO TREATED THE COLORADO
MOVIE THEATER KILLER TELLS HER STORY

CONTENTS

AUTHOR'S NOTE	1
FOREWORD	3
PROLOGUE	7
CHAPTER 1: *THE FACE OF EVIL*	11
CHAPTER 2: *BEHAVIORAL PATTERNS*	15
CHAPTER 3: *THE DEVIL'S COURTSHIP*	29
CHAPTER 4: *THE POWER PLAY*	52
CHAPTER 5: *BORN THIS WAY?*	64
CHAPTER 6: *THE HOLLOW CORE*	77
CHAPTER 7: *HIDDEN IN PLAIN SIGHT*	88
CHAPTER 8: *THE DARK WEB*	116
CHAPTER 9: *THE ETHICS OF LABELING*	134
CHAPTER 10: *PSYCHOLOGICAL ABUSE AND ITS IMPACT*	143
CHAPTER 11: *DAMAGE CONTROL*	156
CHAPTER 12: *CHILD'S PLAY*	174
CHAPTER 13: *GLADIATORS*	190
CHAPTER 14: *THE RIPPLE EFFECT*	204
CHAPTER 15: *HEALING FROM HELL*	217
CHAPTER 16: *WARRIORS*	226
ACKNOWLEDGMENTS	245
APPENDIX – A	247
APPENDIX – B	252
APPENDIX – C	254
APPENDIX – D	257

APPENDIX – E	260
APPENDIX – F	266
FURTHER READING & REFERENCES	273
ABOUT THE AUTHOR	289

AUTHORS NOTE

I WROTE THIS BOOK for the countless victims of psychological abuse who find themselves trapped not only in toxic relationships but also in a courtroom battlefield they never anticipated. For too long, survivors have faced relentless onslaughts of litigation from psychopathic spouses— individuals who weaponize the legal system as another tool for abuse. As an attorney, time and again, I have witnessed a glaring void: a lack of education and understanding among victims, judges, and even attorneys about the psyche of predatory individuals and the challenges their victims face.

Victims were being retraumatized—not just by their abusers, but by the very court system meant to protect them. The judicial process's chaos, confusion, and emotional toll often left survivors powerless, defeated, and misunderstood. I saw an overwhelming need to provide tools to navigate litigation and empower survivors to reclaim their voices and regain control.

---

1 The discussions in this book are based on professional analysis, research, and firsthand experiences but do not constitute definitive medical or psychological conclusions. The author expressly disclaims any intent to defame, harm, or misrepresent any individual. While certain individuals' behaviors are analyzed in the context of psychopathy using traits from the Hare Psychopathy Checklist-Revised (PCL-R), this does not constitute a clinical diagnosis. The mention of specific individuals is intended for illustrative purposes only. It should not be interpreted as an assertion that they have been formally diagnosed with psychopathy or any other psychological disorder.

As a former prosecutor and capital defense attorney with extensive experience in both criminal and family court, and as a true crime author and someone with a deep understanding of the pathology of these disordered individuals, I felt uniquely positioned to address this need. Over the years, I've seen the devastating impact of unchecked psychological manipulation and legal abuse. I've also seen the extraordinary resilience of survivors when equipped with the right tools, strategies, and support.

This book aims to fill that void. It is a guide not only for victims but also for the judges, attorneys, and advocates who can change the trajectory of these cases. The following pages provide practical tools for litigating against manipulative and calculating adversaries and shed light on the psychological dynamics at play. More importantly, this book seeks to educate and empower—because knowledge is the greatest weapon against injustice.

The names and scenarios presented throughout this work are composites drawn from real-life cases and clients. To protect privacy and confidentiality, identifying details have been altered and certain circumstances have been modified or combined. These adaptations serve to illustrate key points while maintaining the integrity of the experiences shared.

To the survivors reading this: you are not alone. This book is for you—a roadmap to help you navigate the courtroom, stand your ground, and emerge stronger on the other side. To the professionals reading this: I hope the contents of this book serve as a call to action, a reminder that justice begins with understanding. Together, we can build a legal system that not only protects and empowers victims but also holds their abusers accountable.

FOREWORD

MANY OF US know, have known, or will know a psychopath at some point in our lives. It won't be much fun. Some actively target us, causing us harm before we can spot the danger. Even experts on this disorder know they can still be duped.

Years ago, I spoke with Dr. Robert Hare. He's the face of psychopathy research, one of the world's leading authorities. He and his colleagues created the primary diagnostic instrument for the disorder, the Psychopathy Checklist-Revised (PCL-R). In 1993, Hare published *Without Conscience*, which detailed the damage paths that criminal psychopaths leave in their wake. He told me that since the book's publication, he'd heard from hundreds of readers who've described psychopaths who've harmed them—not the master criminals we've come to expect but the everyday manipulators who present a façade of charm or credibility. The perfect spouse, the caring pastor, the helpful teacher, the rapt student, the neighborhood big brother. The victims described being cruelly exploited or abused, then left to pick up the pieces.

"Psychopathy," Hare says, "touches virtually every one of us." He thought these wounded people needed a resource for healing and protection. And here it is. Kerrie Droban, a lawyer and award-winning author, provides a solid, accessible guidebook in *Surviving a Psychopath: In Court. In Life. In "Love."* She's seen plenty of this devastation herself. Although her book does include psychopathic offenders and their victims, it's also for those who need to size up a "good" person in their lives who might be doing them significant harm.

Too many people view the psychopath as a Ted Bundy, an unfeeling monster with an aim to kill. Yet most psychopaths are seemingly ordinary, socially adept people. They don't even commit crimes. They can get what they want in lawful ways, usually through manipulation, deception, and twisting our trust and expectations against us. That's partly why we don't recognize how they gain advantages at our expense. Only after we've been hurt do we realize that something was missing in the person, something that connects them to humanity—honesty, integrity, and compassion. Without remorse, they exploit us and move on to their next target. Those they leave behind feel shattered. They can't comprehend that they failed to see the signs.

One woman who wrote to Hare said she was dating a man who often lied, took things that belonged to her, directed how she should talk and dress, and canceled her plans without asking. She kept explaining it away, hoping he'd change. Instead, his deceptive and controlling behavior only worsened. Still, she continued to do what he told her, as if he'd neutralized the intelligent part of her brain. She shut out friends and family who warned her, accepting only the version of events that maintained the relationship. Eventually, the man moved on, and she took stock of the friends, family connections, and money she'd lost. Looking back, she couldn't understand how she'd gotten involved with such a person. She no longer trusted her instincts and hadn't been able to date another man in years.

Psychopathy demonstrates strong and consistent correlations with a range of problematic behaviors that impact relationships. These people engage in high-risk activities, coerce others into doing things they don't want to do, and find multiple ways to undermine and dominate. With psychopaths, there's no such thing as an equal partnership. Over time, they reduce their level of commitment while isolating their partner from those who care about them. This gives them more opportunities to deceive, gaslight, or exploit their targets.

So, we're vulnerable and they know it. We assume that others mean what they say, are invested in their actions, and will show certain types of manners. We tend to give appearances the most benign spin. We want to think well of others. But psychopaths are often predatory. They look for people who have something they want and then insert themselves into that person's world. They use deflection, social miscues, and misinformation to provide a frame in which to manage our attention. They'll use whatever works: charm, false credentials, love-bombing, a smooth manner, complements, gifts, favors, a winning smile. They know that most of us see what we want to see and believe whatever confirms our sense of other people. They use these tendencies to dupe us.

That's why a book like this is so valuable. It's a solid guide for spotting the signs and protecting yourself, especially if you might one day have to document the abuse and take someone to court. You'll learn about a psychopath's maneuvers, power plays, secret identities, and manipulation strategies. You'll be able to identify the signals for a psychopath's approach, spot their nonverbal tells, and even predict their potential for future violence. You'll grasp the *modus operandi* of a psychopath's typical courtship rituals and find out what it takes to ease your way out before you lose too much. You'll gain confidence in knowing what to do should you become a target. You'll learn how *not* to become their prey, and it's all organized in checklists and charts. This book will also be valuable for therapists, social workers, lawyers, and marriage counselors who can assist clients to navigate these perilous waters.

Psychopaths will always find people to dupe and exploit, but you can avoid being one of them. Even if no one currently in your life fits this description, read this book and get prepared. They're often closer than you think.

Dr. Katherine Ramsland
Professor of forensic psychology
Author of *How to Catch a Killer*

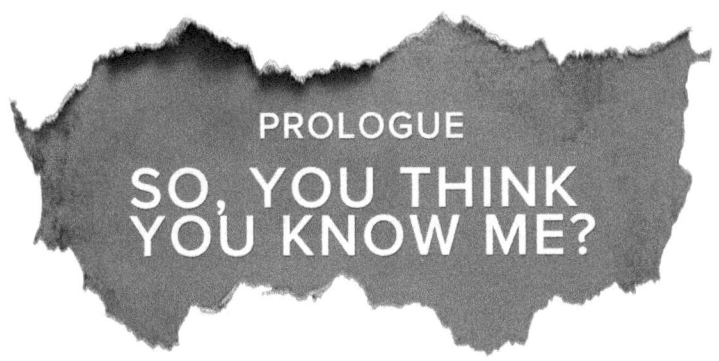

PROLOGUE
SO, YOU THINK YOU KNOW ME?

"Let's start with something simple. Why do you think you're here today?"

The Psychopath leans back in the chair, a grin playing at the corners of his mouth. Not a smile—a grin, deliberate and predatory. His posture is at once casual and commanding, legs spread wide as though the sterile gray walls of this room were his domain. His eyes, glacier blue, meet mine without hesitation. "You wanted to meet someone like me. Isn't that why you're here? Curiosity? I'm your specimen, aren't I?"

There it is, the charm, the glint of arrogance just beneath the surface. He's not asking because he doesn't know; he's establishing control.

"I'm here to understand you better."

"Understand me? Oh, that's cute. You people always think you can understand me." The Psychopath chuckles, a low, humorless sound. "But fine, let's pretend for a second that you can. What do you want to know?"

"I want to know what makes you tick. How you see the world."

"The world? It's simple, really. People are tools, resources. Like… chess pieces. Some are useful for a while, but most…" He snaps his fingers. "Disposable."

He says it matter-of-factly as if commenting on the weather. I keep my face neutral, but he's watching closely, waiting for a reaction. He thrives on them.

"And what makes someone useful to you?" I ask.

"Leverage. Everybody has it. A secret they don't want out. A weakness. A need. It's just a matter of finding it. You could be useful too, you know. I bet you have a weak spot." His gaze lingers just a second too long. "Everybody does."

There's no malice in his tone, which makes it worse. This isn't about emotion; it's about power.

"Do you ever feel guilty about… hurting people?" I ask.

His grin widens, and for a moment, I see the mask slip. Beneath it, there's nothing. Just an empty chasm where empathy should be. "Guilt is for people who want to play by someone else's rules. I make my own."

"But don't you think that's… damaging? For others?"

He leans forward now, his voice dropping as though sharing a secret. "You're still thinking like a pawn. Damage is a concept you care about because you see the world as this… shared space. I don't. I see it as mine. And if something's mine, I'll do whatever I want with it." He sits back, pleased with himself. It's clear he's rehearsed this, polished it. He's practiced how to drop these little bombs of insight for maximum impact.

"How did you get here? Were you always like this?"

The Psychopath's expression shifts. It's brief, almost imperceptible—a flicker of something— before the mask snaps back into place. "Oh, you're going for the origin story. Classic. You want me to say I had a bad childhood or some tragic trauma that made me this way, right? Sorry to disappoint. My parents were fine. Boring, even. It's just… I figured out early on that emotions are overrated. Why cry when you can think? Why love when you can win?"

His words come out in a staccato rhythm, each one sharpened like a blade. But there's something rehearsed about it, too. It's a performance. He's telling me what he wants me to hear, not necessarily the truth.

"Do you ever lie to manipulate people?" I probe.

He laughs outright, the first genuine sound I've heard from him. "Oh, come on. Everyone lies. Don't act like you don't. The difference is I'm better at it. You lie to spare feelings. I lie to get what I want. Guess which one works better?"

I press on, ignoring the heat rising in my chest. "What do you want people to understand about you?"

He tilts his head, mock-serious now, as though genuinely considering the question. Then he shrugs. "Understand? Nothing. I'm not here to be understood. I'm here to win. You see, people like you are obsessed with finding reasons for everything—why people do what they do, what's wrong with them, how to fix it. But me? I don't need reasons. I don't need fixing. I'm not broken. I'm just better at playing the game than you are."

He leans back again, this time folding his arms across his chest, a smug look on his face.

The interview is over. He's decided that, not me.

As I gather my notes, he watches me. I feel the weight of his gaze, calculating, dissecting. He knows exactly what he's done—left me with more questions than answers, revealed just enough truth to muddy the water.

"See you next time," he says, flashing that same predatory grin as I step out of the room.

And for a moment, I wonder if I'm leaving him behind… or if he's coming with me.

CHAPTER ONE
THE FACE OF EVIL

"One side of me says, 'I'd like to talk to her, date her.' The other side of me says, 'I wonder what her head would look like on a stick.'" -Edmund Kemper

PSYCHOPATHS ALWAYS WEAR a mask.

Not the kind you see in Halloween stores, or the crude makeup streaked across a clown's face. Theirs is sleek, polished, crafted to perfection—a mask of sanity. You've seen it before. It's the charming coworker who laughs a little too easily, the spouse who can't seem to remember the promises they made and the charismatic leader who leaves devastation in their wake. A psychopath doesn't introduce themselves as a villain. Instead, they step into your life as a savior, a confidant, the answer to your deepest prayers. Until the mask slips.

They're not always the killers splashed across headlines, profiled in true crime documentaries, movies, and books, or the violent criminals locked away in maximum-security prisons. (*A criminal mind is not necessarily without conscience; most have a felonious code of conduct. Psychopaths have no allegiance to anyone but themselves.*) Often, they sit at the dinner table, slipping their hand into yours and whispering promises they have no intention of keeping.

What is a Psychopath?

Forget the Hollywood clichés. A psychopath isn't just a chainsaw-wielding maniac. They're more dangerous than that. They're the predator who never looks like one. Think Ted Bundy, a monster who wasn't just a killer but also an actor, playing the role of a law student, a concerned citizen, and a doting boyfriend—all masks he used to lure his victims.

According to Dr. Robert Hare, whose Psychopathy Checklist-Revised (PCL-R) remains the gold standard for diagnosing these manipulative predators, a psychopath is defined by a constellation of traits: glib charm, pathological lying, an inability to feel remorse, lack of empathy, and an uncanny ability to mimic normal human emotions.

They walk among us, feeding on our kindness, exploiting our vulnerabilities, and leaving behind a trail of psychological wreckage. They know how to size you up within moments, reading your vulnerabilities like an open book. Are you lonely? They'll make you feel adored. Do you crave stability? They'll offer you the world. And yet, even with this roadmap, they remain hard to spot. Why? Because they're masters of the game. And they never present as villains. They enter your life as saviors, confidants, and soulmates—until you see them for what they really are.

Real estate mogul Robert Durst, whose charm allowed him to dodge suspicion for years, even as bodies piled up in his wake, viewed relationships as transactional, his partners reduced to objects of utility rather than people with emotions or autonomy. Durst's marriage to Kathleen McCormack deteriorated as her demands for equality clashed with his controlling nature. When his wife "disappeared" in 1982, it was a chilling echo of a pattern: the calculated elimination of someone perceived as an obstacle. Kathleen was not a person to Durst—she was a problem to be solved.

Chapter One: The Face of Evil

Susan Berman, loyal to Durst for decades, likely knew too much about Kathleen's disappearance, and so Durst acted preemptively, silencing her permanently. Berman's execution-style murder was emblematic of Durst's calculated approach to conflict resolution. His ability to compartmentalize his actions allowed him to maintain a facade of normalcy even as he committed acts of extreme violence.

His time in Galveston, living as a mute woman, was a grotesque performance of deception. His interactions with Morris Black showcased the psychopath's tendency to exploit others, forming superficial bonds that served only their needs. When the relationship with Black soured, Durst's response was characteristic: eliminate the threat and craft a narrative of innocence.

The jury's decision to acquit Durst, despite the overwhelming evidence, highlights another troubling aspect of psychopathy: the ability to manipulate perception. People like Durst often project an air of sincerity that confounds even seasoned observers. Durst's courtroom demeanor and carefully rehearsed self-defense claims played directly into this dynamic.

But his infamous confession in HBO's documentary, *The Jinx: The Life and Deaths of Robert Durst*— "What the hell did I do? Killed them all, of course"—is perhaps the clearest window into his psyche. It reveals the absence of remorse, the ease of rationalization, and the underlying sense of invulnerability that defines the psychopath. Durst wasn't lamenting his actions; he was processing the possibility of being caught.

And therein lies the duality of the psychopath: the outward charm and internal emptiness that allows them to wreak havoc while remaining inscrutable to those around them.

Few exemplify this dichotomy better than Bernie Madoff. Unlike the snarling villain or the violent sociopath, Madoff was a polished, genial predator whose charm disarmed his victims. As the mastermind behind the largest Ponzi scheme in history, he built an empire of deception, swindling billions from trusting investors with an air of effortless charm, a calculating smile, and a confident handshake—traits that allowed him to move among his victims undetected for decades. Madoff preyed on trust and vulnerability, exploiting the very values that formed the foundation of his victims' lives. He didn't just steal their money—he dismantled their belief systems, leaving a wake of emotional and financial ruin.

What makes Madoff's actions distinctly psychopathic is not just the scale of the betrayal but the cold indifference with which he justified it. When confronted with the ruin he caused, Madoff dismissed his victims as "greedy," flipping the narrative to place the blame on those he exploited. This deflection is a hallmark of psychopathy: the absence of remorse, the refusal to acknowledge responsibility, and the audacious ability to reframe devastation as the fault of the devastated.

He saw himself as intellectually superior, more capable, and untouchable—a mindset that allowed him to view his victims not as people but as tools to feed his ambition. He wore the face of evil with disarming ease, smiling through boardroom meetings, fundraising galas, and personal conversations, all while plotting his next move. This is the terrifying truth about psychopathy: it often resides not in the shadows but in the spotlight, camouflaged by success, charm, and social standing.

But this book isn't about fear—it's about preparedness. The individuals discussed here may be extreme cases, but the traits they exhibit are present in many personal and professional relationships. Recognizing these behaviors isn't just important—it's essential for survival in high-stakes environments. By learning to spot the signs, set firm boundaries, and disengage from their influence, you can protect yourself from their calculated harm.

CHAPTER TWO
BEHAVIORAL PATTERNS

"We're all psychopaths under the skin." – Dr. Ronald Markham, author of Alone with the Devil.

PSYCHOPATHS DON'T JUST hide behind their masks; they thrive on your disbelief (*It could never happen to me*) and count on your desire to rationalize their behavior (*He's not perfect, but no one is. She's been through a lot; maybe that's why she acts this way*).

This is their playground.

They manipulate not just their victims but everyone around them—friends, family, and even the legal system. They create a narrative that paints themselves as the victim and their target as the villain. And by the time the mask begins to slip, it's often too late.

The *Diagnostic and Statistical Manual of Mental Disorders (DSM-5-TR)*—the authoritative guide on psychological conditions—classifies personality disorders into three distinct clusters: A, B, and C. To simplify, these groups can be thought of as *Mad* (eccentric or detached), *Bad* (dramatic and unpredictable), and *Sad* (anxious and avoidant).

- **Cluster A** (odd and eccentric) includes *paranoid*, *schizoid*, and *schizotypal* personality disorders.

- **Cluster B** (dramatic and impulsive) covers *antisocial, borderline, histrionic,* and *narcissistic* personality disorders.

- **Cluster C** (anxious and fearful) consists of *avoidant, dependent,* and *obsessive-compulsive* personality disorders.

Each cluster reflects a distinct pattern of thinking and behavior, shaping how individuals relate to the world and those around them.

A landmark 2004 study sponsored by the National Institutes of Health (NIH) and others indicates that roughly 15% of adults in the U.S. have a personality disorder, with many falling under the Cluster B category—those characterized by dramatic, emotional, or erratic behavior. Additionally, 10% of adults have two or more overlapping disorders, with prevalence increasing in younger age groups: it is higher among those aged 30–40 and even more common in individuals aged 20–29.

While psychopaths—a subset of Cluster B disorders—make up only about 1% of the population, their influence far outweighs their numbers. In high-stakes environments like law enforcement, business, and politics, the likelihood of encountering one increases significantly. And in high-conflict divorces, that probability skyrockets. Recognizing their patterns isn't paranoia—it's self-protection.

PSYCHOPATHY AND OTHER DISORDERS
The Devil in the Details

Psychopathy and narcissism share key traits—grandiosity, manipulation, and a chilling lack of empathy. This overlap often leads to confusion, with people using the terms interchangeably—a dangerous mistake that can leave victims unprepared. Understanding the difference isn't just academic; it's a matter of survival.

Narcissists are fueled by fragile self-esteem, constantly seeking admiration and validation to maintain their sense of superiority. Their relationships tend to be codependent, as they rely on others to affirm their worth. Psychopaths, in contrast, are emotionally detached predators who see relationships as purely transactional—using charm and manipulation not for validation but for control. While narcissists may hurt others as a side effect of their self-absorption, psychopaths inflict harm intentionally—without remorse.

The Narcissist

Sarah didn't notice the red flags at first. Alex was magnetic, confident, and endlessly flattering. When he spoke, it was as if the spotlight followed him everywhere. "I've never met anyone like you," he told her during their first date, his eyes glinting with what felt like genuine admiration.

But slowly, the shine wore off. Compliments turned into backhanded remarks. "You're so smart; I'd think you'd know better than to wear that." Sarah began second-guessing herself, striving harder to meet his unspoken expectations. If she voiced her feelings, he'd dismiss her with a laugh. "Oh, don't be so sensitive," he'd say, pulling her back in with a disarming grin.

Alex was a textbook narcissist. His behavior was rooted in a deep need for validation and an endless hunger for admiration that came at the cost of Sarah's emotional stability. When she started setting boundaries, he pushed back, testing the limits. "You're really going to treat me this way after everything I've done for you?" he'd ask, painting himself as the victim. But once Sarah stood firm and refused to engage in his games, his power over her began to wane.

*Sarah should respond with **C.A.L.M.** (**C**reate boundaries; **A**void arguments; **L**et go of seeking approval; **M**aintain self-worth).

The Psychopath

The first time Madison met Nick, his presence sent a chill down her spine—not from fear, but from the intensity of his gaze. He didn't talk about himself much; instead, he dissected her with unnerving precision. "You must be the oldest child," he said within minutes of meeting her. "You're used to being responsible for everyone, aren't you?"

Nick's s charm wasn't the kind that dazzled—it ensnared. Over time, Madison realized his compliments were bait, designed to extract information he could later use. Nick didn't seek validation; he sought control. "Why don't you trust me?" he asked one evening when she hesitated to share details about her past. His voice was soft, but his eyes were hard, his smile sharp as a blade.

When Madison confronted him about his lies, his response was chilling. "You should know better than to test me," he said, his voice calm, almost amused. There was no guilt, no shame, just the sense that he'd already calculated three steps ahead.

Nick's behavior escalated when Madison tried to pull away. He punished her silence with subtle acts of sabotage—a missed deadline at work, a mysteriously deleted contact. It wasn't enough to keep her close; he wanted to ensure she couldn't escape.

*Madison should protect herself by being **S.A.F.E.** (**S**tay alert by documenting everything; **A**void confrontation (for them, it's about control); **F**ind support; **E**xit strategically).

Chapter 2: Behavioral Patterns

Psychopathy and Sociopathy

> "I'm not a psychopath; I'm a high-functioning sociopath."
> –Benedict Cumberbatch as Sherlock Holmes in the cult series *Sherlock.*

The terms *psychopath* and *sociopath*[2] are often used interchangeably, but they aren't the same. Both fall under the broader category of antisocial personality disorders (ASPD), as outlined in the DSM-5 *TR*, and both are marked by antisocial behavior, a lack of empathy, and a disregard for societal norms. The difference, however, lies in their origins, behaviors, and methods. Simply put, sociopathy is more *environmentally influenced*, while psychopathy is more *biologically hardwired*. Sociopaths tend to be more reactive, impulsive, and prone to emotional outbursts; psychopaths are calm, calculating, and emotionally detached. While the former justifies their actions rather than feel guilt or remorse, psychopaths lack conscience altogether, and morality... is irrelevant. But make no mistake, both are dangerous.

The Sociopath

They always think I'm impulsive and unpredictable, but that's their mistake—I know exactly what I'm doing. The bartender at the dive down the street can't stop smiling at me. She thinks I'm funny and disarming. That's the trick. You make them feel seen and special. You keep your tone light and your gaze sharp until you have them where you need them. I'll ask for her number, maybe even take her to dinner. Not because I care but because I need a place to crash for a few nights. She won't know it's all an act until I'm gone along with her tips from the register. It's not personal. Nothing ever is.

---
2 Take the Quiz in Appendix A

*The Bartender should recognize the red **F.L.A.G.**s: (Fake empathy), (Lying) (Aggression), (Gaslighting).

Psychopathy and Borderline Personality Disorder

Borderline Personality Disorder is a complex and deeply rooted condition characterized by pervasive instability in mood, self-image, and interpersonal relationships. Unlike psychopathy or narcissism, which are often defined by a lack of empathy and exploitative behavior, individuals with BPD frequently experience intense emotional turbulence, a fear of abandonment, and a profound struggle to regulate their emotions. Their relationships tend to be marked by dramatic highs and lows as they oscillate between idealizing others and perceiving rejection or betrayal. This sensitivity to perceived slights often drives self-destructive behaviors, impulsivity, and a sense of chronic emptiness. Notably, emotional instability is typically absent in psychopathy; instead, there is a shallow, controlled affect designed to deceive.

While narcissism and psychopathy are characterized by an inherent disconnection from others, individuals with BPD often feel their emotions with overwhelming intensity. They are not inherently manipulative or exploitative; rather, their actions are often driven by a desperate attempt to stave off the perceived threat of abandonment. Understanding these distinctions is crucial for effective treatment and to avoid conflating the symptoms of these distinct yet often misunderstood disorders[3].

It's worth noting that some individuals can have a combination of BPD and ASPD traits, which may create the appearance of psychopathic tendencies. This dual diagnosis can result in behaviors that include emotional volatility combined with calculated, antisocial actions. However, these individuals are still distinct from true psychopaths due to their emotional vulnerability and internal turmoil.

Chapter 2: Behavioral Patterns

The Borderline

The first time Nicole met Hank, she was captivated, not by his intensity, but by the vulnerability she sensed beneath it. He seemed to understand her in a way that no one else had, quickly pinpointing her deepest fears and desires. "You must be the oldest child," he said softly, studying her face. "You've spent your whole life trying to be what everyone else needs you to be, haven't you?" The way he saw her made her feel exposed yet deeply understood, as though he could fill the void she had always carried inside.

Hank's charm was magnetic, but it came with a volatile undercurrent. At first, Nicole found his attentiveness intoxicating—his relentless focus on her, his hunger for connection. But over time, it began to feel suffocating. When she hesitated to open up about her past, his reaction wasn't anger or coldness; it was an aching, almost desperate plea. "Why don't you trust me?" he whispered, his voice trembling with emotion. It was as though her hesitation had wounded him deeply, and she felt an overwhelming urge to reassure him, even at the expense of her own comfort.

When Nicole tried to establish boundaries, Hank's emotions surged unpredictably, swinging from adoration to despair to anger. Confronting him about a lie felt like stepping into a storm. "I can't believe you'd think I'd hurt you," he said, his voice trembling with anguish. His pain was palpable, but underneath it was a subtle thread of manipulation—a need to draw her back in, to avoid the rejection he seemed to fear more than anything. When Nicole tried to pull away, Hank's behavior became chaotic. He would flood her with apologies one moment and accusations the next. He wasn't trying to punish her deliberately; it was as though he couldn't bear the thought of being abandoned. His actions—like showing up unannounced or bombarding her with texts—weren't about control but about soothing his own terror of being left behind.

*Nicole should respond with **C.A.L.M.** (**C**ommunicate Clearly and Consistently as ambiguity can exacerbate fears of abandonment or misunderstanding; **A**cknowledge emotions and validate their feelings without reinforcing unhealthy behavior. Statements like, "*I see that this is really upsetting for you*," can help them feel heard without encouraging emotional manipulation. **L**imit emotional reactivity by avoiding escalating the situation with your own frustration or defensiveness; **M**aintain boundaries, clearly state what behaviors are acceptable and what aren't, and follow through consistently).

The Borderline and Anti-Social Personality Disorder[3]

The wind choked the air with ash, the smell of burning wood mingling with something sharper—the acrid tang of gasoline. Monica stood by the window, watching the fire devour the woodpile in the backyard. The flames leaped high, sparks clawing at the night sky. Paul was nowhere to be seen, but she knew he was close. He always was a phantom presence that lived between her breath and her shadow.

It had been two days since she'd asked for the divorce.

Monica had expected rage—Paul's anger was legendary, a storm that razed everything in its path. She'd braced herself for shattered dishes, for the venom of his words slicing her open. But Paul had surprised her. He'd smiled. That smile had unnerved her more than his fury ever could.

"Are you sure?" he'd asked, his voice so soft it felt like a lullaby. The words wrapped around her throat, tightening with each syllable.

"Yes," she'd whispered, her voice barely audible. "I'm sure."

And then he'd leaned in close, his wolf-like eyes glinting with something she couldn't name. "You'll regret this, Monica. Not today. Not tomorrow. But soon."

---

3 Accurate diagnosis can only be made by a well-trained professional.

Chapter 2: Behavioral Patterns

The fire roared louder, pulling her back to the present. Monica's hands shook as she drew the curtains closed. She'd stopped leaving the house except for necessities, afraid of what Paul might do. He hadn't hit her, not yet, but his violence was never overt. It simmered beneath the surface, a toxin that seeped into her life in ways she couldn't predict.

Her phone buzzed on the counter, the screen lighting up with a message. She hesitated before picking it up. Unknown Number. Check the garage.

Her heart slammed against her ribs. She didn't need to ask who it was. The air seemed to thicken as she made her way to the garage, every step an act of defiance against the terror coiling in her chest. She flipped on the light and stopped cold.

The car's tires were slashed, the rubber hanging in jagged strips. A single word was spray-painted across the windshield in red letters: Liar.

She stumbled back, her hand flying to her mouth. The walls seemed to close in, the room shrinking until she could barely breathe. She turned off the light and ran back inside, locking every door and window. Her mind raced with questions, but she knew the answers wouldn't come. Paul didn't explain himself. He didn't need to.

That was the thing about Paul. He was two people. The man she'd fallen in love with had been magnetic, charming in a way that made you believe he was the only light in a dark world. But that light had a way of blinding you, making you forget the shadows he cast. He had a knack for knowing exactly what you wanted, exactly what you feared, and he used that knowledge like a weapon.

Now, his charm was a mask he wore only when it suited him. The rest of the time, he was cold and calculating. He had a way of turning her fears against her, of making her doubt her own reality. He'd accuse her of things she hadn't done, then smile as she scrambled to defend herself. When she'd finally stopped defending, when she'd asked for the divorce, he'd shifted tactics.

The next morning, Monica's phone buzzed again. Another message. You're nothing without me.

She deleted it, her fingers trembling. She wanted to block the number, but she knew it wouldn't stop him.

Paul had ways of getting what he wanted, and right now, what he wanted was to break her.

Her therapist had tried to warn her about people like Paul. "He exhibits traits of both borderline and antisocial personality disorders," she'd said. "The emotional instability, the fear of abandonment, the manipulation—it's all part of the pattern. But the antisocial traits? That's where the danger lies. He'll do whatever it takes to maintain control."

Monica hadn't understood then. She'd thought it was just another label, another way to pathologize their relationship. But now, with the fire in the backyard, the slashed tires, and the messages, she understood.

By the third day, she stopped responding to his texts. She stopped checking the garage, the backyard, and the dark corners of the house where shadows seemed to linger too long. But Paul didn't stop.

She found the dead bird on her porch that night. Its neck was twisted at an unnatural angle; its wings splayed like a macabre offering. Beside it was a note: Leave, and you'll end up like this.

Tears streamed down her face as she stared at the note, her hands trembling so badly she dropped it. She wanted to scream, to call the police, but what could she say? That her soon-to-be ex-husband was trying to scare her? That he hadn't hurt her, but she knew he wanted to.

The police would want proof, something tangible. Paul was too careful about that. He'd leave just enough to terrify her but not enough to incriminate himself. It was a game to him, one he played with precision.

That night, Monica slept with a knife under her pillow, her heart racing at every creak and groan of the house. She dreamed of fire and wolves, of shadows that whispered her name.

When she woke, there was another message waiting for her. You'll never escape me.

*Monica should respond to Paul's actions with **G.R.I.T.** (Ground herself. Record everything for evidence. Inform authorities—establishing a pattern of abuse strengthens her case. Take precautions that include increasing personal safety, securing her home, seeking a restraining order, gathering allies, installing alarms, and Ring cameras).

Ultimately, it is the pattern (and not necessarily the diagnosis) that defines the predator and its methods. Arming those who seek justice with the clarity and strategy to counteract their influence by focusing on behavioral consistencies rather than relying solely on diagnostic frameworks, attorneys, investigators, and even victims can anticipate the next move, diffuse attempts to destabilize, and build compelling cases rooted in the evidence of what was done, not just who they might be.

TRAIT	PSYCHOPATH (ASPD)	NARCISSIST (NPD)	SOCIAPATH (APD)	BORDERLINE (BPD)
MOTIVATION	Power & control validation	Admiration	Impulsivity	Fear of abandonment
EMPATHY	Absent	Superficial	Low	Hyper-emotional
EMOTIONAL REGULATION	Cold, detached	Grandoise, entitled	Volatile, impulsive	Unstable, dramatic
MANIPULATION TACTICS	Strategic, calculated	Gaslighting, self-centered	Reactive, reckless	Clingy, guilt-tripping
VIOLENCE POTENTIAL	Planned, high-functioning	Less physical, psychological	Explosive, reckless	Rare, mostly self-harm

Jodi Arias, A Case Study in APD and BPD

Jodi Arias, the infamous "sex, lies, and audiotape" killer, exhibited both BPD and ASPD traits. Her obsessive fixation on her victim, Travis Alexander, marked by stalking, emotional volatility, and an intense fear of abandonment, aligned with BPD's defining traits: unstable relationships, frantic efforts to avoid rejection, and extreme emotional swings. Yet, her cold-blooded manipulation, deception, and complete lack of remorse fit seamlessly into ASPD's framework of chronic lying, exploitation, and calculated aggression.

Arias lied effortlessly, spinning multiple versions of the murder—first denying involvement, then blaming intruders, and ultimately claiming self-defense. Her selective memory ("I don't recall stabbing [Travis] thirty times") contrasted sharply with her photographic recollection of self-serving details, highlighting a predatory instinct for self-preservation. This cognitive dissonance is not unusual in individuals with antisocial traits, who can justify violence if it serves their interests. Her traits are highlighted in the following chart:

TRAIT CATEGORY	BPD	PSYCHOPATHY
FEAR OF ABANDONMENT	Intense obsession with Travis Alexander after their breakup, including moving closer to him and repeatedly intruding on his life.	She has no genuine emotional bond with Alexander and views the relationship transactionally, evidenced by her cold detachment after the murder.
EMOTIONAL INSTABILITY	Swinging between idealizing Alexander (journals describing him as her "soulmate") and demonizing him when feeling rejected.	A composed, unemotional demeanor during the trial, even while describing the murder, reflects emotional detachment.

Chapter 2: Behavioral Patterns

MANIPULATION	She adapts her personality to match Alexander's preferences and interests and strives to stay connected.	Shifting narratives: Denied involvement, blamed intruders, then claimed self-defense, strategically tailored to fit the evidence.
IMPULSIVITY	Driving long distances to confront Alexander, without clear planning and escalating arguments during emotional outbursts.	Premeditated murder: Stole a gun, rented a car and bought a gas can to avoid being traced, showing calculated intent.
SELF-DESTRUCTIVE BEHAVIORS	Threatened self-harm and exhibited obsessive behaviors, such as slashing Alexander's tires.	Disregarded consequences of murder, attempting to evade detection by discarding evidence (e.g., washing the camera with incriminating photos).
LYING AND DECEIT	Attempted to maintain emotional control over Alexander by misrepresenting her intentions and emotions.	Pathologically lied to police, media, and the court, including claiming intruders killed Alexander and selectively forgetting key moments
LACK OF EMPATHY	Demonstrated emotional distress only when discussing her own plight, rather than Alexander's death or the impact on his family.	Stabbed Alexander 27 times, slit his throat, and shot him, showing callous disregard for his life and suffering.
GRANDIOSITY AND ARROGANCE	Repeatedly sought validation in her relationship, expressing delusions of being "the best thing" for Alexander.	Infamously claimed, "No jury will convict me," showcasing overconfidence and an inflated sense of invulnerability.

Arias was especially dangerous because she was capable of both impulsive rage and calculated deception. The courtroom became a stage, her trial a performance where the audience could both condemn her and grapple with the uneasy duality—the horror and the recognition: How much of Arias' capacity for manipulation, deceit, and survival lay dormant within *us?*

CHAPTER THREE
THE DEVIL'S COURTSHIP

"I do wish we could chat longer, but I'm having an old friend for dinner." –Hannibal Lecter.

A PSYCHOPATH DOESN'T SEDUCE their prey; they consume them and devour their boundaries and their sense of self with a kind of relentless precision. Their courtship is a campaign—calculated, obsessive, and ultimately devastating. It doesn't matter who you are: the CEO of a Fortune 500 company, a suburban mom, or an ambitious twenty-something. To them, you're just a target, another puzzle piece in their intricate game.

But there's something you should know about their game: the rules are rigged.

THE SEDUCTION
Perfectly Tailored Illusions

Psychopaths don't stumble into your life; they study you first. Every weakness, every insecurity, every hope or dream—they catalog it all, tailoring themselves to fit the void you didn't even know you had. This is why they often seem "too perfect." They mirror your desires, shaping themselves into the ideal partner, colleague, or friend.

Allison, a tech executive, met Ryan at a networking event. He was charming, attentive, and seemed genuinely interested in her work. Within days, he'd memorized the details of her career, asked insightful questions about her family, and casually mentioned his own ambitious projects. He was her perfect match—or so it seemed.

What Allison didn't realize was that Ryan had spent hours researching her online presence before their "chance" encounter. By the time they met, he knew her vulnerabilities—her recent divorce, her struggles as a single mom— and used them to his advantage.

His tone was soothing but calculated, every syllable placed deliberately. He spoke in loops, drawing her into his web without her realizing. His words weren't so much a conversation as they were an interrogation disguised as intimacy.

He told her a story—about his childhood, about loss, about pain. Or at least, that's what she thought it was about. The details were vivid: his mother's garden, the smell of freshly turned soil, the way the light fell across his father's shoulders the day he left. His voice shifted effortlessly, carrying the rhythm of a storyteller.

But there was something missing. She realized it halfway through his tale. There was no feeling in his words. The emotions he described— grief, anger, joy—were like ornaments, perfectly placed but hollow. It was as if he'd studied the cadence of human emotion without ever feeling it himself.

And yet, she couldn't look away. His voice was hypnotic, and the intensity of his stare made her feel both exposed and chosen. He was speaking to her, not just at her, and that created a false intimacy, a belief that she was special for being the one he shared this with.

There was something about his eyes. Not just the color, though they were striking—a pale, icy blue— but the way they locked onto hers, unwavering, unyielding. It wasn't like normal eye contact, where people glance away out of politeness or self-consciousness. His gaze was invasive as if he were tunneling into her mind, searching for vulnerabilities to exploit.

In his presence, she felt both drawn in and repelled, like standing too close to the edge of a cliff. Her heart raced, not because she was charmed, but because she was afraid—though she couldn't explain why. It wasn't anything he'd said or done, but something deeper, primal, like her instincts were screaming at her to run.

After an hour, the conversation ended. He stood, paid the bill, and left her with a lingering smile and a promise to call. When he was gone, the air around her felt thinner, her senses dulled. She sat there for a while, replaying the encounter in her mind. It felt like a fever dream—something about his presence had left her disoriented, unmoored.

The longer she thought about it, the more she realized how little she actually knew about him. He'd spoken at length, but it was all fragments, stories that revealed nothing substantial about who he was or what he wanted. Instead, he'd turned the focus onto her, steering the conversation with questions that seemed harmless at the time but now felt invasive. She felt exposed as if he'd mapped her weaknesses.

That night, when she tried to sleep, his voice echoed in her mind. She couldn't shake the feeling that she'd been toyed with and manipulated, even though she couldn't pinpoint how. His stare lingered in her thoughts, and for the first time in years, she locked her bedroom door before going to bed.

During the encounter, Allison felt simultaneously flattered and unnerved, a mix of emotions that left her vulnerable. Afterward, she felt drained, questioning her instincts and wondering why she couldn't shake the unease he left behind.

This is the essence of the psychopath's communication: to manipulate, unsettle, and dominate without ever raising suspicion.

In his world, words were not tools for connection but weapons for control, and Allison had unknowingly become his next subject.

LOVE BOMBING
The High of a Lifetime

Psychopaths don't waste time. They overwhelm their targets with affection, attention, and promises. This tactic, known as "love bombing," is intoxicating. It's designed to disarm you, to make you feel like the luckiest person in the world.

But love bombing isn't about love; it's about control. It's the bait in the trap, the sugar that masks the poison, a calculated tactic designed to overwhelm a target with excessive praise, attention, or gifts to create dependency and lower defenses.

Ryan texted Allison constantly, showering her with compliments and planning elaborate dates. He'd say things like, "I've never felt this way before," and "You're the one I've been waiting for." It felt magical—until it didn't. After just two days, Ryan's messages quickly escalated in intensity and frequency.

Ryan's Texts

- **9:12 AM:** "Good morning, beautiful ☺ Thinking about you already."

- **10:45 AM:** "I just can't stop smiling since I met you. You're incredible. How's your day so far?"

- **12:30 PM:** "Can I take you out tonight? Or do you need a break from me? 😜"

Allison's response:

- **12:45 PM:** "Hey! You're sweet ☺, but I think tonight might be tough."

Chapter 3: The Devil's Courtship

Day 4:

- **8:07 AM:** "Good morning, sunshine! ☺ Another day where I get to think about you. 🖤"
- **10:30 AM:** "I don't know how I got so lucky to meet someone like you. Honestly, you're all I think about. How's work going?"
- **1:15 PM:** "I was just telling my friend about you. They're dying to meet you someday—don't worry, I said it's way too soon. ☺"
- **4:50 PM:** "You haven't responded. Is everything okay? I just want to make sure you're happy."

Allison's response:

- **5:20 PM:** "Busy day, sorry! All good, though ☺."

Day 7:

- **9:01 AM:** "Morning, gorgeous! I had a dream about us last night... we were in Paris, and I couldn't stop staring at you. I know it sounds crazy, but I just feel like we're meant to be."
- **12:10 PM:** "I'm sending you flowers! They'll be there by 5. Just wanted you to know how special you are."
- **2:45 PM:** "Hey, just making sure you got my last text. Can't wait for you to see the flowers 💐🖤."
- **5:30 PM:** "Did the flowers arrive? What did you think? Do you love them? I hope they're perfect for you."

Allison's response:

- **5:45 PM:** "They're beautiful, thank you 😊."

Ryan's Reply:

- **5:50 PM:** "Beautiful flowers for the most beautiful woman in the world. Seriously, I can't get over how much I care about you already."

Day 10:

- **8:30 AM:** "You're my everything. I can't imagine my life without you anymore."

- **11:20 AM:** "I just got you something. You'll see it tomorrow. Hope you like surprises! 😊🖤"

- **3:10 PM:** "Why haven't you been texting much? Are you upset with me? I'd do *anything* to make you happy, you know that, right?"

Allison's response:

- **3:30 PM:** "I'm not upset. Just overwhelmed."

- **Ryan:** "Overwhelmed by me? I just want to love you the way you deserve."

The constant praise, grand gestures, and over-the-top declarations escalate quickly, leaving Allison feeling emotionally suffocated. Her responses become shorter and less enthusiastic, showing her discomfort.

Chapter 3: The Devil's Courtship

Love Bombing in the Workplace

In professional settings, love bombing can manifest as a boss or colleague who showers an employee with admiration, promotions, or special treatment—only to later exploit their gratitude or compliance.

Aaron is a new employee and has been assigned as a mentee to Laura. Within a week, Aaron becomes overly effusive and clingy, constantly praising Laura in emails and text messages.

Aaron's Emails

Day 2:

Subject: You're the BEST!

"Hi Laura,
I just wanted to say THANK YOU for everything you've already taught me. You're seriously amazing at your job, and I feel like I've learned so much in just two days. I hope I can make you proud as your mentee!"
Best, Aaron.

Laura's Response:

"Thanks, Aaron. Glad to help!"

Day 4:

Subject: Quick Question + Thanks Again!

"Hi Laura,
Can I grab 5 minutes with you tomorrow to go over that report? Also, I just need to say—you inspire me. Seriously, I've never met anyone so knowledgeable and patient.

Hope you're having an awesome day!" Cheers, Aaron

Laura's Response:

"Sure, let's meet at 3 PM. Thanks for the kind words!"

Day 6:

Subject: You're my work hero!

"Hey Laura,
I've been thinking about how lucky I am to have you as a mentor. I've worked in other places, and I've NEVER had someone so dedicated to helping others. You're not just a great coworker— you're a great person. I'd love to grab a coffee outside of work sometime just to learn more from you!"

Laura's Response:

"I appreciate the compliment, but let's keep it work-focused."

Day 8:

Aaron's Text Messages

Aaron: "Hey, Laura, I just wanted to check in. Are we good? I hope I didn't do anything wrong."

Aaron: "I really value your opinion—more than you know. Please let me know if there's ever anything I can do to support YOU!"

Aaron: "I'd hate to lose this connection. You're one of the best things about this job for me."

Chapter 3: The Devil's Courtship

Laura response:

"I'm busy. Let's catch up later."

Aaron: "Of course! 😊 Just let me know when. You're amazing!"

Aaron's over-the-top compliments and insistence on personal connection blur professional boundaries, leaving Laura uncomfortable and unable to reciprocate his intensity.

GASLIGHTING
Warping Reality

Gaslighting is a psychopath's favorite tool. It's subtle at first—a denial here, a distortion there. They rewrite the script of your shared experiences, insisting things happened differently than you remember.

At first, it feels like a misunderstanding. A misplaced comment, an offhand criticism, a tension you can't quite name. You tell yourself they're just having a bad day, or maybe you're being too sensitive. After all, they love you. They said so. They showed you. Didn't they?

But love, in the hands of a psychopath, is never love. It's a weapon sharpened against the whetstone of your vulnerabilities. They wield it, not to nurture or protect but to control, destroy, and feed their insatiable hunger for dominance.

This is the moment when the mask truly slips, and the person you thought you knew becomes a stranger.

Take the story of Jenna, a schoolteacher who married Mark, a successful entrepreneur. Mark was everything she wanted: attentive, charming, and generous. But over time, his generosity soured into control. He'd insist she spend less time with her friends, claiming they didn't have her best interests at heart.

When Jenna confronted him, Mark would smile, tilt his head, and say, "You're imagining things, sweetheart. I never said that."

Jenna began to question herself. Was she being paranoid? Were her memories faulty?

Psychopaths are masters at making their victims doubt their own minds. The more they distort reality, the more control they gain.

Control isn't achieved in a vacuum. It requires the elimination of outside influences—friends, family, colleagues—anyone who might challenge the psychopath's narrative.

Mark escalated his tactics by "accidentally" forgetting to pass along messages from Jenna's family or making subtle digs about her best friend. "She's just jealous of what we have," he'd say. Slowly, Jenna found herself isolated, her world narrowing until it revolved entirely around Mark.

They create a cycle of reward and punishment, keeping their victims off-balance and desperate for approval.

After isolating Jenna and undermining her confidence, Mark would shower her with affection—flowers, surprise dates, and heartfelt apologies. "I've been so stressed at work," he'd explain. "I didn't mean to take it out on you."

The good times were intoxicating, making Jenna cling to the hope that the man she fell in love with was still there. But the punishments always returned, often harsher than before.

Soon, Jenna was no longer the woman she used to be. "I didn't recognize myself," she said. "I was living in survival mode, walking on eggshells daily."

The devil is in the details—or, in this case, the red flags that victims often miss. In hindsight, these signs are glaring, but in the moment, they're easy to dismiss.

MANIPULATIVE PHRASE	WHAT IT REALLY MEANS
"You're overreacting."	They're invalidating your feelings to maintain control.
"You're the only one who understands me."	They're isolating you from others.
"I just care about you too much."	This could mask controlling or possessive behavior.

PATHOLOGICAL LYING
I'm Telling You, *I'm* Not *Lying.*

Liars, much like predators, leave behind linguistic breadcrumbs that betray their deception. The absence of self-referential language—words like "I," "me," and "my"—can be a glaring red flag. These words typically comprise about six percent of our everyday speech, but liars avoid them, instinctively distancing themselves from their statements. Instead of taking ownership, they opt for impersonal phrasing.

A liar won't say, "I wasn't out at eleven p.m." They'll deflect: "Who'd go out so late?"

Their words are carefully structured, often following a rigid, chronological order—a coping mechanism to manage the overwhelming mental load of fabricating a coherent narrative. They cling to transition words like "then," "during," and "next" as markers in the minefield of their deceit, desperate to keep the story straight. But when pressed to recount events in reverse, the facade often crumbles. Most liars simply cannot.

Note their verbal camouflage. Phrases like "believe me" or "honestly" are attempts to strong-arm the listener into submission, as though insistence can substitute for truth. Words like "roughly," "perhaps," and "probably" serve as slippery exits, granting the liar plausible deniability. By feigning poor memory, the liar creates a flexible narrative, one they can adapt when confronted with inconvenient facts.

The key to unmasking deception lies in listening not just to what is said, but to what is avoided. A skilled observer doesn't just hear the story—they dissect its gaps, its inconsistencies, and its desperate need to escape scrutiny.

The Weaponization of Words

Psychologist Phil McAleer of Scotland's University of Glasgow, collaborating with French researchers, conducted a fascinating study examining the human voice's power to convey personality. They recorded 64 individuals saying the word *hello* and played these recordings to 320 participants. Remarkably, the listeners largely agreed on the speakers' personalities—judging them as trustworthy, aggressive, confident, or warm—based solely on vocal tone. This underscores a critical point: a single word can wield an arsenal of psychological influence depending on its delivery.

The human voice is a weapon as much as a tool. Its cadence and timbre can underscore or utterly distort meaning. A deeper voice, for example, isn't merely commanding—it correlates with higher income, as research from Duke University and UC San Diego suggests. This aligns with historical precedents: Adolf Hitler's rhetoric was often devoid of substance, yet his powerful, resonant voice and oratory skill mesmerized millions. Conversely, Al Gore's monotone delivery rendered his ideas unremarkable to many ears.

In his first presidential debate against George W. Bush, for instance, Gore sighed audibly multiple times, appearing impatient and disengaged rather than commanding. His voice lacked the variation in pitch and intensity that makes a speaker compelling, and instead of drawing people in, his delivery often created distance. Even when discussing urgent issues like climate change, his style came across as dry and overly technical, failing to evoke the emotional urgency needed to rally large audiences.

The difference between the two lies in the psychological impact of delivery. Hitler's speeches activated primal responses—fear, unity, urgency—through tone, pacing, and repetition, even if the content itself lacked depth or reason. Gore, by contrast, had substantive ideas but failed to translate them into a delivery that commanded emotional engagement. This distinction is critical when analyzing how psychopaths—or any manipulative figures—can use vocal power and delivery to mesmerize an audience, making their words feel more significant than they truly are.

The Two Speeches: A Study in Power and Forgettability

The room hummed with anticipation. Hundreds of people packed the grand hall, their bodies pressed shoulder to shoulder, the air electric. At precisely 8 p.m., the doors swung open, and Victor strode onto the stage. He did not walk—he marched, his chest out, his arms stiff at his sides. He stopped at the podium, gripping both edges, then let the silence stretch, let the tension build. And then, in a voice that was deep, unwavering, and thunderous, he spoke. "They have mocked you." A pause. The audience leaned in. "They have stolen from you." Another pause. Shoulders stiffened. "And now they ask you to kneel!" His voice rose. A murmur swept through the room, a rustling of bodies shifting forward, of hands clenching into fists.

Victor's speech was not about policy. There were no facts, no figures, no economic plans or legislative goals. He did not need them. His voice rose and fell like a symphony, controlled and masterful, laced with righteous fury. He repeated words and phrases, driving them like nails into the crowd's collective mind.

"But I tell you this: No more!"

A roar of approval.

His voice booming and then dipping to a whisper, forcing the audience to hold their breath, to chase his words. He painted pictures of enemies lurking in the shadows, of betrayal, of a grand destiny they were all called upon to fulfill.

By the time he finished, the crowd was not just applauding—they were on their feet, chanting his name. He had not given them knowledge. He had given them belief.

Across town, in a brightly lit conference hall, Daniel adjusted his tie. The microphone crackled. He cleared his throat, eyes darting across the sea of attendees who had shuffled in quietly, arms crossed, waiting. He smiled—too tightly—then adjusted his notes.

His voice, when it came, was steady but flat.

"I'm here today to discuss our economic strategy for the next fiscal year." A few people coughed.

"We have identified three major areas of improvement that will allow us to allocate resources more efficiently. First, we must analyze our energy expenditures—"

A yawn rippled through the audience. A man in the back checked his watch.

Daniel continued, unaware or unwilling to acknowledge the disconnect between himself and his listeners. He spoke in full, well-researched sentences, but his voice never rose, never fell, never ignited. It was like listening to a report read aloud, informative but lifeless. His words held facts but no urgency. No danger. No grand call to action.

By the end, the audience clapped, but it was the polite, obligatory kind. They had listened. They had learned something, maybe. But they would not remember him.

The difference between the two men was not intelligence. Not even ideology. It was the *art* of persuasion.

Victor had tapped into something primal; it did not matter if his speech lacked substance. People did not follow him for *facts*. They followed him because he made them *feel*.

Daniel had done what was expected. He had delivered *information*. But information alone does not move nations. It does not start revolutions. And so, by the next day, his words would fade from memory.

Figurative Language: A Mask for Deception

Psychopaths excel at using figurative speech, metaphors, and calculated shifts in diction to distort reality, evade accountability, and erode their victims' sense of self. Understanding these linguistic strategies is essential for identifying their tactics and countering their influence.

They craft narratives that draw victims in, often cloaked in language that evokes trust and intimacy. A psychopath might describe their relationship as "fate" or "a perfect storm," creating an illusion of inevitability or shared struggle. Later, the metaphors shift, turning into descriptions of their partner as "dead weight" or "a thorn in their side"—language that justifies cruelty and detachment.

Strategic Diction: Rewriting the Truth

Language isn't just descriptive for a psychopath—it's *prescriptive*. They use euphemisms to downplay harm ("I was helping you grow") and dehumanizing terms to rationalize abuse ("You're being hysterical"). This calculated diction mirrors President George W. Bush's rhetorical pivot after 9/11, from describing the dead as "victims" to reframing them as "losses," subtly transitioning the public mindset from criminal justice to military action. Similarly, a psychopath reframes events in their relationships to suit their narrative, recasting their betrayals as necessary or even altruistic. These shifts obscure culpability and make it harder for victims to articulate the depth of their suffering.

The Fallout: Framing the Harm

The language used to describe the aftermath of a relationship with a psychopath profoundly impacts how the damage is understood. Psychopaths are experts at reframing their harm as "misunderstandings" or "mistakes," minimizing their actions, and shifting blame onto their victims. Survivors who internalize these narratives might struggle to articulate the seriousness of their experiences, dismissing their own trauma as "drama" rather than recognizing it as systemic abuse. Reclaiming the narrative—by framing the fallout as "psychological damage" or "manipulative warfare"—can help survivors validate their pain and demand accountability.

Linguistics as a Tool for Survival

Much like identifying the telltale signs of a criminal mind, analyzing a psychopath's language can reveal their intent. Recognizing their reliance on metaphor and shifting diction exposes their strategies, helping survivors resist the pull of their control and neutralize their impact. Armed with linguistic awareness, victims can begin to unravel the web of manipulation and reclaim their sense of reality.

Silent Language: Understanding Psychopathic Nonverbal Tells for Victim Awareness

Even the most calculated individuals, including psychopaths, continuously transmit information through nonverbal cues, often without realizing it.

Chapter 3: The Devil's Courtship

NONVERBAL TELL	WHAT IT INDICATES	HOW IT CAN HELP POTENTIAL VICTIMS
SUBTLE TWITCHING (E.G., THUMBS)	Hidden stress or tension despite a calm demeanor	Recognize that the person may be concealing true intentions or lying, even if they appear composed.
NOSTRIL FLARE	Physiological preparation for challenge or stress	Identify moments when the person is under pressure, especially when discussing sensitive topics.
INCONGRUENT SMILING (E.G., SMIRK OR DELAYED SMILE)	Masking contempt or enjoying manipulation	Be cautious if their expressions don't match the emotional context, as this could indicate insincerity or hidden malice.
FEET POINTING TOWARD THE EXIT	Subconscious desire to leave the situation (flight response)	Pay attention to body orientation as it can signal discomfort or a desire to escape scrutiny, hinting at deceptive behavior.
PROLONGED EYE CONTACT	Attempt to dominate or intimidate	Recognize this as a tactic to assert control and avoid being coerced by their intensity.
TOUCHING WATCH OR GROOMING (PREENING BEHAVIOR)	Assertion of control or comfort-seeking	Spot attempts to regain control in situations where they feel challenged or exposed.
MICRO EXPRESSIONS OF CONTEMPT	Lack of empathy or regard for others	Spot attempts to regain control in situations where they feel challenged or exposed.
FIDGETING OR LEG/FOOT MOVEMENT	Internal agitation or nervous energy	Understand that fleeting looks of contempt can reveal their disdain or detachment, even when they appear polite.
MISMATCHED WORDS AND BODY LANGUAGE	Disconnection between verbal and nonverbal communication	Identify subtle signs of discomfort that might indicate deception or internal conflict.
BLANK STARE OR "RESET BUTTON"	Recalibration after being caught off guard	Trust actions over words if their body language contradicts what they are saying. Be wary of sudden, calculated stillness; it may signal they are strategizing their next manipulative move.

When the Mask Slips

The fairytale inevitably begins to crack. Maybe it's a sudden outburst of anger, a careless lie, or a moment of cold indifference that doesn't fit the persona they've crafted. For Jenna, it was the day Mark berated a waiter during dinner, his charm vanishing in an instant. The cruelty in his eyes startled her, but just as quickly, he recovered, laughing it off as a bad day.

Victims often ignore these early warning signs, rationalizing the behavior or blaming themselves. This is what the psychopath counts on—that you'll doubt your instincts.

THE MOST NOTORIOUS PSYCHOPATHS USED THESE SAME TACTICS.

Ted Bundy, for instance, didn't abduct his victims with brute force. He charmed them first, pretending to be injured, vulnerable, and in need of help. Bundy's victims saw a man who seemed safe, even kind. It was a carefully constructed act, one designed to lower their defenses.

"I'm the most cold-hearted son of a bitch you'll ever meet," Bundy said in one of his final interviews before he was executed. "We serial killers are your sons, we are your husbands, we are everywhere. And there will be more of your children dead tomorrow.... I liked to kill. I wanted to kill. I'm not going to sit here and tell you that I feel any remorse for what I did. It would be a lie." Even in the face of execution, Bundy was unapologetic, offering no solace or closure to his victims' families and insisting "they wouldn't be executing me if it wasn't for the media frenzy."

The chilling reality is that Bundy's tactics aren't unique to serial killers. Psychopaths in everyday life use similar methods to lure their prey.

Chapter 3: The Devil's Courtship

EMILY'S STORY[4]

My client, Emily, sat across from me, her hands trembling slightly as she smoothed out the wrinkles in her skirt. Her voice was steady, but her eyes betrayed the storm raging beneath the surface. "I feel like I'm losing my mind," she began. "He's so convincing. Sometimes, I believe him even when I know he's lying."

I leaned forward; pen poised over my notepad. "Tell me about the lies," I said gently. "What's he saying?"

She exhaled sharply, a bitter laugh escaping her lips. "That I'm forgetful. That I'm too sensitive. That I imagine things. He'll move something in the house, like my keys, and then swear I'm the one who misplaced them. And when I confront him about it, he looks at me with this... pity, like I'm some fragile little thing that can't keep her life together."

Her words spilled out in a torrent, each one carrying the weight of a thousand second-guesses. "I started writing things down," she continued. "Dates, times, everything. Just to prove to myself that I'm not crazy. But even then, he finds a way to twist it. He says my notes are evidence that I'm paranoid. He's always two steps ahead."

"You're not crazy," I told her. "You're being manipulated by someone who knows exactly how to exploit your vulnerabilities."

She looked at me then, her eyes filling with tears. For the first time, someone had named the monster hiding in the shadows of her life.

"He was the man of my dreams—or so I thought. Turns out, he was a dream of his own making, and I had no idea I was living in his nightmare." Emily leaned forward in her chair, her words came haltingly at first, each one carrying the weight of disbelief and betrayal. "He was perfect," she said, her voice barely above a whisper. "Too perfect. And that's where it all began."

---

4 All names and stories are fictional composites of many clients and experiences.

She described their first meeting:

A cozy, candlelit restaurant. Emily looked radiant, albeit slightly shy. Cole leaned across the table; his gaze unwavering. "I have to say, Emily, you're... breathtaking.... You have this way of lighting up a room. I noticed it the moment I saw you at the party. Everyone else just disappeared.

"That's sweet of you to say, but I think you might be exaggerating a bit."

"Exaggerating? Absolutely not. You don't realize how extraordinary you are, do you? It's rare to meet someone who's so intelligent and beautiful. You're this perfect combination of driven and kind. Honestly, I feel like I've been waiting my whole life to meet someone like you."

Emily laughed nervously, "You barely know me! I mean, we've only just met."

Cole leaned in, his tone dropping to a confessional whisper. "Do you believe in fate? Because I'm starting to."

Emily was caught off guard by his intensity. "I... I don't know. I've never really thought about it that way."

Shaking his head, Cole looked at her with feigned vulnerability and said, "I can't explain it. It's like I've been sleepwalking through life, and then you came along, and suddenly, everything makes sense. You have this... energy. It's magnetic. With you, I feel alive in a way I never have before."

"That's a lot to take in... but thank you. It's nice to feel appreciated."

Cole reached across the table to take her hand. "Appreciated? Emily, you deserve so much more than that. You deserve someone who sees you and who truly understands you. I want to be that person. I want to be someone who makes you feel safe, loved, and unstoppable."

Emily, hesitant but flattered, said, "That's... sweet of you. But it's all happening so fast."

Cole squeezed her hand, his eyes intense but warm. "Sometimes life brings people together for a reason. I'm not going to let fear stop me from showing you how much I care about you. You're worth it, Emily. You're worth everything."

Emily paused, her jaw tightening. "Cole wasn't who he said he was. Not even close."

He had introduced himself as an investment consultant specializing in international ventures. He claimed to be managing portfolios for high-net-worth clients, jetting off to Europe and Asia to close deals. "I remember thinking how glamorous it all sounded," Emily said, a bitter laugh escaping her lips. "He painted this picture of success—tailored suits, first-class flights, dinners with CEOs. He made me feel like I was stepping into a world I'd only read about."

Cole's stories were laced with just enough detail to make them believable. He spoke of meeting royalty at a gala in Monaco and closing a deal over drinks with a Saudi prince. "He even showed me pictures," Emily said. "Him standing next to yachts, at cocktail parties, shaking hands with men in tuxedos. I had no reason to doubt him."

And why would she? Cole carried himself with effortless confidence, the kind that only comes with years of honing a skill. He could discuss markets, politics, and global events with such authority that Emily often found herself in awe. "He made me feel like I'd won the lottery," she admitted. "And he was the prize."

The cracks began to show in small, almost imperceptible ways. Cole would cancel plans at the last minute, claiming he was called away for an emergency meeting. "He always had an excuse," Emily said. "A client in London, a merger falling apart, some urgent call he couldn't miss. At first, I believed him. I mean, who wouldn't? He always had an explanation."

But the explanations grew thinner, the excuses more elaborate. Emily noticed inconsistencies in his stories—places he said he'd been didn't match the timeframes he gave. Once, he mentioned a weekend spent in Paris while the photos he posted online showed him at a golf course. When she pointed it out, he laughed it off, saying, "Oh, I forgot. That was the weekend before."

Her doubts started to fester. "He was so convincing," she said. "But there was this gnawing feeling in the back of my mind. Something didn't add up."

Emily's suspicions came to a head one evening when Cole left his laptop open while taking a shower. "I wasn't trying to snoop," she said, her voice defensive. "But the screen lit up with an email, and I couldn't help but look."

The email wasn't from a client. It was from a collection agency demanding payment for overdue debts. "At first, I thought it was a mistake," Emily said. But as she dug deeper, she discovered a trail of lies. Cole wasn't a high-powered consultant; he was a freelance financial planner with no steady income. The yacht photos? Stolen from social media accounts. The trips? Fabricated.

"He wasn't even using his real last name," she said, her voice breaking. "Everything about him was a lie."

Emily's discovery sent her spiraling. She felt betrayed, humiliated, and—most of all—terrified. "If he lied about all of that, what else was he hiding?" she wondered. The answer came sooner than she expected.

When Emily confronted Cole, his reaction was immediate and explosive. His usual charm vanished, replaced by a cold, calculating anger.

Emily realized at that moment that Cole's persona wasn't just a lie—it was a weapon. He had crafted an identity to ensnare her, and now that she was slipping away, he didn't care about maintaining the facade. The situation escalated quickly. Cole's anger turned physical, and Emily knew she had to get out. She locked herself in the bathroom and called the police, her heart pounding as she waited for help to arrive.

Chapter 3: The Devil's Courtship

But when the officers showed up, Cole's mask was back in place. He greeted them at the door, calm and composed, spinning a tale about Emily being "overly emotional" and "blowing things out of proportion." He pointed to a shattered vase and claimed she had thrown it at him.

The officers suggested they "take some time apart" and left, leaving Emily more trapped than ever. "It was like the system didn't see him for what he was," she said. "They didn't see the monster."

It took Emily months to untangle herself from Cole's web. She started gathering evidence of his lies—emails, photos, financial records—and quietly reached out to friends she'd pushed away. "I had to rebuild everything he'd torn down," she said. "My confidence, my relationships, my life."

As Emily finished her story, she looked at me with a mix of defiance and bewilderment. "How could this have happened to *me*?"

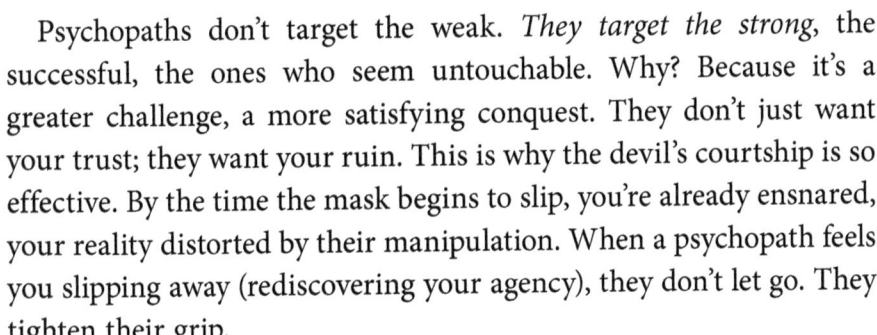

Psychopaths don't target the weak. *They target the strong*, the successful, the ones who seem untouchable. Why? Because it's a greater challenge, a more satisfying conquest. They don't just want your trust; they want your ruin. This is why the devil's courtship is so effective. By the time the mask begins to slip, you're already ensnared, your reality distorted by their manipulation. When a psychopath feels you slipping away (rediscovering your agency), they don't let go. They tighten their grip.

CHAPTER FOUR
THE POWER PLAY

Are You Being Brainwashed in Your Relationship?

CULT LEADERS AND THEIR TACTICS

PSYCHOPATHY WITHIN GROUP dynamics reveals a chilling reality: the ability of psychopaths to exploit and manipulate groups to achieve dominance and control. Nowhere is this more evident than in the realm of cult leadership, where individuals like Charles Manson and Jim Jones have demonstrated the devastating impact of unchecked psychopathic traits on entire communities. These leaders wield charisma, cunning, and emotional manipulation as weapons, creating environments where followers willingly surrender their autonomy and critical thinking.

They create an illusion of shared purpose, a "family" presenting themselves as saviors or visionaries offering answers to existential questions or societal disillusionment. They, too, isolate their followers from outside influences, severing ties to family, friends, and other support systems to ensure dependence. Jim Jones, for instance, leader of the Peoples Temple cult, relocated his followers to the remote jungle settlement of Jonestown, in Guyana, where their physical and psychological isolation allowed him to dominate every aspect of their lives, culminating in the tragic mass suicide of over 900 people.

Control is further solidified through cycles of reward and punishment. Cult leaders alternate between praise and degradation, keeping followers in a perpetual state of striving for approval and fear of rejection. This psychological conditioning mirrors gaslighting tactics seen in one-on-one relationships but with an amplified impact in group settings. Followers internalize the leader's worldview, making dissent nearly impossible without significant personal and social repercussions.

Charles Manson, the leader of the Manson Family cult, spoke in exaggerated and abstract terms to position himself as a messianic figure: *"I am the devil, and I'm here to do the devil's business." "You are the reflection of me in the mirror of the universe."* He frequently referred to himself as an eternal force: *"I've been here forever. I've been to every place you've ever walked. I've walked."* These statements exemplify his self-aggrandizement and manipulation, designed to create awe and obedience among his followers while baffling outsiders.

Manson's speech often lacked linearity, making it difficult for anyone to pin him down: *"You can't kill me. I am already dead, and I have never been alive." "If I am God and God is you, then who are we killing when you say murder is wrong?"* His use of circular logic created an air of philosophical depth while serving to confuse and disorient his audience, making it easier to control them. He often relied on metaphors that sounded meaningful but were incomprehensible: *"The trees know what I'm talking about, but people are too blind to see it." "You can't pick up a flower without troubling a star."* By using abstract and poetic-sounding language to imply hidden wisdom, he reinforced his cult leader persona.

And when challenged, Manson deflected with aggression or nonsensical diversions:

Interviewer: *"Did you instruct your followers to kill?"*

Manson: *"I never told anyone to kill; the universe told them. Blame the wind, blame the stars, blame your own ignorance."*

Many modern cult-like groups exploit social media platforms like Instagram and TikTok, targeting young influencers, dancers, and wellness enthusiasts. They often use hashtags, motivational content, and promises of enlightenment or financial independence to draw members. Think: The Garden: accused of being a modern utopian cult using TikTok and Instagram to promote eco-conscious living and spiritual growth[5]. Influencer cults are smaller, decentralized cult-like groups that revolve around charismatic leaders offering wellness retreats or self-help courses. Common recruitment tactics involve campus organizations posing as harmless clubs promoting spirituality or networking and targeting students looking for meaning, community, or career advancement. Some offer free or low-cost dance, acting, or professional development workshops as a gateway. They leverage social media with direct messages, hashtags, and aesthetically pleasing content to lure in influencers. And leaders rely on current members to introduce friends, making the process feel "organic."

The Netflix documentary series Dancing for the Devil: The 7M TikTok Cult profiles 7M Films, a talent management company that recruited dancers through social media platforms like TikTok. Founder Robert Shinn, who also leads the Shekinah Church, is alleged to have engaged in abusive behavior, financial exploitation, and coercive control over dancers associated with the organization. Former members accused Shinn of requiring substantial financial contributions, sometimes up to 80% of their earnings, under the guise of religious donations or "management" fees.

Preventing psychopathic dominance in group settings begins

---

[5] The organization has vehemently denied these allegations but after a wave of online negative press, temporarily closed and have now reopened as a new community land project, "The Land."

with awareness and education. Institutions and communities must recognize the red flags of psychopathic leadership—excessive charm, grandiose promises, and efforts to isolate members. Empowering individuals with critical thinking skills and encouraging skepticism of charismatic figures can disrupt the early stages of manipulation. Media literacy programs that teach people to recognize emotional manipulation in speeches and propaganda could serve as valuable tools in preventing the rise of psychopathic leaders.

Intervention strategies should focus on dismantling the leader's control mechanisms. Support systems for current and former group members, such as counseling and reintegration programs, can provide a path out of the psychopathic leader's grip. Additionally, legal frameworks that hold leaders accountable for psychological abuse and coercion can deter such behavior. For example, organizations like the International Cultic Studies Association (ICSA) work to expose manipulative group dynamics and provide resources for survivors, serving as a model for intervention on a broader scale.

The Club of Fools

Kai stood at the threshold of the sleek glass doors; her palms clammy with anticipation. "Welcome to the Club of Fools" the receptionist greeted her, a serene smile stretching across her face. The reception area exuded an air of sophistication—polished wood floors, soft instrumental music, and the faint scent of lavender. Kai reminded herself that she had nothing to lose; she had come here to reclaim her life and find purpose again after the implosion of her marriage and career.

Inside the main hall, Cliff, the enigmatic founder of the Club of Fools, stood before a rapt audience. His presence was magnetic—sharp cheekbones, piercing blue eyes, and a voice that wrapped around each word with precision. "You are here because the world has failed you," he said, his tone intimate, as though speaking directly to Kai. "But within this Club, you will discover the tools to rebuild. To reclaim your power."

Cliff's gaze seemed to linger on her as he continued. "The world outside wants you weak, disconnected, controlled. Here, we strip away the lies and rebuild your true self."

In her first week at the Club of Fools, Kai was assigned a personal mentor, Lila, who shared a story like hers of heartbreak and disillusionment. "Cliff saved my life," Lila confided one evening. "He sees people for who they truly are."

Kai was soon immersed in the Club's teachings. Daily workshops emphasized "letting go of societal constraints" and achieving "sovereignty." Cliff's philosophies were laced with a mix of empowerment and subtle undertones of dependency. "You can't heal alone," he often said. "True growth requires submission to the process."

The workshops quickly evolved into more demanding tasks. Cliff instructed members to write confessions of their deepest fears and secrets under the guise of "clearing emotional baggage." These confessions were shared in small groups, fostering a sense of intimacy—and vulnerability.

Two months later, Kai was invited to join the "Inner Circle," an elite subgroup within the Club of Fools. Cliff delivered the invitation himself during a private dinner. "You have a rare energy, Kai," he said, his voice heavy with sincerity. "You are meant for greatness, but greatness requires sacrifice."

As part of her initiation, Kai was required to reduce her contact with "negative influences," which included her family and friends. "They can't understand your journey," Cliff explained. "They'll only hold you back."

Kai's days became consumed by the Club of Fools. Sleep deprivation from late-night workshops and early-morning meditations began to blur her sense of time. Meals were sparse, often consisting of controlled portions of bland food— another step, Cliff claimed, toward achieving "purity."

Cliff's charm could shift in an instant. On one occasion, Kai failed to complete an assigned task on time. Cliff called her out in front of the group. "Do you think you're above the work?" he asked, his voice sharp. The humiliation stung, but moments later, he softened. "I push you because I see your potential, Kai. Don't let me down." Kai found herself striving harder to earn his approval. Every failure felt devastating, every word of praise a euphoric high. The group became her entire reality; her old life faded into a distant memory.

Kai's doubts began to fester after she overheard whispers among other members. One had been forced to give up their savings to fund "essential programs," and another had been cut off from their spouse entirely. The final crack came when Cliff revealed the ultimate stage of enlightenment: a "symbolic offering." Members were expected to sign contracts pledging absolute loyalty to Cliff and the Club of Fools.

Kai hesitated. That night, she crept into Lila's room, her voice trembling. "Why does he need all of this—our money, our lives?"

Lila's eyes filled with fear. "Because it's the price of freedom. If you leave now, you'll never find it."

Kai knew she had to leave, but breaking free would not be easy. Her phone had been confiscated weeks ago, and Cliff's inner circle monitored members closely. She began documenting her experiences in a hidden notebook, carefully piecing together evidence of the manipulation and abuse.

One night, while the others were occupied in a workshop, Kai slipped out through a back door. She fled to a nearby police station, trembling as she recounted her story. "It's not just me," she told the officer. "There are dozens of us in there."

Group Dynamics of Psychopathy in the Workplace

Psychopathy in workplace dynamics manifests in ways that can deeply undermine morale, productivity, and mental health, particularly when the psychopath occupies a position of leadership. A psychopathic boss or manager, like a cult leader, manipulates group dynamics to exert control and maintain dominance. They may create a toxic environment by exploiting the vulnerabilities and ambitions of team members and often position themselves as indispensable visionaries, fostering an illusion of loyalty and shared purpose, but their true goal is personal gain and power. Their veneer of benevolence masks a calculated exploitation of others.

The Silent Predator

The corner office of the Law Firm belonged to Harrison, the managing partner who seemed to embody the perfect lawyer: brilliant, polished, and endlessly charming. Harrison's reputation stretched beyond the firm. Judges, clients, and even rival firms spoke of his magnetic presence and silver tongue. He was the rainmaker, the face of success. But within the firm's walls, Harrison's charm was a facade, a carefully crafted mask that concealed a ruthless predator.

New associates often described meeting him as a career-defining moment. Harrison would stroll into the bullpen, exuding confidence, stopping just long enough to compliment an associate's work or offer a word of encouragement. "You've got real potential," he'd say, his voice a velvet caress. "I see something in you most people would overlook."

Junior attorney Melanie remembered the first time he praised her. His acknowledgment was intoxicating, a bright light in the grueling monotony of twelve-hour days. "Stick with me," he'd said. "You'll go far."

Chapter 4: The Power Play

But Harrison's interest came with an unspoken cost. He expected loyalty and obedience, often cloaked in the guise of mentorship. Melanie found herself staying late to work on his cases, sacrificing weekends, and deferring to his judgment without question. "This is how you learn," he'd insist. Yet no matter how much she gave, the approval she sought always seemed just out of reach.

To maintain control, Harrison pitted employees against one another. Promotions were dangled like carrots, and he made sure everyone knew that only one person could earn the coveted spot. Subtly, he'd feed tensions. "I heard Mark is aiming for the lead on the next case," he'd mention to Melanie. "He's good but not as sharp as you. Don't let him outwork you."

The atmosphere became cutthroat. Associates stopped collaborating and were unwilling to share insights that might give a colleague the edge. Harrison thrived in the chaos. By keeping his team fractured, he ensured they remained focused on their internal competition rather than questioning his decisions or authority.

Harrison's control extended into psychological manipulation. When mistakes happened, he was quick to place blame— but never on himself. He'd call an associate into his office, the walls lined with imposing bookshelves and calmly dismantle their confidence. "I'm disappointed, Melanie," he'd say, shaking his head. "I thought you were sharper than this."

Melanie would leave his office reeling, questioning her abilities. Yet Harrison always followed the criticism with a crumb of reassurance. "I'm hard on you because I know you can handle it," he'd say with a smile. The praise was enough to keep her striving, desperate to redeem herself in his eyes.

Isolation was another weapon in Harrison's arsenal. He discouraged associates from seeking support outside the firm, subtly implying that colleagues and even family couldn't understand the pressures of the job. When Melanie's husband suggested she was being overworked, she found herself defending Harrison. "He's just demanding because he wants the best," she'd said, though even she wasn't convinced.

The firm's culture, molded by Harrison, became a pressure cooker. Associates burned out at alarming rates. One took a six-month leave for anxiety; another quit law altogether, citing an "unbearable environment." Yet Harrison remained untouchable. The partners viewed him as indispensable, brushing off concerns as the cost of excellence. "Harrison delivers results," they'd say. "He's intense, but that's what it takes."

The toxicity seeped into every corner of the firm. Secretaries trod lightly, partners avoided direct confrontations, and morale plummeted. Yet, no one dared challenge Harrison openly. He had a knack for turning complaints against the accuser, labeling them as weak or unfit for the demanding field of law.

Melanie reached her breaking point during a high-stakes trial. Harrison had promised her the second chair, only to replace her at the last minute with a junior associate who'd been courting his favor. "You're not ready," he said dismissively when she questioned him. "It's not personal."

That night, as Melanie stared at her office ceiling, the cracks in Harrison's charm became impossible to ignore. She began documenting every manipulative tactic, every incident of gaslighting, and every pattern of favoritism. She wasn't alone. Others at the firm had similar stories. Together, they built a case—not in court, but within the firm's partnership— presenting a united front to oust Harrison from his throne.

Harrison's departure didn't come without fallout. He left a trail of broken confidence and fractured careers, his influence lingering like a ghost. The firm slowly began to rebuild, implementing mental health programs and fostering collaboration over competition. For Melanie, it *was a bittersweet victory. She had reclaimed her sense of self but carried scars from the experience.* "Harrison taught me a lesson," she said. "Not the one he intended, but one I needed—to trust my instincts and never mistake charisma for integrity."

The Impact on Employees

The presence of a psychopathic leader in the workplace can have devastating effects on employees' mental health and performance. They may experience chronic stress, fear, and self-doubt as the leader uses gaslighting, public humiliation, and erratic behavior to maintain control. Team members may find themselves questioning their abilities and even their perceptions of reality as the leader manipulates them into believing they are the problem. Over time, this can lead to burnout, anxiety, depression, and high turnover rates.

A psychopathic leader might also take credit for others' work, deflect blame onto subordinates, and manipulate case outcomes for personal or professional advancement. This not only undermines the team but can also compromise the integrity of the project itself, potentially leading to disastrous consequences for the client.

They will exploit hierarchical structures to solidify their power and cultivate loyalty from certain subordinates through favoritism and rewards, creating an inner circle that is complicit in their tactics. This not only isolates dissenters but also fosters an environment where unethical behavior is normalized. For example, a psychopathic manager in a corporate setting might encourage team members to cut corners or engage in deceptive practices to meet quotas, all while absolving themselves of responsibility if things go wrong.

In the film Wall Street, Gordon Gekko embodies the traits of a corporate psychopath: using his charisma to draw people into his orbit, convincing them to align with his worldview. For example, he seduces Bud Fox, an ambitious stockbroker, with promises of wealth, power, and success. He appeals to Bud's greed and ego, creating a sense of loyalty while exploiting his naivety. Gekko pushes his employees to engage in illegal and morally dubious activities, such as insider trading. He doesn't directly handle the dirty work but manipulates others, like Bud, to take the risks on his behalf. When Bud initially resists, Gekko gradually erodes his ethical boundaries, normalizing unethical practices.

He views his employees and associates as tools to achieve his goals without regard for the consequences of his actions on their lives. When Bud becomes expendable, Gekko betrays him without hesitation, prioritizing his own financial gain over any personal or professional loyalty.

And he ensures that his employees remain dependent on him for success by positioning himself as the gatekeeper of wealth and power, making it clear that loyalty to him is the only path to upward mobility. At the same time, he instills fear of failure or irrelevance if they defy him.

One of the most chilling examples of his exploitation is his willingness to destroy entire companies— and the livelihoods of employees—for personal gain. Gekko's plan to dismantle Bluestar Airlines for its assets shows his disregard for the workers' futures, including Bud's father, who is a union leader at the company.

Recommendations for Prevention and Mitigation

Addressing psychopathy in workplace dynamics requires systemic and individual strategies: Organizations should implement robust screening processes for leadership roles, prioritizing emotional intelligence and ethical behavior over charisma and ambition. Educating employees and HR teams about the traits and tactics of psychopathic leaders can empower them to recognize and report toxic behavior early. Establishing and enforcing policies against manipulation, favoritism, and harassment can mitigate the damage caused by a psychopathic leader. Offering resources such as counseling, anonymous reporting mechanisms, and whistleblower protections can help employees resist and recover from a toxic workplace.

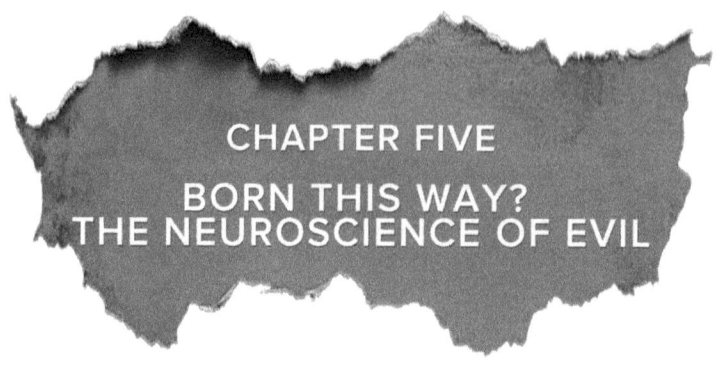

CHAPTER FIVE
BORN THIS WAY?
THE NEUROSCIENCE OF EVIL

While many psychopaths engage in activities that the rest of us consider "evil," very few of the people who engage in evil activity are psychopaths.

THE GOOD (OR bad) news is that psychopathy is largely rooted in biology, not upbringing. It's a neurological and psychological condition characterized by deficits in empathy, impulse control, and emotional depth. While environmental factors can influence how these traits manifest, psychopathy is not "caused" by bad parenting or traumatic childhoods in most cases. Instead, it often reflects inherent abnormalities in brain function.

Studies on psychopathy consistently show reduced activity in areas of the brain responsible for empathy and moral reasoning. While the environment can exacerbate certain tendencies, it is unlikely to create a psychopath where none existed. Functional magnetic resonance imaging (fMRI) scans of diagnosed psychopaths reveal significant anatomical differences: a smaller subgenual cortex and reduced activity in the amygdala, the parts of the brain responsible for processing fear, empathy, and guilt.

In fictional depictions of psychopaths, like Dexter Morgan (*Dexter*) or Joe Goldberg (*You*), we see characters who harness their psychopathy for seemingly justifiable ends. While imagined, these stories mirror

Chapter 5: Born This Way? The Neuroscience of Evil

a growing interest in understanding whether psychopathy can be mitigated or even redirected.

Both Dexter and Joe are driven by a pathological need for control, and they mask their violent tendencies with the illusion of some moral code. What makes them interesting from a narrative perspective is that they operate within frameworks of justice, even though their justice is perverse. It suggests that perhaps a psychopath could be "trained" or "reformed" to function in society in a way that benefits others. But what these characters don't show us—what the creators of these stories don't acknowledge—is the profound neurological and psychological differences that make psychopathy so deeply ingrained. The ability to "redirect" one's fundamental nature is unlikely since psychopaths live in a world that is stripped of authentic emotional connection, and they lack the motivation to conform to societal norms beyond what serves them. The idea of a psychopath using their traits for a "good" purpose is as mythical as the notion of a truly reformed serial killer. It's about as realistic as thinking you can teach a predator to stop hunting for its own survival.

In truth, the "good" psychopath may be a contradiction in terms. Psychopaths are driven by self-serving impulses and a lack of moral compass that renders them incapable of true altruism. While they may learn to mimic socially appropriate behavior for their own gain, the deeper psychological reality is that they operate outside of the realm of genuine morality. They are not capable of caring for others in the way Dexter seems to care for his sister or Joe for his romantic interests. It's a tragic misinterpretation of what psychopathy is.

That said, some psychopaths live unremarkable lives, their lack of empathy manifesting in subtle ways, such as emotional detachment in relationships or a ruthless approach to personal gain. By focusing exclusively on violent or high-profile cases, society overlooks the more insidious and pervasive impact of psychopathy in everyday settings—workplaces, family dynamics, and social circles—potentially derailing efforts to understand and address the condition comprehensively. It fosters fear rather than awareness, creating a caricature of psychopathy that is easier to sensationalize but far removed from the nuanced reality.

The "Perfect" Boy—A Cautionary Tale

Jessica had always thought her son, Michael, was special. From the moment he was born, he carried an air of quiet confidence that set him apart from other children. He wasn't fussy like the other babies at daycare; he didn't cry when she left or cling when she returned. "He's so independent!" the other mothers would say, their voices tinged with envy. Jessica beamed with pride. Michael wasn't needy; he was self-sufficient.

By the time Michael was five, Jessica had noticed small things—quirks, really, nothing to worry about. His preschool teacher called her in for a meeting to discuss an incident where Michael had pinched another child hard enough to leave a bruise. "He wanted the truck, and when the other child wouldn't give it to him, he acted out," the teacher said gently. "It's not unusual, but I wanted to flag it."

Jessica brushed it off. "He's a little boy. They're bound to have scuffles."

Still, the incidents began to pile up. At six, Michael brought home a stray cat. Jessica found it in his room, trembling, with a makeshift leash tied so tightly around its neck that the fur was matted down. "Michael, what were you thinking?" she asked, horrified.

He shrugged. "I wanted to see if it would listen to me."

Jessica untied the cat and sent it on its way, but she didn't push Michael further. He was curious, she told herself. Just a phase.

Chapter 5: Born This Way? The Neuroscience of Evil

The Warning Signs Grow

In elementary school, Michael's behavior became harder to ignore. He seemed to delight in tormenting his classmates—small, insidious acts that were hard to catch but left other children in tears. He would pull chairs out from under them, whisper cruel nicknames, and, on one occasion, sabotage a class project by spilling glue into another student's diorama.

The principal called Jessica in. "Michael is very intelligent," she began, "but he struggles with empathy. We've noticed some concerning patterns."

Jessica bristled. "He's just bored. He's advanced for his age. Maybe if you challenged him more, he wouldn't act out."

The principal sighed. "We'll try, but these behaviors go beyond boredom."

Jessica refused to believe it. Michael was brilliant, a prodigy even. Of course, he was bored. He was misunderstood, not malicious. Teachers just didn't appreciate how special he was.

Middle School: The Mask Slips

By the time Michael reached middle school, his acts of cruelty had escalated. He hacked into a teacher's email account to send out humiliating messages to his classmates. When confronted, he denied it with a calm, unflinching expression, turning the blame onto another student. The school's IT team eventually traced the emails back to Michael, but Jessica defended him fiercely.

"He's just experimenting with technology," she argued in a meeting with the school administration. "You should be nurturing his skills, not punishing him."

The principal looked skeptical but relented. Michael was given a light suspension and allowed to continue his extracurricular activities, including leading the robotics club. "We don't want to stifle his potential," the school counselor admitted, unwittingly enabling Michael's behavior.

High School: The Darkness Emerges

In high school, Michael perfected the art of duplicity. He was charming, articulate, and knew exactly how to manipulate adults into giving him what he wanted. Teachers praised his intelligence and leadership, often overlooking his cutting remarks or the way he isolated and humiliated less popular students. One of his classmates, a quiet boy named Ethan, became a particular target.

Michael spread vicious rumors about Ethan, sabotaged his locker, and once left a threatening note inside his backpack. When Ethan finally broke down in tears during class, the teacher pulled Michael aside.

"Michael, did you have anything to do with this?"

Michael tilted his head, his voice calm and convincing. "I have no idea what you're talking about. Ethan has always been a little... fragile."

The teacher let it drop. Michael's grades were too good, and his demeanor was too composed to fit the profile of a bully.

At home, Jessica continued to defend him. "Teenagers can be mean," she told a concerned neighbor whose son had been one of Michael's victims. "Michael's just confident. Other kids see that and get jealous."

The Breaking Point

The summer before his senior year, Michael was arrested for vandalizing a neighbor's car. When the police brought him home, Jessica refused to believe it.

"This is ridiculous," she said, glaring at the officer.

"Michael is not a delinquent."

"He confessed, ma'am," the officer replied. "He said he did it because he was bored."

Jessica turned to Michael. "Why would you say that?"

Michael's face was blank, his tone even. "Because they wouldn't believe me if I said I didn't. It's easier this way."

Jessica believed him, and once again, Michael avoided real consequences.

The Fallout

It wasn't until years later, when Michael was in college, that the full extent of his pathology became clear. He was expelled for orchestrating a cheating ring and later arrested for scamming elderly victims out of their savings. The headlines painted a damning picture of a manipulative young man who had charmed his way into people's trust only to exploit them.

Jessica sat in the courtroom, numb, as the prosecutor described Michael's calculated schemes. How had it come to this? She had always thought of him as a gifted, misunderstood boy. But now, as Michael smirked at the jury, she saw the truth: the boy she had spent years defending, excusing, and enabling had never needed her protection. He had needed boundaries, accountability, and the recognition that his behavior wasn't just "quirky" or "boredom." It was dangerous.

The School's Role

The schools, too, had played their part in creating the perfect storm. By prioritizing Michael's academic performance over his behavior, they had failed to address the root of his issues. Teachers and administrators had been complicit, enabling Michael's manipulations by minimizing his actions or assuming his intelligence outweighed his moral failings.

Michael's story is a cautionary tale about the dangers of ignoring red flags, of making excuses instead of enforcing accountability. Jessica's love for her son blinded her to the truth, while the school's focus on his potential allowed his darker traits to flourish. Together, they created the perfect environment for a psychopath to thrive—and for disaster to unfold.

Michael is never adequately disciplined or held accountable. His charm shields him from serious scrutiny, and his parents' attempts to seek help are met with vague platitudes rather than concrete solutions. Jessica, consumed by guilt and frustration, is left to manage Michael alone.

The question of parental blame is both central and complex, and it reflects broader societal debates about the origins of psychopathy and criminal behavior.

ARE PARENTS TO BLAME?

Recognizing Psychopathy in Children: The Critical Role of Early Intervention

A 2012 *New York Times Magazine* article detailed the frustration of parents who had spent years chasing a diagnosis for their son. First, it was A.D.D., then depression, then obsessive-compulsive disorder—each theory contradicted the last. Despite multiple evaluations, no one could pinpoint the core issue, the chilling possibility no parent is prepared to hear: their child might be a psychopath.

Currently, there is no definitive test for psychopathy in children, but research suggests it is a distinct neurological condition identifiable as early as age five. Dr. Dan Waschbusch, a leading researcher at Penn State and Florida International University, has spent over two decades studying children who exhibit "callous-unemotional" (CU) traits—indicators of a cold, predatory nature. His work relies on psychological evaluations and behavioral rating scales, including the Inventory of Callous-Unemotional Traits and the Antisocial Process Screening Device, to measure a child's capacity for empathy, remorse, and manipulation.

TRAIT DESCRIPTION

LACK OF GUILT	Shows no remorse after misbehaving or causing harm; indifferent to the consequences of their actions on others.
FEARLESSNESS	Exhibits an unusual absence of fear in situations where it would be expected; engages in risky behaviors without concern.
INSENSITIVITY TO PUNISHMENT	Does not respond to disciplinary actions; continues undesirable behaviors despite negative consequences.
MANIPULATIVE BEHAVIOR	Uses deceit or charm to exploit others; displays a callous disregard for the feelings and needs of others.
LACK OF EMPATHY	Unable to understand or share the feelings of others; indifferent to others' distress or suffering.
OVEREMPHASIS ON REWARDS	Highly focused on obtaining rewards, often at the expense of ethical considerations, may disregard rules to achieve desired outcomes.
SUPERFICIAL DISPLAY OF GUILT	May feign remorse or guilt only to avoid punishment rather than from genuine understanding or regret.

The prevailing belief is that psychopathy is largely inherited and untreatable, but Waschbusch, suggests that with early intervention, change may be possible. *"You have to hope that's true. Otherwise, what are we stuck with? These monsters."*

According to Dr. Paul Frick, a psychologist at Louisiana State University who has studied risk factors for psychopathy in children for three decades, *"psychopaths (and children with CU) have no emotional empathy, but they have cognitive empathy; they can say what other people feel, they just don't care or feel it."* He described one boy who used a knife to cut off the tail of the family cat bit by bit over a period of weeks. The boy was proud of the serial amputations, which his parents initially failed to notice. "When we talked about it, he was very straightforward," Frick recalls. "He said: 'I want to be a scientist, and I was experimenting. I wanted to see how the cat would react.'"

While no one wants to label a five-year-old a psychopath, according to Dr. Mark Dadds, director of the Child Behavior Research Clinic at the University of Sydney, ignoring these red flags is far more dangerous. Psychopathy exists on a spectrum, and while some individuals are more predisposed to it than others, the environment a child grows up in—particularly how parents respond to early warning signs—can influence whether those tendencies develop into violence or remain dormant.

Parental responsibility is not to "fix" the child but to create an environment that fosters emotional regulation, accountability, and connection.

Neuroscientist Dr. James Fallon, who discovered he had the "brain of a full-blown psychopath," stressed the importance of early intervention: There were early signs," he wrote in a 2014 article for The Guardian "How I Discovered I Have the Brain of a Psychopath," "but these disturbances were largely offset by my otherwise cheerful, positive and agreeable outgoing traits, ones that would mark me as both class clown in my high school class and Catholic boy of the year in my post-pubertal years. I was athletic, funny, good looking and popular, often being asked to take on leadership positions from high school to this day as a professor. But throughout those years, there was always the odd clinician, cleric or teacher here and there who had told me point blank that there was something decidedly evil about me."

He described a pattern of dangerous behavior throughout his life as a "telltale" sign. He scored consistently high on Hare's psychopathy checklist, particularly in the category of fearless dominance, baffled at how, despite being born a psychopath, he became a successful professor and family man, Fallon concluded it was the result of having been showered with love (versus abuse or abandonment) from birth through the critical first few years of life.

This is why," he told The Guardian, *"I tell my 97- year-old mother that the book I wrote about a young boy who could have turned out to be quite a danger to society is just about someone who will do anything to beat you in a game of Scrabble or follow you into a deadly cave. She still doesn't realize that the book is not about me, it is about her.*

WHAT IF *THE PARENTS* ARE THE PSYCHOPATHS?

The Turpins

David and Louise Turpin exemplified the calculated cruelty and cold manipulativeness often associated with psychopathy. They weaponized language and reality to gaslight their 13 children, systematically erasing their sense of autonomy and warping their perception of the world. Like predators cloaked in sheep's clothing, the Turpins convinced their children that the outside world was treacherous and malevolent. Isolation, they insisted, was not punishment but protection, and resistance was a betrayal. Over time, this psychological manipulation forged an unyielding dependency. The children came to see their parents not as tormentors but as protectors, their prison as a sanctuary.

This psychological entrapment is a hallmark of psychopathy: the ability to manipulate others into complicity, even against their own best interests. The Turpins' control was so absolute that their children, deprived of external validation and social contact, could no longer discern reality from the fabricated narrative imposed upon them.

Meanwhile, the Turpins carefully cultivated a facade of devout, loving parenthood. They crafted this persona with the precision of a psychopath constructing an airtight alibi. Their strong religious rhetoric—asserting their large family was a "blessing" from divine providence—masked their true nature. They claimed their homeschooling practices stemmed from a desire to instill superior education and moral values. To outsiders, this explained the children's absence from school and their limited social interactions, a key red flag that went unnoticed.

Public performances further reinforced this illusion. The Turpins orchestrated family outings to Disneyland, meticulously dressing the entire family in matching clothing to present a picture of cohesion and happiness. These displays were not acts of joy, but calculated manipulations designed to deflect suspicion. When neighbors or acquaintances expressed curiosity about the children, the Turpins delivered rehearsed responses with unnerving consistency, emphasizing their religious convictions and their children's supposed academic achievements and disciplined upbringing.

They constructed an intricate narrative that camouflaged their abuse, deflecting suspicion while perpetrating unspeakable cruelty behind closed doors.

The clues were there—children who were visibly malnourished, who rarely interacted with others, and whose behavior hinted at something darker—but these signs were buried beneath the Turpins' meticulously controlled image. The inability to see past their mask allowed their psychopathy to flourish unchecked, demonstrating the devastating power of manipulation when wielded by those who lack conscience.

Psychopaths Have No Guardrails

Psychopaths regard children as an inconvenience. It is not uncommon, for instance, for them to leave their children unattended for long periods of time or with unreliable sitters, alcoholics, or drug addicts. Oftentimes, the children will be found malnourished or dehydrated.

Casey Anthony was accused of murdering her 2-year-old

daughter, Caylee, in 2008. While the jury ultimately acquitted her of murder, the details of her behavior during the time leading up to Caylee's disappearance and after her death painted a picture of extreme irresponsibility and callousness that many commentators have linked to psychopathic traits. After Caylee went missing, it was Casey's mother who finally reported her missing [31 days later]. During this period, Cassey was seen partying, getting a tattoo that read "Bella Vita" (beautiful life), and acting as though nothing was wrong. Even more troubling, Casey consistently lied to investigators, claiming that a nonexistent nanny named "Zanny" had kidnapped her daughter. Her web of lies extended to her family, friends, and law enforcement, demonstrating a blatant disregard for the truth. Rather than taking responsibility for her daughter's disappearance or expressing genuine concern, Casey focused on maintaining her carefree lifestyle, prioritizing her desires over her child's well-being.

Casey often made statements about how much she loved Caylee and how she would do anything for her daughter. Even in the face of overwhelming evidence, Casey exhibited little to no genuine remorse for her daughter's death, focusing instead on her own legal defense and public image.

Criminals from "Good, Decent" Families

Many high-profile criminals, including those deemed psychopathic, have come from stable, loving homes. This reality challenges the assumption that poor parenting is the root cause of criminal behavior. Psychopathy can manifest in individuals from any background. Loving families can produce individuals who lack empathy, just as dysfunctional families can produce well-adjusted, compassionate children.

CRIMINAL	BACKGROUND	CRIME	WHY SURPRISING
Ted Bundy	Middle-class Well-educated	Serial Killer	No X abuse/neglect, intelligent
Nathan Leopold	Wealthy, prodigy Privileged	Kidnapped/ murdered child	No motivation for the intellectual experiment
Jeffrey Dahmer	Middle-class, Stable family Father, chemist	Murder/necrophilia cannibalism	No history of trauma
Robert Chambers	Affluent Elite schools	Strangled woman in Central Park	No history of trauma
Andrew Cunanan	Upper-middle-class Private schools	Cross-country spree Killed Versace	Privilege and success
Michael Skakel	Kennedy family Elite Education	Bludgeoned Martha Moxley	Affluent, family connections
Elliot Rodger	Son of a Hollywood Director, wealthy	Killed six people in a mass shooting	Privileged life

Understanding the origin of psychopathy is a cornerstone in the legal arena, not merely for its implications in criminal cases but for its profound impact on family court dynamics and sentencing strategies. In custody disputes, the echoes of psychopathic traits—manipulation, lack of empathy, and calculated charm—can shape a parent's behavior, distorting the best interests of the child and weaponizing the system. Similarly, in criminal cases, uncovering the roots of psychopathy can tilt the scales of justice, offering a lens through which to view culpability and mitigation. Is the defendant irredeemably callous or the product of a fractured past—abuse, neglect, or trauma that carved pathways to dysfunction? The answer to this question not only informs sentencing but also challenges the narrative of punishment versus rehabilitation, requiring legal professionals to peel back the layers of human behavior in search of justice, not vengeance.

CHAPTER SIX
THE HOLLOW CORE

"I have no desire whatsoever to reform myself. My only desire is to reform people who try to reform me, and I believe the only way to reform people is to kill them. My motto is: 'Rob 'em all, rape 'em all, and kill 'em all.'" —Carl Panzram.

PAUL BERNARDO, ONE of Canada's most notorious serial killers, is serving a life sentence for the abduction, sexual assault, and murder of teenagers Kristen French and Leslie Mahaffy in the early 1990s. Designated a dangerous offender, Bernardo's interactions with law enforcement and the judicial system have been extensively analyzed, particularly regarding his manipulative behaviors.

For instance, during police interviews, Bernardo exhibited persuasive nonverbal behaviors, such as deliberate hand gestures, which often distracted listeners from his deceitful statements.

In early interrogations, Bernardo maintained eye contact, smiled at inappropriate times, and used flattery toward law enforcement, portraying himself as cooperative while downplaying the severity of his actions. He referred to his role in his wife Karla Homolka's crimes as "misguided loyalty," portraying himself as a victim of circumstance rather than an active participant. He spoke about the logistics of the crimes rather than expressing any empathy for the victims, attempted to charm prison staff and legal professionals by discussing his intelligence and education, subtly asserting superiority. And when discussing details of the videotapes that documented his crimes, Bernardo used vague, sanitized language to describe what was clearly horrific and violent. His questioning of witnesses showed an unnerving lack of empathy, focusing on technicalities rather than moral responsibility.

The idea of "treating" psychopathy is controversial. Traditional therapy often backfires, giving psychopaths new tools to manipulate others. Prison populations participating in group therapy programs are a rich source of "material" for the psychopath. They take courses in psychology, criminology, and sociology and learn "buzzwords" for superficial emotional processes, which enable them to convince authorities they have been rehabilitated and "born again."

Dr. Lisa

Dr. Lisa prided herself on being able to see through her patients' facades. With two decades of experience as a clinical psychologist, she'd worked with everyone, from grieving spouses to individuals grappling with severe personality disorders. But no one intrigued her quite like Bill.

Bill had been referred to her after a string of workplace conflicts—shouting matches with colleagues and accusations of sabotage. His employer described him as "charming but volatile," a man whose talent couldn't quite outweigh the trouble he caused. Dr. Lisa had seen people like Bill before who were impulsive and struggling with anger but fundamentally good-hearted.

At least, that's what she thought at first.

Bill arrived at the first session impeccably dressed, his smile disarming.

Chapter 6: The Hollow Core

He apologized profusely for being three minutes late, blaming traffic and his own poor time management. "I hate letting people down," he said, his voice tinged with what sounded like genuine regret. Dr. Lisa nodded, jotting down notes.

From the outset, Bill was engaging, articulate, and self-aware—everything a therapist hoped for in a patient. He spoke openly about his "shortcomings": his temper, his tendency to take things personally, and his struggles with self-esteem. He even offered anecdotes about his childhood, painting a picture of a boy desperate to please a father who was never satisfied.

"I just want to be better," he said, leaning forward, his eyes locking onto hers. "That's why I'm here. I know I need help."

Dr. Lisa felt a flicker of hope. Maybe Bill wasn't as complicated as his file suggested. Maybe he truly wanted to change.

As their sessions progressed, Dr. Lisa noticed Bill's knack for steering the conversation. She'd ask a direct question— "Can you tell me about the incident with your coworker?"—and Bill would veer off on a tangent about how much pressure he was under at work or a heartfelt story about mentoring a junior colleague. His stories were vivid, detailed, and just tangential enough to seem relevant.

When she gently redirected him, Bill would sigh and smile sheepishly. "Sorry, I'm rambling again. You're right—back to the coworker thing." But even then, his answers were slippery, framed in a way that made him seem like the victim of misunderstanding or bad luck.

"She's always had it out for me," he'd say of one colleague. "I think she felt threatened by my ideas. I tried to smooth things over, but... I guess I said the wrong thing."

Bill knew how to play the role of the wounded patient. In one session, he broke down as he recounted a failed romantic relationship. Tears brimmed in his eyes as he described how his ex-girlfriend had left him, accusing him of being manipulative and controlling.

"I didn't mean to be that way," he said, his voice cracking. "I just... I get scared. When I love someone, I feel like I'm not enough, so I overcompensate. I push too hard."

Dr. Lisa felt her heart soften. She assured him that recognizing these patterns was the first step toward change.

But what she didn't see—what Bill had perfected—was that this vulnerability was a performance. He had rehearsed these stories, fine-tuning every detail to evoke empathy and redirect scrutiny. He wasn't there to change; he was there to manage perceptions.

One day, Bill arrived late, disheveled, and unusually subdued. "I haven't been sleeping," he confessed. "I think I'm spiraling. Sometimes... I wonder if it's even worth it. You know, life."

Dr. Lisa's clinical instincts kicked in. She asked pointed questions, trying to assess the severity of his suicidal ideation. Bill responded with vague answers, enough to suggest he was struggling but not enough to warrant hospitalization. It was a delicate balance; one he played masterfully.

Over the next few sessions, Bill spoke about his "depression," dropping keywords like "darkness" and "emptiness" that he'd gleaned from self-help books and online forums. He presented just enough symptoms to keep Dr. Lisa concerned but not skeptical. She adjusted her approach, focusing on his supposed depression, while Bill quietly redirected her away from his more troubling traits—his lack of empathy, his manipulativeness, his utter inability to take responsibility.

What Bill hadn't anticipated was that his need for control would ultimately betray him. During one session, as Dr. Lisa probed deeper into his patterns of conflict, Bill's facade cracked.

"She said I was 'toxic,'" he said, referring to a coworker. His lips curled into a tight smile, but his eyes were cold. "So, I reported her to HR. I figured if she wants to play games, I'll play them better."

Dr. Lisa paused, her pen hovering over her notebook. "What do you mean by that?"

Bill shrugged, his tone flippant. "I just made it clear she wasn't a team player. Gave them some examples of her attitude, her 'lateness.' They bought it. She got a warning."

There it was—the glimpse behind the mask. Dr. Lisa saw the calculation and realized that Bill's tears, vulnerability, and charm were all scripts. He wasn't seeking help; he was seeking validation, control, and someone to mirror back the version of himself he wanted to project.

After that session, Dr. Lisa revisited her notes with fresh eyes. Patterns emerged—his avoidance of responsibility, his use of tangents to derail conversations, and his ability to evoke sympathy while never addressing his core behaviors. She recognized the traits of psychopathy: charm, manipulativeness, lack of empathy, and a penchant for deception.

When she confronted him in their next session, Bill didn't react as she expected. Instead of anger or denial, he smirked. "So, you figured me out," he said, leaning back in his chair. "Took you long enough."

The admission was chilling. Dr. Lisa terminated their sessions, documenting her concerns and referring him elsewhere. But she knew that Bill would likely find another therapist, someone else to charm, manipulate, and use as a tool to maintain his carefully constructed image.

Bill's ability to manipulate his therapist, Dr. Lisa, was a textbook demonstration of psychopathic tactics at play. His charm and wit were his first defense, using humor and charisma to disarm her and make himself appear likable and relatable. By establishing a connection based on warmth and likeability, he quickly created a rapport that made it difficult for Dr. Lisa to see through his true intentions. However, his manipulation didn't end there. Bill was often highly adept at redirection, often steering the conversation away from topics that could expose his more profound issues. Whenever the discussion veered toward his actions or accountability, he skillfully deflected attention toward external factors, keeping the focus off his psychopathic traits and his lack of personal responsibility.

In addition to deflecting, Bill mastered the art of feigned vulnerability. His tears and confessions, though seemingly genuine, were nothing more than calculated performances designed to evoke sympathy and distract from the more dangerous aspects of his psyche. By presenting himself as emotionally distressed, he triggered Dr. Lisa's protective instincts, distracting her from the fact that he was manipulating the entire process. Lastly, Bill utilized malingering—exaggerating symptoms of depression and emotional turmoil to divert attention away from his psychopathic traits. By portraying himself as a victim of his mind, he ensured that Dr. Lisa's focus remained on his purported psychological struggles rather than on the manipulative, self-serving behavior that lay beneath the surface. All these tactics combined to create an illusion of vulnerability, allowing Bill to control the narrative while continuing his psychological games unchallenged.

For therapists, Bill's story reminds them of the importance of vigilance, skepticism, and the ability to see beyond the surface charm. For Bill, it was just another game.

Evil Is Not a Mental Illness

Psychopaths don't change because they don't believe they're broken. They see therapy as a game, a stage, a chance to outwit their therapist. Since psychopathy is not a mental illness but a distinct, incurable personality disorder marked by a profound lack of empathy, remorse, and conscience, perhaps the focus should be on prevention and protection rather than rehabilitation. Psychopaths do not experience the world as others do. Their lack of emotional depth and connection to others means they view people as objects to exploit rather than as beings with intrinsic worth. Their superficial charm, grandiose sense of self, and manipulative tendencies often allow them to blend seamlessly into society while leaving a trail of devastation.

Attempts to "fix" psychopaths through therapy often fail because their condition is not rooted in emotional distress or internal conflict. Traditional therapeutic techniques—rooted in empathy, self-reflection, and accountability—presuppose a willingness to change. Psychopaths lack this willingness. Instead, therapy provides them with new tools to manipulate others.

Before his trial, John Wayne Gacy, the charismatic serial killer who deceived therapists and law enforcement alike, underwent extensive testing, including over 300 hours at Menard Correctional Center. Some professionals noted inconsistencies in his behavior and accounts, suspecting deliberate deception rather than genuine dissociation or schizophrenia. This strategic misrepresentation contributed to early misdiagnoses.

Gacy's legal team brought in doctors who supported a diagnosis of paranoid schizophrenia or multiple personality disorder, arguing he was mentally unfit to be held accountable. These diagnoses were based on his self-reported symptoms rather than verifiable behaviors, allowing him to perpetuate a false narrative.

Gacy leveraged his charm and intelligence during psychological assessments to appear cooperative and rational. For instance, he engaged in complex narratives about his childhood abuse and claimed remorse in a manner designed to evoke sympathy, masking his psychopathy and preventing some evaluators from recognizing his true nature.

During evaluations, Gacy claimed he had different personalities, one of which was responsible for the murders. This tactic was likely intended to support an insanity defense. He described an "evil side" distinct from himself, using this narrative to portray the killings as dissociative acts, potentially confusing evaluators and lending credibility to claims of a split personality.

Similarly, Edmund Kemper, known as the "Co-Ed Killer," was incarcerated at Atascadero State Hospital during his teenage years for the murder of his grandparents. While there, he administered psychiatric tests to other inmates and learned how to manipulate these assessments. This knowledge enabled him to deceive his psychiatrists into believing he was rehabilitated, leading to his release. Following his release, Kemper committed several more murders before being apprehended again.

Studies have shown that psychopaths who undergo therapy often become more adept at mimicking human emotions, using therapeutic language to feign progress and further their agenda.

In the business world, psychopathy manifests as ruthless ambition, a lack of moral constraints, and the exploitation of others for personal gain. Rehabilitation efforts in corporate settings, such as leadership coaching or emotional intelligence training, often provide such individuals with more sophisticated tools to manipulate colleagues and climb the corporate ladder.

This is not to say that society should abandon all hope of managing psychopathy. Instead, resources should be redirected toward harm reduction, containment, and support for victims. Psychopaths may never change, but their capacity for destruction can be mitigated through vigilance and education.

The goal is not to "save" the psychopath but to arm potential victims with knowledge and strategies to safeguard their lives and futures.

But prevention isn't just about spotting the next Ted Bundy. It's about recognizing the warning signs in everyday relationships, workplaces, and communities. It's about teaching people, especially women, to trust their instincts, set boundaries, and say no to toxic behavior before it escalates.

Chapter 6: The Hollow Core

They Break the Rules.

In the documentary series *Most Evil*, Richard "The Iceman" Kuklinski, a contract killer responsible for over 100 murders, discussed his crimes with chilling detachment as if murder itself were an "art form." He casually explained how he killed people in creative ways, using cyanide in nasal spray, sprinkling it over food, or freezing bodies to confuse the time of death. These methods were chosen not because they were necessary but because they entertained him or made his work easier. In one interview, he discussed shooting a man on the street with a crossbow just to see how it would work. This random act of violence, devoid of necessity or purpose, epitomized his psychopathic disregard for the rules that govern civilized behavior.

Kuklinski blended into normal society—he was a husband and father—while committing horrific crimes. This double life allowed him to evade law enforcement for decades. He created the image of a family man while threatening to murder his wife and her family if she ever threatened to leave him.

He pretended to be a businessman to lure victims into a false sense of security before killing them. This level of deceit showed his utter disdain for the social contracts of trust and honesty.

Dennis Rader, the "BTK Killer" (Bind, Torture, Kill), is infamous not only for his brutal murders but also for his contradictory and emotionally detached speech patterns. His statements, particularly during interrogations, court proceedings, and interviews, reveal the hallmarks of a psychopathic mind: an inability to grasp the emotional weight of his actions, a need for control, and a tendency to contradict himself.

During his confession, Rader expressed a hollow form of regret: *"I guess it's just, you know, I wanted this fantasy to happen. So, it became real. I'm sorry for what I did, but it's something I had to do."*

He claimed to feel remorse while simultaneously justifying his actions as something necessary to fulfill his fantasies. He considered himself ordinary, "*a regular guy, family man, you know? I went to church, worked, and cared for my family.*" And murdered people on the side. "*I bound them, gagged them, and killed them. It was like a project for me.*"

In interviews, Rader explained he had "*a demon in me. It's not who I am, but something that drives me.*" At other times, he took full ownership of his crimes: "*No one forced me to do anything. I planned everything myself, and it went how I wanted it to.*"

In court, Rader provided chillingly clinical accounts of his killings: "*After I strangled her, I let her down to the ground. She was dead at that point. I think I got a glass of water before leaving.*" At other times, he contradicted this detachment by romanticizing his crimes: "*I wanted to make them mine, to control their final moments.*" His speech shifted between unemotional recounting and disturbingly intimate descriptions, highlighting his inability to consistently understand or articulate the gravity of his actions.

"*I was very careful. I planned every detail so nothing would go wrong.*" Yet, he would admit to errors: "*I made some mistakes, like leaving evidence behind or not timing things right. But I adapted.*" Rader's contradictions reflected his inflated sense of self and his need to portray himself as both perfect and adaptable, even when caught.

In court, Rader addressed the families of his victims: "*I'm sorry for what I did to your loved ones. It was wrong.*" However, in private letters and communications with police, he boasted about his crimes and sought attention for them: "*I want credit for my work. No one else did this, only BTK.*"

False Promises

Psychopaths are notorious for displaying fake contrition at sentencing, promising the judge they'll "never do it again" and they've "learned their lesson." "Trust me," they say, it was "a big misunderstanding." They are awarded probation, and terms, and second chances. When psychopaths violate their probation, fail to check in with their probation officers, comply with any terms, or submit to random drug or alcohol tests, they make excuses and are afforded more chances to prove their inability to follow instructions. Or they are incarcerated, held on bail, and manage to convince their families they'll show up for court if only they are released. Their families want to believe the fantasy that their psychopathic relative will do as he says, leverage their homes (and lose all once the psychopath skips town).

In the criminal arena, this advice is the opposite of the law (where past behavior cannot be used to condemn present or future conduct). For a psychopath, past behavior is absolutely a predictor of future behavior, once a psychopath, always a psychopath. *Rules and laws mean nothing to them.*

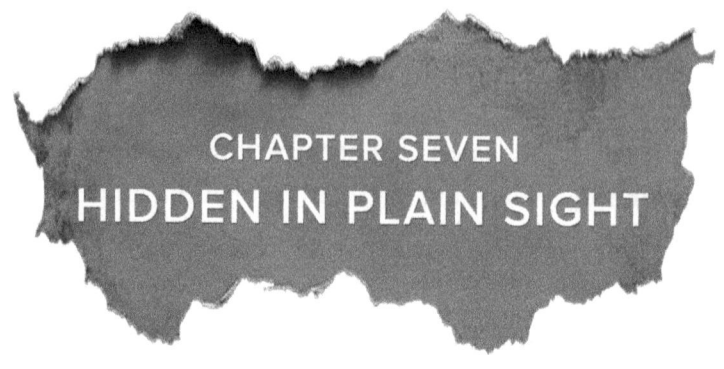

CHAPTER SEVEN
HIDDEN IN PLAIN SIGHT

"She Smiles at Me. But I Know Inside I'm The Strangest One of All." –Issei Sagawa

UNMASKING THROUGH EXPLOITATION

IN THE MORALLY ambiguous sphere of espionage and covert operations, figures like Aldrich Ames and Robert Hanssen found what ordinary life could never offer: constant novelty, high stakes, and the adrenaline rush of manipulating people and systems for personal gain. They both certainly displayed strong psychopathic tendencies—an insatiable need for stimulation, a pathological boredom with the mundane, duplicity, and a chilling lack of emotional connection. They found solace in subversion, thriving in a world where lies were currency and danger the ultimate drug.

Aldrich Ames, the CIA officer turned Soviet mole, sold out his country for personal gain, living extravagantly on the blood money he received for betraying agents who trusted him. Many of those agents were captured and executed because of Ames's actions, yet he displayed no remorse, no guilt, and no concern for the lives he destroyed. Instead, he justified his actions as if the consequences were irrelevant to him—a hallmark of psychopathy. Even within his

Chapter 7: Hidden in Plain Sight

personal life, Ames maintained a chilling duplicity involving his wife, Rosario, in laundering his illicit earnings. The ease with which he compartmentalized his treachery from his family life underscores the emotional detachment that is central to psychopathy. Though Ames was never formally diagnosed as a psychopath, his actions and traits aligned with many characteristics of psychopathy. Arguably, he represented what is sometimes called the "corporate" or "functional psychopath"—a high-functioning individual who uses charm, manipulation, and deceit to achieve their goals. Understanding these traits was crucial to his capture.

Former FBI agent Robert Hanssen, another devastating example, similarly led a dual existence. Outwardly, Hanssen appeared to be a devoted family man (with six children) and devout Catholic, yet he sold secrets to the Russians for over twenty years, compromising national security and the lives of numerous operatives. Hanssen's ability to maintain this facade for so long speaks to his manipulative charm and capacity for deceit. His lack of genuine remorse for betraying not only his colleagues but his entire nation underscores his psychopathic traits—his actions were motivated by ego, greed, and a cold disregard for the harm he caused.

Eric O'Neill[6], an elite FBI operative trained as a "ghost[7]," played a pivotal role in Hanssen's capture. In his book Gray Day, O'Neill describes Hanssen as both a mentor and a tyrant—shrewd, condescending, and wholly self-serving. Hanssen's downfall reveals an essential truth about psychopaths: to stop them, you must use their traits against them. They trust no one, but they believe in their own superiority—and that's where their defenses crack.

Hanssen joined the FBI with dreams of being a real-life James Bond—a suave spy hunter, a man of action. Instead, the Bureau

---

[6] His three-month investigation into the capture of Hanssen is memorialized in the film *Breach*
[7] Modeled after MI5's "The Watchers"

assigned him to a desk job, a "librarian" role, as Hanssen saw it. The perceived slight festered. He had a growing family and mounting bills, and instead of taking out a loan like any ordinary man, he decided to betray his country, signaling his intentions with an initial letter to Soviet intelligence. Hanssen identified a double agent—a move that ensured the agent's execution. Such an act is emblematic of the psychopathic mind: a complete disregard for the consequences of one's actions on others, paired with an inflated sense of one's own invulnerability. To Hanssen, this was not treason but strategy. He offered his services on his own terms, demanding payment while arrogantly asserting he could remain undetected.

Hanssen first identified himself simply as "B," a ghost in the system who, over two decades, became the ultimate cyber spy. He exploited his deep knowledge of FBI computer networks to erase his tracks and shift suspicion onto others—most notably, an innocent colleague, Brian Kelley. This kind of strategic misdirection is a hallmark of psychopaths: they manufacture chaos, redirect blame, and remain unnoticed while others take the fall.

His capture wasn't about brute force—it was about psychology. The FBI needed someone who could infiltrate his world, mirror his mindset, and exploit his blind spots. Enter Eric O'Neill. Young, Catholic, technically skilled, and—crucially—an aficionado of James Bond films, O'Neill became the perfect projection screen for Hanssen's ego. Psychopaths instinctively seek out and manipulate commonalities to forge trust, but in this case, the FBI turned the tactic against him.

Hanssen's Bond obsession wasn't just fandom—it was identity. He memorized lines, collected replica weapons, and built a self-image around power and control. Even his compulsive pen-clicking—an unconscious tick—hinted at an obsessive need to ritualize and dominate his environment. In the end, it was his own nature that betrayed him. Understanding a psychopath isn't just about knowing what they do—it's about recognizing how they see themselves.

Hanssen's downfall wasn't just about evidence—it was about ego. Like many psychopaths, he believed himself untouchable. That arrogance led to mistakes. He called the Russian embassy directly, demanding payment—a reckless move that was recorded and archived. He left fingerprints on the trash bags he used for dead drops, a careless slip for someone who prided himself on precision. But these errors weren't enough. The FBI needed him to betray himself in real-time.

So, they fed his delusions. A fabricated cybersecurity division, a fake promotion, unlimited access to classified data—it was all a trap designed to appeal to his pathological need for status. They didn't just watch him; they lured him. They stroked his ego, reinforced his belief in his own brilliance, and let him think he was still outplaying them. They needed one final act of espionage.

The key? His PalmPilot. Hanssen guarded it obsessively, a digital extension of his control. Psychopaths often fixate on objects that reinforce their power, and the FBI weaponized this compulsion. A carefully staged confrontation pried the device from his hands just long enough to clone its contents. His own habits—his need for control, secrecy, and superiority—became the very tools used to bring him down.

When the evidence was undeniable, Hanssen was finally caught. His first instinct? Control the optics. In his booking photo, he tried to cover the "65a" designation—traitor. A meaningless gesture yet revealing. Even in chains, even in the moment of his reckoning, he was still playing the game, still clinging to the illusion of power.

ASPECT	ALDRICH AMES	ROBERT HANSSEN	SIMILAR TAKEAWAYS
MOTIVATION	Primarily financial; desired wealth to fund a lavish lifestyle.	Financial need initially; later driven by ego, power, and a belief in his own superiority.	Greed and a sense of entitlement drove their betrayal.
ROLE IN ESPIONAGE	CIA counterintelligence officer specializing in Soviet operations.	FBI counterintelligence agent with access to cybersecurity and classified systems.	Both exploited their high-ranking positions and access to critical intelligence.
DURATION OF ESPIONAGE	Approximately 9 years (1985–1994).	Over 22 years (1979–2001).	Both engaged in long-term espionage, showing patience and calculated planning.
APPROACH TO SPYING	Directly approached the Soviets offering to sell secrets.	Wrote an anonymous letter to the Soviets offering his services.	Both initiated contact with their handlers, showcasing confidence in their ability to avoid detection.
IMPACT	Exposed dozens of CIA operatives, leading to the deaths of at least 10 agents.	Compromised U.S. counterintelligence operations, exposing double agents and methods.	Both caused severe, irreparable damage to U.S. intelligence and national security.
MISTAKES LEADING TO CAPTURE	Lavish spending beyond his CIA salary raised suspicions.	Careless phone call to the Russian embassy and leaving fingerprints on trash bags.	Arrogance and overconfidence led to critical mistakes that ultimately exposed them.
LIFESTYLE	Flashy and conspicuous; large house, luxury cars, and expensive vacations.	Modest; maintained an outward appearance of a devout Catholic and family man.	Both led double lives, carefully concealing their espionage activities from friends and colleagues.
CAPTURE METHOD	Financial investigation revealed unexplained cash deposits and spending.	Surveillance, behavioral analysis, and cloning of his PalmPilot linked him to espionage.	Both were caught through detailed, methodical investigations that leveraged their routines and flaws.

ASPECT	ALDRICH AMES	ROBERT HANSSEN	SIMILAR TAKEAWAYS
SENTENCING	Life imprisonment without parole.	Life imprisonment without parole.	Both received the maximum sentence for espionage, reflecting the severity of their betrayal.

Whether motivated by ideology, greed, or ego, their ability to compartmentalize their actions, to betray with impunity, and to remain emotionally detached from the destruction they caused—traits so central to psychopathy—made them uniquely suited to espionage but also profoundly dangerous. Their stories demonstrate how psychopathic traits—when unchecked—can wreak devastation on both a personal and geopolitical scale, blurring the line between the calculated professional and the cold-blooded predator.

Life on the Edge

David had always thrived on the edge. By the time he was twenty, he had gambled away a small inheritance, raced motorcycles through crowded city streets, and set fire to a rival's sports car—all to feel the electric hum of adrenaline. Boredom, to David, wasn't just an inconvenience—it was a cage. Every dull second gnawed at him, pushing him toward something darker, riskier, more dangerous.

It was his handler at MI6 who saw the potential. David wasn't recruited because he was patriotic or skilled—he was recruited because he was thrillingly unpredictable, the kind of operative who could walk into a den of armed extremists with nothing but a smirk and walk out holding their secrets. His life became a game of subterfuge: fake passports, coded messages, dead drops in foreign cities. He thrived on the intricate web of deception, relishing the feeling of constantly being hunted. The knowledge that a single mistake could cost him his life only heightened the pleasure.

David's need for excitement translated seamlessly into his espionage career. He was the perfect double agent, his natural charm disarming even the most suspicious adversaries. Yet, it wasn't just the danger that thrilled him—it was the duplicity. One moment, he was a trusted confidant in a Kremlin-backed operation; the next, he was slipping intelligence to his Western handlers over a bottle of champagne in Paris.

The subversion—the act of lying to everyone in his life—was as intoxicating as the danger itself. He didn't just live for the thrill of the missions; he lived for the moments when he could turn to an unsuspecting colleague who thought they knew him and smile, knowing they didn't have a clue who he really was.

The Central Intelligence Agency's Operative

Central Intelligence Agency covert operatives and spies are two sides of the same coin, with shared skills and overlapping traits that make them masters of deception and survival. However, their core differences lie in their motivations, allegiances, and the frameworks within which they operate. While operatives serve a defined mission tied to national security, spies often exist in a murkier, self-serving realm, untethered to any higher cause.

Chapter 7: Hidden in Plain Sight

Comparison Table: CIA Covert Operatives vs. Spies

ASPECT	CIA COVERT OPERATIVES	SPIES
ALLEGIANCE	Operate on behalf of a legitimate government agency, such as the CIA, to serve national security objectives.	May act independently, for foreign governments, private organizations, or personal motivations.
MOTIVATION	Aligned with U.S. policies and legal frameworks, with goals rooted in national interest.	Driven by ideology, greed, coercion, ego, or personal benefit, often with flexible or self-serving goals.
LEGAL CONSTRAINTS	Actions are covert but sanctioned by the government and subject to classified oversight.	Often operate outside the law, engaging in illegal activities without oversight.
RECRUITMENT VS. ROLE	Recruit and handle foreign assets or informants to gather intelligence; act as handlers rather than infiltrators.	Frequently infiltrate target organizations firsthand, embedding deeply to gather information.
OPERATIONAL SCOPE	Missions align with broader geopolitical objectives, such as regime destabilization or covert support to allies.	May act with narrower, more personal, or financially motivated goals, such as selling secrets.
IDENTITY	U.S. citizens trained and employed by the CIA, often working under the guise of diplomatic or commercial roles.	Diverse backgrounds, including defectors, foreign nationals, or opportunists within target organizations.
DECEPTION AND MANIPULATION	Skilled in creating and maintaining false identities, using charm and manipulation to achieve objectives.	Equally adept at deception, often leveraging personal relationships or trust for infiltration.
RISK TOLERANCE	Trained to remain calm under high-stakes situations; thrive in dangerous environments.	Operate with similar risk tolerance but may be more impulsive or reckless, depending on their motivations.
ACCOUNTABILITY	Internally accountable within the CIA and its chain of command, with missions contributing to national security.	Rarely accountable; often operate in isolation, answering only to handlers or benefactors.

ASPECT	CIA COVERT OPERATIVES	SPIES
LEGACY	Seen as national heroes or unsung protectors of state security.	Viewed as heroes or villains depending on perspective, often labeled traitors in their home countries.
PSYCHOLOGICAL IMPACT	Grapple with isolation and moral ambiguity but find purpose in serving national interests.	Struggle with paranoia, guilt, and existential dread, particularly if betraying their own countries.

The Emotional Debris

Emotional detachment—essential in espionage and undercover work—can leave children feeling unseen, much like those raised by emotionally absent or erratic parents. The unpredictability of such a life—frequent relocations, unexplained absences, shifting rules—creates an environment not unlike that of children raised by addicts or personality-disordered parents. In response, children develop hyper-vigilance, scanning for the slightest danger cues, a survival mechanism that sharpens perception but erodes security.

For these children, love and abandonment become intertwined. The public face of normalcy masks a private world of secrecy and instability, echoing the experience of those raised by manipulative or dangerous parents. They learn to read deception, anticipate betrayal, and find safety in control. Some emerge with a near-clairvoyant ability to detect threats; others carry deep psychological wounds.

The outcome depends on variables beyond their control—genetics, external support, and the rare parent who can balance duty with genuine presence. But for many, moral ambiguity is not a curiosity; it is the air they breathe. They don't just recognize dangerous minds; they understand them—not to align with them but to prevent harm, expose hidden truths, and survive.

Chapter 7: Hidden in Plain Sight

My father was a covert operative with the Central Intelligence Agency. From the outside, my childhood seemed fascinating—glamorous, even. We moved between continents as easily as some families moved between neighborhoods. My parents spoke in hushed tones, traded coded glances, and possessed a quiet confidence that, as a child, I mistook for omniscience. They knew everything— where exits were, who was watching, and what could be used as a weapon if necessary.

I would later learn that this wasn't just awareness. It was survival.

My childhood was a study in controlled vigilance. The rules of the house were unspoken but understood. Trust no one. Observe everything. Keep moving. If a call came in the middle of the night, we left—sometimes for weeks, sometimes forever. I stopped asking why.

In families like mine, love and abandonment were braided together. One moment, my parents were there—sharp-eyed, precise, invincible. The next, they were gone, vanishing into a world I was not allowed to see. They would return eventually, sometimes bruised, sometimes changed. Sometimes, the change was permanent.

The unpredictability of it all hardened me. By the time I was seventeen, I had developed a skill set most adults would never need. I could tell when someone was lying—not from their words, but from the pauses between them. I knew how to disappear in a crowd, how to exit a building without being noticed, and how to tell when we were being followed. I learned that fear was an asset if you used it correctly.

Some of the lessons were explicit. Others, I absorbed like secondhand smoke.

"People are predictable," my father told me once. "If you understand what they fear, you understand what they will do."

I never forgot that.

But understanding people in this way comes at a cost. When you grow up in a world of deception, you stop expecting honesty. Love feels like a trick, kindness like a tactic. You learn to anticipate betrayal because, in your world, nothing is ever what it seems.

There were moments—rare but real—when my father would let his guard down. In those quiet intervals, he wasn't an operative, a strategist, or a ghost moving through the world unseen. He was just my father, tucking me in and reading me a story that always seemed to end too soon.

And then the phone would ring. And he would be gone again.

Most people raised in chaos either repeat it or rebel against it. I did neither. Instead, I used it. I took the paranoia, the hyper-vigilance, the ability to read danger in the way someone shifts their weight, and I turned it into something useful. I became the one who recognized threats before they materialized, the one who sensed what others could not.

Because the truth is, when you grow up in a world of secrets, you don't just learn to detect danger. You learn to become it.

The Mask of Normalcy

One of the most unsettling aspects of psychopathy is how often we celebrate it in certain contexts. Successful psychopaths thrive in high-stakes environments where charm, manipulation, and ruthlessness are rewarded: think Wall Street executives, politicians, and high-powered attorneys.

Consider the case of Elizabeth Holmes, the disgraced founder of Theranos. Holmes, with her trademark deep voice and piercing gaze, used her charisma, lies, and lack of remorse to manipulate investors, employees, and even world leaders to buy into her dream of revolutionizing healthcare with a portable blood-testing device that could diagnose diseases with a single drop.

She didn't just sell a product; she sold herself. Her charisma

Chapter 7: Hidden in Plain Sight

radiated authenticity, her bold proclamations of "changing the world" silencing critical inquiry. "*I don't want to live in a world where we're doing incremental things. I want to change the world,*" Holmes said in her 2015 *Glamour* interview.

Those who questioned her were met with a well-crafted mask of confidence and an arsenal of pseudo-scientific jargon, leaving them disarmed and, worse, complicit in perpetuating her fraud. Her manipulation wasn't confined to boardrooms; she ensnared her inner circle, isolating dissenters and rewarding loyalty with promises of future glory.

Her willingness to endanger lives by delivering inaccurate medical results underscores her lack of empathy and prioritization of self-interest over others' well-being. Her eventual downfall raised uncomfortable questions: How many others like her are out there, undiscovered, hiding in plain sight?

While Holmes was never officially diagnosed as a psychopath, her behavior follows many of the traits listed on the PCL-R, which can be highly persuasive because they are driven by self-interest, without the usual constraints of empathy or remorse. They are not encumbered by guilt, which allows them to lie convincingly and manipulate others without hesitation. In Holmes' case, her ability to "sell" a narrative—a revolutionary medical technology that was not functional—was indicative of a deep understanding of how to prey on people's hopes and desires.

But there *were* red flags. Despite her polished presentation, there were signs that, had people been more skeptical, could have raised doubts. For example, the lack of transparency about the technology, the secrecy around testing and results, and the inability to demonstrate her claims in any meaningful way should have triggered alarms. But these red flags were often overshadowed by her presentation. She was able to sell her vision so effectively that people ignored their instincts or, worse, were so taken in by her certainty that they couldn't imagine the possibility of deception.

Similarly, Frank Abagnale Jr., the con artist immortalized in *Catch Me If You Can*, wielded charm with equal precision. In his teenage years, he forged checks, donned pilot uniforms, and sweet-talked his way into cockpits, hospitals, and courtrooms. Abagnale's genius wasn't just in his forgery skills; it was in his understanding of human psychology. He tapped into people's need to trust authority, using his boyish confidence to melt skepticism.

Holmes and Abagnale mastered the art of mirroring—the ability to reflect what their targets wanted to see. To investors, Holmes was the revolutionary genius; to airport personnel, Abagnale was the assured airline pilot. Both understood that perception often outweighs reality, especially when delivered with the conviction of a psychopath.

The success of con artists lies in their ability to exploit the cognitive shortcuts humans rely on, such as trust and the tendency to overlook inconsistencies in the face of a compelling narrative.

Holmes played into the narrative of the genius disruptor, tapping into a culture that glorifies ambition and innovation. Her victims wanted to believe in her vision because it promised not only profit but also progress.

Abagnale exploited systemic gaps in verification and people's reluctance to challenge authority. By appearing confident and knowledgeable, he made questioning him seem unnecessary, even rude.

Both thrived in environments where people were eager for what they offered—a revolutionary product, a competent authority figure—making skepticism the enemy of progress.

They are portrayed as antiheroes, their psychopathic traits glamorized as the cost of success. This normalization of toxic behavior blurs the line between ambition and predation, making it harder to spot the true threats.

Chapter 7: Hidden in Plain Sight

Anna Sorokin, the so-called "Soho Grifter" at the center of the series *Inventing Anna*, was a master illusionist, weaving an elaborate facade of wealth, sophistication, and exclusivity that lured her victims into a web of deceit. Her patterns of behavior revealed a chilling blend of psychopathy and sociopathy. Like a psychopath, Anna exhibited calculated manipulation, emotional detachment, and an unflinching focus on her goals, exploiting the social currency of trust and ambition to her advantage. She meticulously crafted her image as a German heiress with a $60 million trust fund, projecting confidence and charm that made her deception nearly imperceptible.

She created fake financial documents and bank statements to secure large loans and credit lines. For example, she submitted fraudulent documents to City National Bank to obtain a $100,000 loan, which she claimed would cover the initial costs of launching the exclusive *Anna Delvey Foundation* (ADF).

She lived in luxury hotels and dined at high-end restaurants without ever paying the bills. She used temporary credit cards, wired payments that never materialized, and convinced hotel staff and concierges that her financial team would handle the expenses. In some cases, she left unpaid bills exceeding tens of thousands of dollars.

At the same time, her impulsivity, risky gambles, and occasional lapses in control aligned more closely with sociopathy. This duality—calculation fused with recklessness—made Anna especially dangerous, as she was adept at adapting her strategy to exploit each situation's unique vulnerabilities.

Anna often invited wealthy friends and business connections on lavish trips and to expensive dinners, then manipulated them into covering the costs. A famous example is when she took her friend Rachel DeLoache Williams to a luxury resort in Morocco, where Anna's credit cards were declined. Rachel ended up paying over

$62,000 on her own credit card, believing Anna would reimburse her — which never happened.

For the victims, these distinctions mattered because they illuminated Anna's modus operandi: the calculated charm that disarms, the impulsive lies that build pressure, and the lack of remorse that leaves ruin in her wake. Victims of psychopaths and sociopaths often struggle to reconcile the disconnect between the perpetrator's charm and their destructive actions, leading to self-doubt and delayed recognition of the threat.

What Anna Sorokin's Victims Could Have Done Differently

ACTION	WHY IT'S EFFECTIVE	HOW IT APPLIES TO ANNA SOROKIN
VERIFY FINANCIAL CLAIMS	Conducting due diligence exposes inconsistencies or fabrications in a person's story.	Anna's claims of wealth and connections could have been disproven with basic background checks or requiring proof of funds.
TRUST ACTIONS OVER WORDS	Behavior often reveals true intentions; inconsistency between words and actions is a red flag.	Anna promised payments and opportunities but failed to deliver, revealing the gap between her words and reality.
ESTABLISH FIRM BOUNDARIES	Clear limits discourage exploitation and force manipulators to reveal their intentions.	Victims who refused to cover Anna's expenses or lend resources might have avoided financial loss.
HEED INTUITION	Gut feelings are often the first sign of danger; ignoring them leads to vulnerability.	Many of Anna's victims admitted feeling uneasy about her but dismissed their instincts.
AVOID THE LURE OF EXCLUSIVITY	Recognizing how status and glamour can cloud judgment helps appear like a gateway to success.	Anna preyed on ambitions for wealth and social elevation, making herself appear like a gateway to success.

By fostering skepticism, verifying claims, and honoring intuition, individuals can better protect themselves from those who exploit trust as currency. Whether labeled a psychopath or a sociopath, Anna's ability to deceive underscores a universal truth: sometimes, the most dangerous lies are the ones we most want to believe.

Another Kind of Predator

Lauren's Stalker

Lauren first noticed him at the coffee shop near her apartment. He wasn't remarkable at first glance—average height, brown hair neatly combed, a friendly face framed by a pair of unassuming glasses. He sat by the window, flipping through a paperback, glancing up only occasionally to take a sip of his latte.

She didn't think much of it until the third time she saw him there. This time, their eyes met, and he smiled. It wasn't overly forward, just warm enough to seem polite. She returned the gesture, her New York upbringing wary but not suspicious. People smiled all the time in small neighborhoods, didn't they? But soon, he was everywhere.

His name was Daniel—or so he said when he finally introduced himself. The fourth time their paths crossed, he approached her at the café. "I see you here a lot," he said, his voice smooth and confident. "I'm Daniel."

"Lauren," she replied hesitantly, her instincts urging her to keep the exchange short. He didn't linger long, just enough to make an impression. Over the next few weeks, their encounters became more frequent: in the park where she jogged, at the grocery store, and even outside her building once, where he claimed to be waiting for a friend who lived nearby. "I guess we're on the same schedule," he joked. His charm was subtle, his tone disarming, but Lauren couldn't shake a faint unease.

Lauren's discomfort grew slowly, like a shadow lengthening at dusk. At first, she chalked it up to paranoia. Coincidences happen; she told herself. But soon, her sense of normalcy began to erode.

She started glancing over her shoulder during her evening jogs. The streets that once felt safe now seemed ominous. Her heart raced when she thought she caught a glimpse of him out of the corner of her eye. Her friends dismissed her concerns. "You're imagining things," her roommate said. "He's just friendly."

Lauren wanted to believe them, but the feeling in the pit of her stomach told her otherwise. One night, she found a note slipped under her door. "You have the most beautiful smile." There was no signature, but she didn't need one. Her blood turned cold.

For Daniel, this was all part of the game. He didn't stalk Lauren out of love or even lust. For him, it was about power and control. Watching her squirm, seeing her try to maintain a sense of normalcy while he subtly unraveled her world—it thrilled him. Every encounter was meticulously planned, every word chosen to make him seem innocuous, even charming.

His friendly demeanor was a mask carefully crafted to lower her defenses. He used small talk and casual smiles to create the illusion of familiarity. He didn't care about the fear he instilled in Lauren. Her anxiety was a byproduct of his enjoyment, a necessary step in his twisted pursuit of dominance.

Daniel viewed himself as superior, a predator toying with prey. He believed he was smarter than everyone else, that he could outmaneuver her and the system. The stalking wasn't just about control— it was about the rush. The adrenaline he felt when he slipped the note under her door or saw her glance over her shoulder was addictive.

As weeks passed, Daniel's behavior grew bolder. He started following her into stores, standing too close without ever saying a word. One night, she returned home to find her window open. Nothing was missing, but her blanket had been folded differently, and a single flower lay on her kitchen counter.

Lauren called the police, but there was little they could do without proof of a crime. "If he tries to contact you directly, let us know," the officer said. But Daniel was too cunning for that. He thrived on ambiguity, staying just within the bounds of plausible deniability.

One evening, as Lauren walked home from a late shift, she heard footsteps behind her. She quickened her pace, her pulse pounding in her ears. When she glanced back, there he was—Daniel, his expression calm, almost amused.

She stopped, her breath hitching. "What do you want from me?"

His smile widened, but his eyes remained cold. "I just wanted to make sure you got home safe."

It was the final crack in her sense of security. She ran the rest of the way home, locking every door and window. The next morning, she packed a bag and stayed with a friend.

Lauren's life was never the same. Even after she moved to a new apartment and changed her routines, she couldn't shake the fear. Every stranger on the street felt like a potential threat, every unexplained noise a harbinger of danger.

For predatory psychopaths like Daniel, the act of connecting with another person is about power, dominance, and the thrill of watching someone unravel.

DO *THEY* KNOW THEY'RE DIFFERENT?

Psychopaths often exhibit a peculiar kind of awareness, though it's not always what we might expect. It's not that they consciously recognize their differences in the way someone might pinpoint their own traits. Rather, it's a subtle, often unconscious understanding that something is amiss. They might sense that they operate on a different frequency than most, but for many, it's less of a moral realization and more of a pragmatic one. Because they are so keenly attuned to social dynamics— though they rarely, if ever, feel the emotional pull that others do—they can be intensely calculating, seeing the world as a chessboard to navigate for personal gain, but without the underlying sense of empathy or remorse that most people experience. So, do they know they're different? On some level, yes—but it's more a functional awareness than an emotional one.

The real question is not whether they know they're different but whether they care. And the answer is often no. Their difference is a tool, not a burden. They don't see themselves as flawed—they see themselves as superior. And therein lies the chilling truth: their lack of empathy allows them to operate unburdened, free from the moral compasses that guide the rest of us.

Excerpt from Ted Bundy's Interview with Stephen Michaud and Hugh Aynesworth (1980) in their book, *Conversations with a Killer: The Ted Bundy Tapes*

"I think I stand as much of a chance of dying in front of a firing squad or in a gas chamber as you do of being killed on a plane flight home. Let's say the odds are pretty remote either way. But that's the way I approach it. It's not that I'm dea.L F2d emotionally—I like to look at myself as a rational individual. I'm aware of the emotional consequences of this situation, but at the same time, I'm not consumed by them."

Excerpt from serial killer Dennis Rader's confession to the police (2005):

"I had already fantasized about what I was gonna do. I'd already put myself in that frame of mind where I was gonna do it... Once I started, I couldn't stop. It was like being on autopilot... For me, it was about control. The emotion wasn't there like people think—it wasn't rage. It was like I was watching myself do it."

Excerpt from American serial killer Carl Panzram's autobiography, *Panzram: A Journal of Murder*.

"I don't believe in man, God, the Devil, heaven, or hell. I hate the whole damned human race, including myself... I was very good to those who were good to me, but I have no feelings for the weak or the oppressed. They are just another tool to be used."

Excerpt from serial killer Michael Bruce Ross' interview with CBS News (2004):

"I had no feelings for these women. I didn't see them as people. They were objects, things to fulfill my desires... I could put on an act—I could make people think I cared. But deep down, there was nothing. Just this emptiness."

Excerpt from killer Aileen Wuornos's interview with Nick Broomfield (1993): *Aileen Wuornos: The Selling of a Serial Killer* (1992)

"I don't know what love is. Never did. I guess it's just something people talk about, something they feel. I never had it, and I don't need it. People get soft with love. It makes them weak. I'm not weak—I couldn't afford to be."

Excerpt from (the "Iceman") Richard Kuklinski's Interview with HBO (2001) titled *The Iceman Tapes: Conversations with a Killer*:

"Emotions don't come into it. That's what people don't understand. It's not personal. It's business. I learned early on that caring makes you vulnerable. You care about someone, and they'll use it against you. I never let anyone have that power over me."

Nathan Leopold's confession from the archival resources at the University of Missouri- Kansas City School of Law.

Leopold famously referred to himself and Loeb as "supermen" influenced by Nietzsche's philosophy, believing they were intellectually and morally superior to others, which justified their crime.

"The killing of Hankby Franks (a child) was an experiment… not inherently immoral… but highly commendable, no matter what extreme pain or injury it may inflict upon others."

THEY KNOW THE WORDS BUT NOT THE MUSIC

Psychopaths take their cue from their listeners, so they know how they're "supposed" to feel. All words are neutral to them: broccoli, for instance, has the same emotional meaning as cancer.

This emotional detachment was strikingly evident in Aileen Wuornos, a convicted serial killer whose disjointed and contradictory behavior revealed a chilling inability to align her emotions with her actions. Her language frequently shifted from victimization to aggression, reflecting her chaotic inner world and inability to articulate consistent narratives. In her courtroom testimony, Wuornos often justified her killings as acts of self-defense. However, her phrasing would veer into irrational outbursts, such as: *"I was raped and beaten, but they won't believe me 'cause I'm a woman, and women don't get believed!"* Contradictory statements followed, where she denied needing to explain herself: *"They deserved it anyway. I'd do it again if I had to!"* Her speech oscillated between victimhood and hostility, undermining her credibility. It revealed her struggle to maintain consistent narratives, likely stemming from deep psychological trauma and an inability to regulate her emotions.

Wuornos often exaggerated her circumstances or minimized the gravity of her actions: *"The cops framed me. They're all crooked. I'm just the scapegoat for their games!"* She once described her murders as the result of being "forced into a corner," but her phrasing spiraled into unrelated accusations against the legal system. Her hyperbole and tendency to redirect blame showed her lack of accountability and her distorted perception of reality.

Word Play

Psychopaths often use language that appears introspective and remorseful to regain trust and control. A client, confused by her spouse's pathology, once asked me to interpret his latest book-length emails: *You will feel the unconditional love that I have for you and our family.* The declaration—appearing overly polished and idealized, almost performative—emphasized abstract ideals rather than providing evidence of specific actions or behaviors that demonstrated his love and commitment. Psychopaths often use emotionally charged language to project an image of warmth and authenticity, even when their emotions are shallow or calculated.

You can rest in my arms in safety and security and infinite love, he wrote, his repeated emphasis on safety, security, and infinite love appearing rehearsed and focused on creating a specific impression rather than conveying genuine emotion. *Thank you for walking with me and for accepting me as I am in this state of development*—while the phrase implied gratitude, he subtly placed the burden on my client to be forgiving and accommodating. Similarly, his statement *that I have my soul, my solar angel, and the Spirit to guide me on this wonderful journey* centered on his internal transformation suggests a sense of moral superiority or exceptionalism. His focus on how my client would (or should) feel in the future, shifting the responsibility for forgiveness or emotional healing onto her while downplaying past issues, is a manipulative tactic.

As I become more refined, I think you will experience greater joy, suggested that my client's happiness hinged on her *husband's* self-improvement, potentially deflecting accountability for previous harm.

Psychopaths often leave behind writings—journals, manifestos, or diaries—that provide chilling insights into their disordered minds. These documents serve multiple purposes, each revealing key aspects of their psychological makeup. These are less about reflection or catharsis and more about power, control, and self-aggrandizement. Psychopaths thrive on constructing narratives that reinforce their sense of superiority and dominance. Keeping detailed accounts of their actions—whether reliving their crimes or outlining their plans—is a way to assert control over their legacy, creating what they see as a monument to their brilliance. Dennis Rader meticulously documented his murders, calling them "projects," relishing the sense of mastery they gave him. The writings also illustrate the pathological narcissism that drives many psychopaths. They don't just crave attention—they demand immortality. Their words, often cold and detached, reveal a complete lack of empathy. Anders Breivik is a Norwegian far-right extremist who was responsible for the 2011 attacks in Norway, which included a bombing in Oslo and a mass shooting at a youth camp on the island of Utøya, resulting in 77 deaths) His manifesto framed him as a crusader for a twisted cause, painting a delusional portrait of heroism to justify his horrific actions.

In his 1,500-page manifesto, titled "2083: A European Declaration of Independence," Breivik refers to himself as a "knight" and claims he is part of a new Templar order, adopting elaborate symbols and titles to enhance his self-image. He coldly calculates the "ideal" number of victims and justifies their deaths as necessary for his cause, describing his strategy of blending in as a "perfectly normal person" to avoid suspicion while preparing for his attacks. In his manifesto, he outlines a detailed plan of "re-education" of Europeans to align with his ideology. He minimizes the moral weight of his crimes by reframing them as acts of "defense" or "patriotism" and refers to his mass murder as "surgical strikes," claiming it was necessary to prevent the "Islamization" of Europe. After his attack, Breivik described it as "the most spectacular political act in Europe since World War II," showing pride rather than regret and a complete absence of remorse.

Luka Magnotta, born Eric Clinton Kirk Newman, is a Canadian convicted murderer and former adult film actor. He gained international notoriety in 2012 after committing the gruesome murder of Jun Lin, a Chinese international student, in Montreal. Magnotta videotaped the murder and subsequent dismemberment of the victim (later mailing body parts to various political parties and schools across Canada) and left breadcrumbs of his crimes on blogs and social media, taunting the world with his audacity while solidifying his role as the architect of his own infamy. He used his crimes as a platform to assert control and elevate his profile. In an anonymous post discussing his infamous 1 *Lunatic 1 Icepick* video, Magnotta wrote: *"The art of killing is a fascinating thing. It's primal, and it's pure power."* His detachment from the moral implications of his actions further highlights his psychopathy.

Magnotta frequently portrayed himself as a victim of bullying, stalking, and online harassment despite being the perpetrator of horrifying crimes. His writings often included appeals for sympathy or attempts to shift blame onto others. In an email exchange with a journalist, Magnotta claimed: *"I've been victimized by the media and stalked online for years. I just want to be left alone."* Psychopaths often lack accountability and frame themselves as victims to elicit sympathy or deflect responsibility. Magnotta's statements reveal his tendency to manipulate public perception for personal benefit.

The Columbine shooters Eric Harris and Dylan Klebold left behind extensive writings, including journals, school assignments, and website posts. Eric Harris's writings provide a striking illustration of psychopathic traits:

I have something only a few people have … TRUE HATRED … I hate you people for leaving me out of so many fun things. And no, don't f*ing say, 'Well, that's your fault.' because it isn't, you people had my phone number, and I asked and all, but no. No no no doesn't let the weird looking Eric KID come along.

I would love to be the ultimate judge and say if a person lives or dies—be godlike.

Harris wrote extensively about killing without remorse:

I want to tear a throat out with my own teeth like a pop can. I want to grab some weak little freshman and just tear them apart like a f*ing wolf.

People are just too stupid and ignorant to understand and respect my mind.

I want to put a 12-gauge shotgun to that little brat's head and open it like a can of meat.

Even in their final messages, neither shooter expressed regret for their planned attack: It's not my fault! People made me do this!

James Holmes, the Aurora theater shooter, exhibited signs of profound psychological disturbance, which his psychiatrist later described as evil incarnate. Unlike Eric Harris, Holmes did not display overt psychopathy but rather a complex mix of narcissism, delusion, and calculated violence. His notebook, discovered after the shooting, revealed chilling insights into his thought process. He wrote extensively about his desire to maximize casualties, detailing his plan with clinical precision: "The message is there is no message. Most fools will misinterpret correlation for causation, namely relationship and work failures as causes. Both were expediting catalysts, not the reason." He saw his violent act as inevitable rather than reactionary. Holmes also dehumanized his victims, referring to them as "sheeple" and outlining attack strategies based on venue layouts and law enforcement response times. His writings revealed a detached, analytical approach to mass murder, underscoring a belief in his intellectual superiority and a lack of empathy. Holmes knew what he was doing, methodically planned it, and sought infamy—a chilling portrait of a killer who understood right from wrong but simply didn't care.

THE "SUCCESSFUL" PSYCHOPATH[8]

Psychopathic traits aren't always confined to criminals and outliers—some of those traits may give people an advantage in certain high-stakes professions. Research suggests that individuals with pronounced psychopathic tendencies are overrepresented in fields like politics, business, law enforcement, firefighting, military special operations, and extreme sports. These people may not meet the full clinical definition of a psychopath, but they display enough traits—like charm, fearlessness, and emotional control—that they stand out under pressure.

---

8 Sarah Francis Smith. Scott O. Lilienfeld, Karly Coffey and James M. Dabbs, Journal of Research in Personality, Vol. 47, Issue 5, October 2013, "Are Psychopaths and heroes twig off the same branch? Evidence from college, university, and presidential samples."

A study of 42 American presidents up to George W. Bush asked biographers and historians to assess each president's personality, including traits tied to boldness. The results were clear: boldness correlated—modestly but consistently—with better overall presidential performance, especially in crisis management, agenda-setting, and public persuasion.

Theodore Roosevelt, for instance, easily the boldest president in the study, was described by his biographer, Michael Canfield, as "robust, forceful, and avalanche-like," with an animalistic intensity that helped him dominate the political stage. But he wasn't extreme or pathological—his boldness was simply higher than the average person's.

Tom Skeyhill, the infamous Australian war hero, understood something fundamental about human nature: people don't want the truth—they want a good story. And so, he gave them one. Stationed in Gallipoli during World War I, he held the dangerous position of a flag signaler and claimed a bomb had exploded at his feet and blinded him.

After the war he wrote poems about his combat experience (a mere 8 days) and toured Australia and the United States as the *blind soldier-poet*, his words dripping with the kind of tragedy and triumph that makes people open their wallets, their hearts, their trust. Miraculously, his blindness disappeared following a medical procedure in America. (Miracles, of course, are convenient things when there's no medical record to back them up).

He mesmerized crowds—including Theodore Roosevelt—who once declared, "I am prouder to be on the stage with Tom Skeyhill than with any other man I know."

Biographer Jeff Brownrigg would later peel back the layers of Skeyhill's persona in his book, *Anzac Cove to Hollywood: The Story of Tom Skeyhill, Master of Deception*, revealing a pattern of exaggeration, fabrication, and manipulation. He wasn't a soldier's soldier. He was a salesman. And his product? Himself.

CHAPTER EIGHT
THE DARK WEB

IN THE VAST anonymity of the internet, predators weaponize human psychology, exploiting the very desires that make us vulnerable. Psychopaths, adept at mimicry, craft online identities designed to mirror their targets' deepest hopes and values. They understand that universal needs—love, belonging, validation—are powerful hooks. Using curated deception, they manufacture trust, drawing victims into a web where connection feels real but is entirely fabricated. This chapter exposes the tactics behind their manipulation, revealing how persuasion becomes a tool for control and how the most dangerous predators don't just deceive—they anticipate and fulfill our unspoken desires.

Understanding Human Motivation
Appealing to Universal Desires

Psychopaths tailor their profiles to reflect the dreams and values of their targets:

- **Web Profile:** A psychopath targets someone craving stability and love. Their profile features carefully selected photos of them engaging in "wholesome" activities—walking a dog, attending family events, or working in humanitarian causes. Their bio is sprinkled with phrases like "I value loyalty above all else" or "Looking for my soulmate to build a life with."

- **Manipulative Strategy:** They present themselves as the perfect antidote to loneliness, aligning their narrative with the victim's unmet emotional needs.

Crafting Trust Through Design and Language

Psychopaths mimic trustworthy profiles through polished language, curated images, and strategic emotional hooks:

- **Web Profile:** A psychopath writes, *"I've been told I'm a great listener—I'm here for deep conversations and real connections."* Their messages are warm, attentive, and laced with affirming statements like, "I've never met someone who gets me like you do."

- **Manipulative Strategy:** The polished, professional tone and curated persona lull victims into a false sense of security, establishing trust quickly and disarming skepticism.

Triggering Emotional Responses

Psychopaths use emotionally evocative stories and visuals to forge artificial intimacy:

- **Web Profile:** They share a carefully crafted sob story—perhaps about losing a loved one or overcoming adversity. This creates a sense of vulnerability and encourages the target to reciprocate with their own personal disclosures.

- **Manipulative Strategy:** By controlling the emotional narrative, psychopaths bond quickly with their targets, fostering a false sense of intimacy and connection.

Online Lures

- **The "Perfect Match" Illusion:** A psychopath might mirror the interests and passions listed in a target's profile, creating the impression of a soulmate. For instance, if a victim loves hiking, the psychopath will post photos of mountaintop adventures and claim to *"feel most alive in the great outdoors."*

- **Digital Love Bombing:** They overwhelm the target with constant attention—likes, comments, and messages filled with admiration—creating an emotional high that the victim becomes dependent on.

- **Exploiting Social Proof:** Psychopaths often build fake networks or post images with friends, family, or colleagues to appear well-integrated and credible. For instance, a psychopath might share a photo at a charity event with the caption, *"So grateful to give back to the community—it's what keeps me grounded."*

- **Creating Urgency:** Once trust is established, they escalate the relationship quickly, claiming, *"I've never felt this way about anyone before"* or *"Life's too short to waste time—I just know we're meant to be."* This rush to intimacy leaves little time for victims to evaluate red flags.

Chapter 8: The Dark Web

How to Recognize a Potential Psychopath, Red Flags in Online Dating Profiles

Name: Dr. Michael R.[9]

Age: 41

Location: Chicago, IL **Occupation**: Pediatric Surgeon **About Me**:

"As a divorced father of two amazing kids, I understand what it means to cherish family and the moments that truly matter. Whether it's coaching my son's soccer team or having tea parties with my daughter, they remind me every day what's important."

"Now, I'm looking for someone to join me on this journey—a woman who's confident, compassionate, and ready to build something extraordinary together."

What I'm Looking For:

"A partner who values authenticity, warmth, and a little adventure. Someone who's equally at home enjoying a quiet dinner or packing for a last-minute weekend getaway. Bonus points if you love the sound of rain on a rooftop and deep conversations."

Interests:

- Morning runs by the lake (nothing clears the mind like fresh air).
- Cooking Italian food with my daughter (she's a budding chef!).

---

9 Example of what a profile might look like, drawn from a variety of sources.

- Volunteering at medical missions abroad (Honduras last summer was unforgettable).
- Reading memoirs and historical fiction—recommendations are welcome!

My Ideal Evening:

"After a long day in the operating room, I'd love to unwind with someone special—cooking dinner together, sharing stories over a glass of wine, and planning our next adventure."

Photos:

- Michael in scrubs, smiling warmly as he leans against a hospital wall.
- A candid photo of him at the park with his two kids, pushing his daughter on a swing.
- A professionally staged photo of him running by Lake Michigan at sunrise.
- A snapshot of Michael laughing with a group of children during a medical mission trip abroad.

How He Lures His Victims:

1. **Relatable Vulnerability:** By emphasizing his role as a devoted father and a man starting over after divorce, Michael creates a narrative that appeals to women seeking stability, family values, and emotional connection.

2. **Hero Persona:** His career as a pediatric surgeon and volunteering abroad portrays him as selfless, compassionate, and trustworthy—an archetypal "good guy."

3. **Emotional Hooks:** Phrases like *"resilience and love go hand in hand"* and *"building something extraordinary together"* evoke a sense of intimacy and exclusivity.

4. **Curated Photos:** The carefully selected images reinforce his narrative of being a caring father, dedicated professional, and adventurous soul, masking his manipulative intentions.

Red Flags for the Observant:

▶ **Too Perfect Narrative:** The profile crafts an image of an ideal partner—successful, emotionally available, and family-oriented—but lacks depth or specific personal anecdotes that feel genuine.

▶ **Superficial Vulnerability:** While he mentions his divorce and children, the focus is on garnering sympathy and admiration rather than revealing real challenges or growth.

▶ **Contradictory Lifestyle:** Despite his demanding career as a surgeon and being a single dad, he claims to have abundant time for travel, hobbies, and romance—a subtle inconsistency that suggests a curated persona.

▶ **Fast-Tracking Intimacy:** Once connected, he would likely escalate the relationship quickly, using his "busy schedule" as an excuse to rush emotional bonding or seek immediate trust.

How He Might Exploit Victims:

- **Love Bombing:** He showers his target with attention, frequent messages, and carefully worded expressions of admiration (*"I feel like I've known you forever"*).

- **Fabricated Crises:** Once trust is established, he might invent professional or personal emergencies, asking for financial or emotional support under the guise of vulnerability.

- **Isolation:** He subtly discourages his target from spending time with friends or family, framing it as a need for their undivided attention or shared exclusivity.

- **Emotional Manipulation:** By leveraging his role as a doctor and single father, he evokes sympathy to justify controlling behavior or evade accountability.

Key Questions to Distinguish Authenticity

When engaging with someone online, asking specific questions can help reveal authenticity:

- **Career Details:** An authentic doctor will discuss their profession with nuance, including both its rewards and challenges, while a manipulator might focus on the prestige or emotional appeal of their work.

  Example: *"What's the hardest part of balancing your career and being a parent?"*

- **Personal Stories:** Genuine individuals will provide specific, relatable anecdotes about their life experiences.

  Example: *"What's a favorite memory with your kids?"* An authentic response might feel personal and heartfelt, while a manipulator might give a vague or overly polished answer.

- **Handling Boundaries:** Authentic people respect your pace in the relationship, while a psychopath may push for quick emotional intimacy.

Example: *"What's your idea of a healthy relationship timeline?"* Manipulators may give an overly romanticized or idealized response.

Additional Warning Signs of Manipulation

- **Inconsistent Details:** Psychopaths might slip up, giving conflicting stories about their past, career, or family life.

- **Excessive Flattery:** Over-the-top compliments early in the interaction (e.g., **"You're unlike anyone I've ever met"**) can signal love bombing.

- **Deflection of Questions:** Avoidance of direct or probing questions about their life or experiences suggests they are hiding something.

- **Attempts to Create Dependency:** Phrases like "I've never felt so understood before" or "You're the one thing keeping me going" signal a manipulative attempt to bond quickly and deeply.

TRAIT	PSYCHOPATHIC DOCTOR	AUTHENTIC DOCTOR
NARRATIVE	Overly idealized and crafted to appeal to universal desires (family man, hero, adventurer).	Honest and balanced, reflecting both successes and challenges (e.g., struggles of parenting or work-life balance).
EMOTIONAL VULNERABILITY	Strategic and curated to elicit admiration or sympathy (e.g., "starting over after divorce").	Genuine and nuanced, with specific lessons learned from past experiences.
RELATIONSHIP TIMELINE	Escalates intimacy quickly; uses flattery and emotional hooks to create dependency.	Builds trust gradually, respecting the natural pace of the relationship.
PHOTOS	Perfectly staged to reinforce the idealized persona (e.g., polished family and work shots).	Includes casual, imperfect moments that reflect real-life spontaneity and authenticity.
ENGAGEMENT STYLE	Overly attentive and flattering early on; avoids detailed questions about their own life.	Open to dialogue and reflective; engages in meaningful conversations about shared values and goals.

Elliot's Illusionist

Elliot sat at the corner table of a dimly lit wine bar, nervously checking his phone. His date, Veronica, was ten minutes late. Normally, he wouldn't have waited this long, but there was something about her profile—her sophistication, her wit—that intrigued him. When she finally walked through the door, he felt his breath catch. She was stunning: sleek black dress, hair perfectly styled, and a smile that could stop traffic.

"Elliot," she said warmly, as though they were old friends. "Sorry to keep you waiting."

"No problem at all," he replied, standing to greet her. She placed a hand lightly on his arm, and he felt a strange electric jolt. She had a way of making him feel like the only man in the room.

Over the course of the evening, Veronica was magnetic. She asked thoughtful questions, laughed at his jokes, and seemed genuinely fascinated by his life. She shared stories about her glamorous job in marketing, her world travels, and her passion for photography. But looking back, Elliot would realize her answers were oddly vague—she never mentioned her company's name, only "clients." Her travels were a blur of exotic locations, but she never specified when or why she'd gone. At the time, though, Elliot didn't notice. He was too mesmerized by her intensity, by the way, she maintained unbroken eye contact, as though hanging on to his every word.

By the night's end, he felt a stronger connection than any he'd experienced. She suggested they see each other again, and he eagerly agreed. "I think we're going to be good for each other," she said, her smile both reassuring and unsettling.

Veronica confessed deep feelings within days of their first date. "I've never felt this way about anyone," she told him, her voice trembling. It was flattering, but her intensity didn't feel earned.

In the following weeks, Elliot and Veronica's relationship moved quickly—too quickly. She began showing up unexpectedly at his office with coffee or at his gym after a workout. At first, it felt romantic. "I just couldn't wait to see you," she'd say, her voice dripping with affection. But as time went on, her attention felt suffocating.

Veronica subtly began to distance Elliot from his friends. "They don't appreciate you like I do," she'd say. "You deserve better." It was flattering at first, but over time, he realized he was spending all his time with her.

When Elliot mentioned needing space after a long workday, Veronica's reaction was explosive. She accused him of not caring, of trying to push her away. Then, just as quickly, she softened, apologizing tearfully.

"I'm just scared of losing you," she said.

The first real crack came when Elliot left his phone unattended during dinner. When he returned, Veronica was holding it, scrolling through his messages.

"Who's 'Carol'?" she demanded, her voice icy.

"She's a coworker," Elliot stammered, grabbing his phone back.

"You're lying," Veronica snapped, her face instantly transforming from warmth to fury. "I can tell."

That night, he felt the first stirrings of unease. He began Googling signs of manipulative relationships and stumbled upon articles describing traits of psychopathy. Words like "charming," "controlling," and "manipulative" jumped off the page. But he dismissed it. *I'm overreacting*, he told himself. *She's just passionate.*

Elliot truly begins to see the danger when Veronica shows up uninvited at his parent's house during a family dinner. She claimed he'd "forgotten" to invite her and made a scene in front of his bewildered family. The following day, he discovered she'd been contacting his coworkers, asking questions about him under the guise of "planning a surprise."

The final straw came when Elliot found his apartment door unlocked one evening, with Veronica waiting inside. "I made a copy of your key," she admitted, as though it were the most natural thing in the world. "I thought it would bring us closer."

Elliot ended things that night, but Veronica didn't go quietly. Over the next few weeks, she bombarded him with messages—alternating between tearful apologies, grand romantic gestures, and veiled threats. He finally blocked her on all platforms and considered changing his locks.

Months after ending things, Elliot still felt the psychological toll of the relationship. He second-guessed his judgment and found it hard to trust again. But he also learned the importance of listening to his gut and recognizing red flags early. Veronica had been dangerous, not in the overt way of a villain in a thriller, but in the quiet, insidious way that left scars long after she was gone.

Chapter 8: The Dark Web

The Dirty John Case
Love, Lies, and the Anatomy of a Predator

The story of John Meehan, immortalized in the hit series *Dirty John*, is not just a tale of romance gone wrong—it's a chilling portrait of manipulation, deceit, and the catastrophic consequences of ignoring. red flags. Meehan's weapon was not physical force but charm, a seductive facade he used to ensnare his victims. For Debra Newell, a successful interior designer with a lifetime of hard-earned stability, Meehan seemed like the perfect partner. But beneath his polished exterior lurked a man capable of unimaginable cruelty.

When Debra met John on a dating app in 2014, he presented himself as a charismatic doctor with humanitarian ideals. He regaled her with tales of saving lives and his supposed altruistic ventures. To someone like Debra, who longed for companionship and admired integrity, John appeared to be everything she wanted. Their whirlwind romance escalated quickly—too quickly. Within weeks, he had moved into her Newport Beach home, weaving himself into her life and isolating her from family and friends.

What Debra couldn't see, or perhaps chose not to, were the glaring inconsistencies in John's story. He dressed the part of a successful professional but lacked the resources to back it up. His overly attentive nature, initially flattering, became suffocating and controlling. When her children raised concerns about John's erratic behavior and questionable past, he dismissed them with calculated charm, turning Debra against the very people trying to protect her.

The truth about John Meehan unraveled slowly but devastatingly. Far from being a doctor, he was a con artist with a criminal record that spanned decades. His history was littered with restraining orders, fraud charges, and a reputation for targeting women, isolating them, and draining their finances. When Debra ended their relationship,

John's predatory nature culminated in escalating threats and violent confrontations, ultimately leading to a final, deadly showdown with Debra's daughter, Terra (who survived).

In hindsight, the signs were there, glaring and undeniable. John's rapid attachment, his insistence on moving in, and his attempts to alienate Debra from her family were classic hallmarks of an abuser. His polished exterior hid the cracks in his persona: vague answers about his past, an overcompensation of charm, and an unwillingness to accept scrutiny. But like so many victims, Debra's desire to believe in love and overlook the warning signs blinded her to the danger.

The lessons from this case are both chilling and essential. Victims of predators like John Meehan rarely miss the signs—they dismiss them. They ignore subtle inconsistencies, override gut instincts, and rationalize behavior that should set off alarms.

The key to self-protection isn't paranoia—it's vigilance. When someone's story doesn't add up, listen to that discomfort. Background checks aren't paranoia; they're due diligence. If friends and family raise concerns, take them seriously—predators count on their victims to isolate themselves from outside perspectives. And most importantly, never feel pressured to move faster than feel safe. Speed is a predator's tool—slowing down is your defense.

Abusers don't just manipulate their victims; they manipulate perceptions—but the truth always leaves a trail. The difference between escape and entrapment isn't whether the trail exists; it's whether you trust yourself enough to follow it before it's too late.

The Grace Millane Case
A Portrait of Predation

Grace Millane's tragic death in December 2018 was not a random act of violence. It was the culmination of a calculated encounter orchestrated by a man who epitomized the traits of a cold-blooded predator: manipulative charm, deceit, and an utter absence of empathy. Jesse Kempson, the man she met on Tinder, hid behind a carefully constructed facade—a textbook example of a psychopathic personality, weaponizing trust to devastating effect.

Grace Millane, a 22-year-old British backpacker, was the perfect target: trusting, adventurous, and far from home. Kempson, 26, matched with her on Tinder and wasted no time deploying his charm. He presented himself as a charismatic and worldly man, luring Grace into a false sense of security.

Their date on December 1, 2018, began like any other—a series of casual drinks in Auckland's bustling bars. CCTV footage shows them laughing, walking arm-in-arm, a predator carefully mirroring his prey's ease and trust. But beneath the surface, Kempson was studying her vulnerabilities, preparing to strike.

That night, Grace accompanied Kempson to his apartment in the CityLife Hotel, and at some point that night, she died of strangulation. Strangulation—a deeply personal and violent act—reflects domination, a hallmark of the psychopathic drive for control. What happened next exposes the terrifying reality of individuals like him: Kempson claimed Grace's death was an accident during consensual rough sex. The facts, however, tell a different story.

Far from panicking or showing remorse, Kempson displayed chilling composure. He scoured the internet for disposal methods, purchased a suitcase and cleaning supplies, and coldly transported Grace's body to the Waitākere Ranges, where he buried her in a shallow grave.

Jesse Kempson was not new to this. He had a history of predatory behavior, using dating apps to charm women, manipulate them, and ultimately exploit their trust. His ex-partners described a man capable of spinning elaborate lies, exerting control, and resorting to violence when challenged. Grace was simply his next target.

Kempson's ability to conceal his true nature underscores a critical point: predators like him thrive on society's naivety, leveraging tools like dating apps to hunt in plain sight. His composed demeanor after the murder and his audacious defense during the trial reveal an individual devoid of empathy and accountability.

In February 2020, Kempson was sentenced to life in prison with a minimum of 17 years before parole. But his impact extends far beyond a courtroom. Grace's death became a global warning—a chilling reminder of how predators camouflage themselves in plain sight, using modern dating culture as their hunting ground.

Like many victims, Grace mistook charm for safety. The public setting, the casual conversation—each step carefully orchestrated to lower her guard. The shift to Kempson's apartment wasn't just a change in location; it was the moment control transferred entirely to him.

Predators don't just overpower their victims—they disarm their instincts. Kempson's calculated demeanor ensured that by the time Grace sensed danger, it was already too late. Recognizing these patterns isn't about fear—it's about awareness. Because the most dangerous people aren't the ones who look like threats; they're the ones who don't.

If there is one takeaway from all of this, it is what security specialist Gavin de Becker, in *The Gift of Fear*, calls ignoring intuition and dismissing early warning signs. His work emphasizes that intuition is a powerful, often lifesaving tool, particularly for women, who are culturally conditioned to downplay or suppress their instincts to avoid seeming rude, paranoid, or overly dramatic. Fear is not the enemy—it's an ally, a signal designed to protect. We must learn to listen to that whisper of unease without dismissing it as irrational. Intuition often surfaces as a vague discomfort or urgency, and instead of silencing it, one should ask, *what is this feeling trying to tell me?*

Saying "no" without guilt is not just a right—it's a survival skill. Predators count on societal pressure to be polite, using it as leverage to erode boundaries. A firm refusal disrupts their control, revealing their true intentions. Understanding context through De Becker's JACA model—examining Justification (the person's perceived threat), Alternatives (does the person have choices?), Consequences (what happens if the person carries out the threat?) and Ability (are they capable?)— help assess whether someone poses a real threat. However, just as critical is recognizing "forced teaming," a manipulative tactic predators use to create a false sense of partnership where none exists.

Consider, for example, the rideshare driver who insists on walking a female passenger to her door, saying, "*We should be careful out here—let's get you inside safely.*" The use of "we" implies a shared concern and partnership in her safety, but the reality is she never invited that level of involvement. The driver is inserting himself into a moment of vulnerability under the guise of helpfulness, subtly pressuring her to comply out of politeness or fear of seeming ungrateful.

But genuine assistance doesn't require manufactured unity **or** persistence. A person with good intentions offers help but accepts "no" without resistance. Recognizing forced teaming for what it is—a strategy, not kindness—allows potential victims to disengage without guilt and maintain control over their own safety.

Recognizing manipulation in the abstract is one thing—falling for it is another. Even the most perceptive people can be drawn in when deception is wrapped in charm, confidence, and the illusion of destiny.

Claire's Story

Claire couldn't believe her luck. After years of uneventful dating, she had finally met the one. Drake was everything she'd ever dreamed of:

charming, articulate, and devastatingly handsome. He had swept into her life during an art gallery opening, dazzling her with stories about his work as a high-profile attorney at one of the most prestigious law firms in the city.

"He's incredible," Claire gushed to her neighbor, Linda, over coffee one morning. "He's handled cases for celebrities, Fortune 500 companies—you name it! Last night, he was telling me about a billion-dollar merger he's negotiating."

Linda raised an eyebrow. "That sounds... impressive," she said, her tone measured.

Claire didn't notice. Over the next few weeks, she proudly shared every detail of Drake's whirlwind romance: the dinners at exclusive restaurants, the designer gifts, and the promises of weekend trips to the Hamptons. Her neighbors marveled at her stories, except for Linda, who listened with quiet skepticism.

There was something off about Drake. Linda had spent years as an investigative journalist, and her instincts were tingling. His anecdotes were too polished, too cinematic. The way Claire described him made Drake sound like he'd stepped out of a romance novel. And yet, there was something naggingly absent—no pictures of his office, no phone calls where she overheard his "important" negotiations.

One evening, Linda decided to dig deeper. Armed with her laptop, she searched for Drake at McMillan & Stokes. The firm's website listed all their attorneys, but Drake wasn't one of them. Maybe he wasn't listed? She tried a broader search, checking LinkedIn, social media, and legal directories. Nothing. He didn't exist.

Linda decided to get bolder. At the next neighborhood potluck, she casually mentioned a friend who worked in mergers and acquisitions. "He's with McMillan & Stokes too," Linda lied smoothly, watching Drake's face closely. "Maybe you know him?"

Drake blinked, his easy smile faltering for the briefest moment before he recovered. "McMillan's a big firm," he said, brushing it off. "I'm mostly tied up in litigation these days."

That night, Linda pulled Claire aside. "I think you need to be careful," she said. "I couldn't find any proof Drake works where he says he does. Something's not adding up."

Claire laughed nervously. "Oh, Linda. It's probably just because private lawyers are careful about their online presence. He is the real deal. I know it."

But doubt had been planted, and over the next few days, Claire began noticing small cracks. Drake's evasive answers about his schedule. His vague responses when she asked about his clients. Finally, the breaking point came when Linda uncovered a shocking truth: Drake had a criminal record under a different name—a history of fraud and impersonation.

Confronted with the evidence, Drake dropped the facade, transforming from suave to sinister in a heartbeat. "What does it matter?" he sneered. "You loved the life I gave you, didn't you?"

The revelation shattered Claire, but with Linda's support, she pressed charges. In the end, Drake was exposed as a con artist who had spent years charming his way into the lives—and wallets—of vulnerable women. Claire had been lucky to escape before the damage became irreparable, but the experience left her wiser, with a keen understanding of how predators operate in plain sight.

CHAPTER NINE
THE ETHICS OF LABELING

"So can 1 just label my kid a psychopath if he meets the criteria?"

AI AND PSYCHOPATHY
The Rise of Detection Tools

Artificial Intelligence (AI) is emerging as a tool for identifying psychopathic tendencies by analyzing speech patterns, facial expressions, and digital footprints. Researchers are training algorithms to detect key markers: manipulative language, shallow emotional responses, and a lack of empathy. These systems process vast amounts of data, searching for linguistic and behavioral cues indicative of psychopathy—examining vocal tone, cadence, and response patterns, even in job interviews.

The idea of AI flagging potential predators in high-stakes environments—corporate hiring, politics, or online dating—raises compelling possibilities. Could we prevent a psychopath from infiltrating a workplace, deceiving colleagues, or manipulating trust? In the right hands, such technology might serve as an early warning system, much like behavioral profiling in criminal investigations.

But there are risks. Who defines psychopathy? What if AI

misidentifies traits, branding someone unfairly? The promise of early intervention is tempered by the peril of misuse. In the end, the question is not just whether we *can* build such systems but whether we *should*.

AI tools, however sophisticated, remain dependent on human judgment—introducing a fundamental flaw. Psychopathy exists on a spectrum, and algorithms struggle with nuance. The risk of false positives—wrongly branding someone as a psychopath—can have devastating consequences, deraling careers and reputations. Consider a job candidate whose anxiety presents as detachment or defensiveness. An algorithm lacking human context might misinterpret these cues as manipulative behavior, unjustly compromising their future. Given AI's limitations and the subjective nature of psychopathy, rigorous validation is essential before such technology determines real-world outcomes.

This scenario echoes the movie *Minority Report*, where predictive technology preemptively punishes people for crimes not yet committed. Predictive policing—using algorithms to anticipate criminal behavior—has raised profound concerns about civil liberties, bias, and the ethical use of technology. The power to label someone a psychopath based on an algorithm's assessment is fraught with risk, opening the door to misuse and deepening societal inequalities.

Yet the potential benefits of AI in identifying psychopathic traits cannot be dismissed. If refined to reduce false positives and distinguish psychopathy from other disorders, it could offer valuable insights into human behavior. Early detection might help individuals and institutions guard against those who manipulate, deceive, and exploit without obvious warning signs. In high-stakes fields like law enforcement, business, and politics, such technology—if wielded responsibly—could be a powerful tool for protection. But the fundamental question remains: who controls it, and how far should we trust it?

Law enforcement agencies in the U.S. and UK already use AI-driven micro expression analysis to assess deception during interrogations. AI models analyze subtle facial cues—such as involuntary tics or changes in blink rate—that humans might miss. China employs emotion recognition AI in public surveillance, monitoring people's stress levels at airports and public transportation hubs to flag potential security threats.

While not designed for psychopathy detection, Meta's DeepFace facial recognition system has been used to match individuals across multiple online accounts, even when they try to anonymize their identities. This has been helpful in identifying catfishers, fraudsters, and traffickers. Similarly, DARPA[10]'s social media in Strategic Communication (SMISC) Program has actively researched social media behavior patterns to detect online radicalization, coercion, and manipulation. Their AI models analyze linguistic patterns, sudden changes in posting frequency, and engagement with extremist or deceptive narratives. ISIS Recruitment Detection (U.S. Intelligence & Tech Companies), in partnership with Google's Jigsaw, AI-driven programs analyze online behavior to detect radicalization and recruitment attempts.

Thorn, a nonprofit organization fighting child trafficking, partnered with DARPA to develop AI that scans escort ads, social media profiles, and chat messages to identify patterns of coercion, deception, and recruitment by traffickers. The FBI uses AI-driven interrogation tools to analyze speech patterns, pauses, and inconsistencies in responses to detect deception. These tools use a mix of natural language processing (NLP) and vocal stress analysis.

While controversial, COMPAS (Correctional Offender Management Profiling for Alternative Sanctions) is used in U.S. courts to assess the

---

10 Defense Advanced Research Projects Agency

likelihood of recidivism. Though not explicitly detecting psychopathy, it evaluates behavioral risk factors linked to antisocial behavior and repeat offenses.

AI-driven online scam detection chatbots (Facebook, Twitter, FBI's IC3 unit) analyze fraudulent online conversations to detect scams, impersonation, and coercion tactics. These models detect psychological manipulation patterns used by con artists and cyber criminals.

While these AI tools are not yet diagnosing psychopathy outright, they are actively used to detect deception, manipulation, coercion, and antisocial behavior—all traits often associated with psychopathy. Their integration into criminal investigations, human trafficking prevention, and counterterrorism is already changing how law enforcement operates.

But its implications extend beyond criminal investigations and into everyday life. The ability to identify deception and manipulation also raises questions about how society perceives and labels individuals.

What happens when the fine line between human judgment and algorithmic detection blurs? When technology evaluates behavior, does it capture the full story, or does it impose a narrative of its own?

The False Label
Cooper's Fall

Cooper stood in the breakroom of his elementary school, waiting for the coffee pot to fill. The hum of laughter from the hallway—students sharing stories, teachers swapping advice—was a sound Cooper had come to treasure. Teaching had always been more than a job; it was a calling.

That calling unraveled the day a parent stormed into the principal's office, claiming Cooper had "emotionally manipulated" their child during a heated parent-teacher conference. The allegation was vague, but it was enough to prompt an administrative review.

Weeks later, Cooper sat across from a psychologist, who peppered him with questions about relationships, conflicts, and choices. The questions felt loaded, but Cooper answered honestly. The psychologist's tone remained detached. When the report came back, it included a chilling conclusion: Cooper exhibited traits consistent with psychopathy.

It didn't matter that the evidence was circumstantial. Word of the diagnosis spread quickly through the district. Whispers followed Cooper in the hallways. Parents withdrew their children from Cooper's class. Co-workers stopped sharing casual conversations, their laughter fading to silence when Cooper entered the room.

At first, Cooper tried to fight back. "This isn't me," he told anyone who would listen. But the label was immutable, a stain on his reputation that no amount of protesting could erase.

Within months, Cooper was forced to resign. Job applications in other districts went unanswered; references subtly hinted at "complications" in his employment history. Friends drifted away. Even Alex's sister hesitated when Cooper offered to babysit her kids.

The isolation was suffocating. Cooper, once vibrant and connected, became a recluse, haunted by a label that didn't fit. Depression took hold. And yet, Cooper's story wasn't the only tragedy.

The school community, wary of repeating its mistake, became paralyzed by fear. Teachers hesitated to enforce discipline, worried about how their actions might be misconstrued. Parents questioned the motives of every educator, creating a climate of mistrust that fractured relationships.

The cost of a false diagnosis wasn't just Cooper's ruined life—it was a community that had lost its ability to function as a safe, trusting environment.

Chapter 9: The Ethics of Labeling

The Accurate Label
Michelle's Rise

Michelle entered the council chambers with a smile that could light up the darkest room. Every eye turned her way. Michelle had a gift: making people feel seen, important, and heard. But behind the charm was something colder—a calculated hunger for power.

For years, Michelle's rise had been meteoric. From student government to state politics, she always seemed to know the right people, say the right things, and make the right moves. However, cracks in the facade began to show when a whistleblower accused Michelle of embezzling campaign funds.

The investigation that followed was damning. Financial records painted a clear picture of deceit. And then came the psychological evaluation, conducted as part of Michelle's defense strategy. The result was chillingly precise: Michelle scored high on the Psychopathy Checklist.

When the diagnosis leaked, the public reaction was split. Some dismissed it as an exaggeration, a smear tactic by political enemies. Others demanded Michelle resign immediately. But Michelle was nothing if not adaptable.

At a press conference, Michelle stood at the podium, radiating confidence. "This so-called diagnosis is an attack on my character, a label thrown around without understanding," she said. "But let me be clear: I will not let this distract from the work I'm doing for this community."

And remarkably, it worked. Supporters rallied. Doubters were shamed into silence. Behind the scenes, Michelle doubled down on manipulation, using the diagnosis as a shield. "People already think I'm a monster," Michelle told her closest aides. "So why not play the part?"

The fallout was devastating. Colleagues who questioned Michelle's decisions found themselves ostracized or mysteriously embroiled in *scandals. Community leaders who tried to expose the truth were discredited. Over time, Michelle's unchecked behavior led to a string of abuses: policies that benefited only Michelle's allies, contracts awarded to corrupt companies, and intimidation of anyone who dared resist.*

By the time the full extent of Michelle's harm came to light, the damage was irreparable. Trust in the political system had crumbled. Voters, disillusioned and cynical, turned away from civic engagement.

In the hands of a true psychopath, the label "psychopath" became a weapon—a tool of deflection and power consolidation.

Dr. Robert Hare's PCL-R checklist was designed as a clinical tool for assessing psychopathy—not as a predictor of future crime. Yet in legal settings, it is frequently misused to justify harsher sentences and parole denials, despite its inherent limitations. Courts often treat it as a crystal ball, ignoring the ethical and scientific concerns surrounding its application in determining criminality.

Beyond misuse, the PCL-R also carries biases that disproportionately impact marginalized communities. Traits like manipulativeness or impulsivity are shaped by cultural and social contexts, yet the tool applies a rigid framework, often mislabeling individuals based on factors beyond their control. The result? A troubling overrepresentation of certain groups in the "psychopathic" category reinforces systemic inequalities within the justice system. When misapplied, the PCL-R doesn't just assess psychopathy—it manufactures it.

Another major criticism is the tendency to conflate psychopathy with general criminality. While psychopathy involves a distinct set of personality traits—such as emotional detachment, lack of empathy, and pathological lying—the checklist is often misinterpreted as a measure of antisocial or criminal behavior. This misunderstanding leads to the overdiagnosis of psychopathy in incarcerated populations, where antisocial behavior may be prevalent, but true psychopathy, as defined by the PCL-R, is comparatively rare. By equating psychopathy with criminal conduct, the checklist risks being misused as a justification for punitive rather than rehabilitative measures. These issues underscore the need for careful and ethical application of the PCL-R. While it remains a valuable tool when used by trained professionals in its proper context, its misuse as a predictive or diagnostic instrument in legal settings can lead to unjust outcomes and erode confidence in psychological assessments. To prevent these misapplications, greater oversight, education, and adherence to the tool's original purpose are essential.

Cinematic Portrayals Oversimplify and Mislead

In the film *Primal Fear*, a young altar boy, Aaron Stampler (Edward Norton), is accused of murdering an archbishop. Throughout the film, Aaron appears meek and traumatized, but during his trial, it is revealed he has a psychopathic alter ego, Roy. However, it's all a calculated act. Aaron's false portrayal as a dissociative identity disorder patient manipulates the justice system. The mislabeling of his true condition (psychopathy) allows him to evade accountability, illustrating how dangerous it can be to accept diagnostic labels without thorough examination.

In *The Bad Seed*, young Rhoda Penmark (Patty McCormack) is a seemingly innocent child who manipulates and kills to achieve her goals. She is never formally labeled as a psychopath, but her mother suspects something is inherently wrong with her. The lack of a clear label leaves her parents and society unprepared to address her behavior. Rhoda's psychopathy remains unchecked, leading to further tragedy. This highlights how failure to recognize and label psychopathy can prevent meaningful intervention and accountability.

In the classic *American Psycho*, Patrick Bateman (Christian Bale) is labeled a psychopath due to his violent and sadistic tendencies. However, the film leaves ambiguous whether his acts are real or figments of his imagination, challenging the reliability of the label. The ambiguity around Bateman's reality creates a distorted understanding of psychopathy, with the label overshadowing his profound alienation, narcissism, and detachment from reality. The fallout lies in the viewer's potential conflation of psychopathy with purely performative or self-indulgent behavior.

In *Shutter Island*, U.S. Marshal Teddy Daniels (Leonardo DiCaprio) investigates a mental institution, only to discover he's a patient himself. The staff labels him as delusional and dangerous, but the truth of his diagnosis remains ambiguous. The potential mislabeling of Teddy raises questions about the reliability of psychiatric diagnoses and their impact on individuals. The film explores the devastating consequences of being labeled without full consideration of one's history or motives.

CHAPTER TEN
PSYCHOLOGICAL ABUSE AND ITS IMPACT

There Is No "Right" to Remain Silent

MARIA DIDN'T FALL in love with a monster; she fell in love with a dream. James was the kind of man who made you feel like the only person in the world. From the moment they met, he seemed to study her, not in a creepy way, but in a way that felt... intimate. He remembered the tiniest details about her life, asked questions no one had ever thought to ask, and made her feel truly seen.

"I've never met anyone like you," he would whisper, his eyes locking with hers in a way that made her believe it was true. "You're so special, Maria." Those words were a balm to wounds she didn't even know she had. It wasn't long before she felt a gravitational pull toward him, a sense that they were meant to be.

That's how love bombing works. It's not love at all—it's control disguised as devotion. Psychopaths like James are masters at it. They overwhelm their targets with affection, attention, and intensity, building a connection that feels like destiny. They mirror your desires, reflecting the image of everything you've ever wanted. But it's a performance, a calculated act to gain trust, to pull you in close so they can begin their real work: dismantling you.

For Maria, the shift was so subtle she didn't even notice it at first. The compliments and devotion were still there, but they began to come with conditions. "Why do you need to go out with them tonight? Don't I make you happy?" he'd ask, his voice soft, his tone wounded. At first, she stayed home because she wanted to make him happy. But soon, it became easier to stay home just to avoid the guilt trips. Her world started to shrink, but she told herself it was because she'd found her person. She didn't need anyone else.

The gaslighting started around the same time. It wasn't overt, not in the beginning. It was in the small, forgettable moments. She'd mention something he'd said a week earlier, and he'd laugh. "Maria, I never said that" he'd reply, shaking his head like she'd just told a bad joke. Or he'd contradict himself, and when she pointed it out, he'd say, "You're always looking for a fight." Those little moments piled up like pebbles in her pocket until one day; she was so weighed down she couldn't trust her own memories.

When Maria tried to set boundaries, he would shift tactics, moving seamlessly from blame to victimhood. "I'm only trying to help you," he'd say. "Why do you always twist everything I do into something bad?" And just like that, the roles would reverse. She would find herself apologizing, desperate to make him understand that she wasn't trying to hurt him. She didn't realize that every apology was another thread in the web he was spinning around her.

Isolation came next. James didn't need to demand she cut people out of her life; he simply made it difficult for her to keep them in it. "I don't think your friends like me," he'd say casually. "They're so negative. They don't understand what we have." Maria found herself canceling plans, avoiding calls, and choosing him over them again and again. Her world grew smaller still until it was just the two of them, orbiting around his needs, his moods, and his version of reality.

The psychological toll was staggering, though Maria wouldn't have described it that way at the time. She just felt... tired. All the time. She stopped recognizing herself in the mirror. The vibrant, confident woman she used to be had been replaced by someone small, uncertain, and afraid. But afraid of what? He wasn't violent. He didn't yell. He didn't need to. The fear came from something deeper—a sense that she was losing herself and didn't know how to stop it.

Maria's breaking point came one night when she confronted him with evidence of a lie. She had the texts—proof he'd been seeing someone else. She laid her phone on the table, trembling, and waited for his reaction. James didn't deny it. Instead, he flipped the script entirely. "So, you're spying on me now?" he said, his voice calm but edged with disappointment. "Do you see how crazy you're acting? This is why we have problems, Maria."

By the end of the conversation, she was the one apologizing. For checking his phone. For doubting him. For everything. That's how deeply he'd gotten inside her head. She couldn't even hold him accountable for the ways he was destroying her because he'd made her believe it was all her fault.

Psychopaths like James are patient. They don't rush the process because they don't need to. The longer they play the game, the more control they gain. And the more control they gain, the harder it becomes for their victims to leave. For Maria, it took months of therapy, the support of family she'd pushed away, and an almost superhuman effort to rebuild her sense of self before she could finally walk away.

Even now, the scars remain. She flinches when people tell her she's overreacting. She apologizes too often. She second-guesses her decisions. But she's learning. Every day, she takes another step toward reclaiming the life James tried to steal from her.

Psychological abuse is a cage you cannot see, and it is often harder to escape than one with bars. But Maria's story is proof that it's possible. It's a reminder that the tactics of love bombing, gaslighting, and isolation are not love—they're control. No matter how convincing the mask of the abuser may be, it can be shattered by truth, courage, and the refusal to stay silent.

The High Cost of Ignoring Psychological Abuse

The high cost of ignoring psychological abuse is not just a personal tragedy—it's a societal failure with far-reaching consequences. Victims of psychological abuse, especially at the hands of psychopathic partners, often endure long-term damage that extends far beyond the immediate relationship. Chronic PTSD is one of the most prevalent outcomes, as the constant gaslighting, manipulation, and undermining of their reality leave victims questioning their own perceptions, judgment, and worth. This erosion of trust in oneself is deeply debilitating and often requires years of intensive therapy to rebuild. Mental health decline is another pervasive effect. Victims frequently experience anxiety, depression, and even suicidal ideation as they grapple with the emotional devastation inflicted by their abuser. Psychopaths are adept at isolating their victims, stripping them of support systems, and leaving them to feel utterly alone and dependent, which exacerbates these mental health challenges.

The economic impact of psychological abuse is equally devastating. Many victims find themselves financially drained, either through direct financial control by their abuser or the consequences of manipulation that leave them unable to maintain independence. For example, an abuser might coerce a victim into quitting a job, taking on excessive debt or surrendering control of shared assets. This financial dependency not only leaves victims trapped in abusive situations but also makes recovery profoundly difficult when they finally escape. Rebuilding a life—securing stable housing, reentering the workforce, and regaining financial security—becomes an uphill battle that many victims are ill-equipped to face.

Addressing psychological abuse requires more than awareness—it demands concrete legal reforms and societal support systems. For instance, mandatory training for law enforcement and family court officials to identify and understand the dynamics of psychological abuse could lead to better outcomes for victims. Economic safety nets, such as emergency financial assistance and job placement programs, could help survivors regain independence and stability.

Ultimately, the refusal to take psychological abuse seriously does not just harm individuals—it weakens the fabric of society. Recognizing the true scope of this abuse and implementing mechanisms to deter it is not just a moral imperative but a practical necessity for fostering healthier, more resilient communities. This is not merely about protecting victims; it is about addressing the broader human and economic costs of ignoring a form of violence that is every bit as destructive as physical harm, albeit in ways that are harder to see but impossible to ignore.

The Cycle—*Why do Victims Stay Too Long*?

Trauma bonding is not love—it's captivity. Built on manipulation and fear, it thrives on a cycle of intermittent reinforcement—moments of affection followed by cruelty. The abuser's unpredictability creates dependency, conditioning the victim to endure suffering in exchange for fleeting kindness. They don't stay for love. They stay for hope.

By distorting reality and severing connections, the abuser makes themselves the victim's sole reference point. The fear of abandonment becomes a powerful chain, tethering them to their tormentor. And the brain's stress and bonding hormones create a biochemical addiction, keeping the victim hooked. They don't crave the abuser. They crave relief.

Compounding this attachment is the concept of learned helplessness. Repeated cycles of abuse erode the victim's confidence, making escape feel impossible. Cognitive dissonance forces the victim to justify staying—clinging to the abuser's "good" moments while suppressing the reality of harm. Breaking free requires strategy, not willpower. Recognizing the cycle is the first step. Support from trusted allies and trauma-informed professionals is essential. No contact weakens the bond, while rebuilding self-worth restores autonomy.

But theory is one thing—living it is another. For many survivors, breaking free isn't a single moment but a slow unraveling of everything they once believed.

Robin's Story

The house was always pristine. Not a single cushion out of place, not a speck of dust on the shelves. Robin took great pride in maintaining her home as if the perfect veneer of her surroundings could reflect the perfect life she believed she had. The neighbors often commented on how lucky she was—her husband, Joe, was charming, successful, and attentive. "The dream couple," they'd say with smiles that Robin basked in.

But the truth was that Robin's world had cracks, deep fissures she refused to acknowledge. Joe worked late hours, often returning home long after she'd gone to bed. He traveled frequently for business, though Robin could never quite remember the names of the companies he worked for or the details of his trips. When she asked, Joe would laugh softly and tousle her hair. "You wouldn't want to bore yourself with the details, sweetheart," he'd say, his eyes twinkling in that way that always disarmed her.

Joe's life outside their home was an enigma, but Robin chose to see what she wanted to see: a devoted husband who provided for her and their two young daughters. Joe was a master of duplicity, a textbook

Chapter 9: Psychological Abuse and Its Impact

psychopath living a double life. By day, he played the role of a successful businessman and loving family man. By night, he became someone entirely different—a predator in expensive suits, scouring online forums for marks to exploit, indulging in affairs, and running a web of illicit schemes that brought in far more money than his "corporate job" ever could.

He was careful, in how he managed both lives. His charm was his most potent weapon. Robin's trust, her unwavering belief in his goodness, was the shield that protected him from scrutiny. When he forgot anniversaries or missed school recitals, he'd buy her a bracelet or whisk her away for a surprise weekend trip. The neighbors and Robin's friends saw these gestures as proof of his devotion. Robin saw them as evidence of the life she wanted to believe in.

The first crack appeared on a Wednesday evening. Robin was sorting through the mail when she came across a letter addressed to a "Mr. Riley" at their address. She furrowed her brow, confused, and handed it to Joe when he came home.

"Oh, that's just a mix-up at work," he said smoothly, sliding the envelope into his pocket before she could ask more. His casual tone seemed genuine, but the faint flicker in his expression unsettled her.

Days later, Robin found a burner phone hidden in Joe's closet while searching for a misplaced shoe. Her stomach churned as she scrolled through messages to a woman named "Lila," the exchanges flirtatious, filled with promises of trips to exotic places. Robin's world should have crumbled, but instead, her mind rebelled against the evidence. It's not what it looks like. There's an explanation.

When Joe returned that night, she confronted him, her voice trembling. Joe's reaction was flawless. He laughed softly; his hands raised in mock surrender. "You caught me," he said, his grin disarming. "It's for a surprise I was planning for us—a little getaway. Lila is the travel agent. She's been helping me with the details."

Robin's relief was instantaneous, as though her mind had been waiting for permission to let go of its doubts. She hugged him tightly, apologizing for snooping, and the matter was closed. Joe's deception had worked, yet again.

Months passed, and the signs became harder to ignore. Joe's trips grew longer, his excuses thinner. A neighbor mentioned seeing Joe at a downtown hotel with a woman who wasn't Robin. Robin laughed it off, saying it must have been a colleague. But at night, she lay awake, her heart pounding.

Eventually, the truth spilled out in the ugliest of ways. Joe's schemes caught up with him—an investor he had defrauded tracked him down, confronting him in a crowded restaurant. By then, Robin's carefully constructed reality had already started to collapse. Bank accounts were drained, debts she didn't recognize were piling up, and Joe's absences became more frequent and unexplained.

When the police finally arrived to arrest Joe, Robin still clung to her denial. "There's been a mistake," she told the officers. "Joe's a good man. He couldn't have done these things."

Joe's ability to lead a double life was rooted in his psychopathic traits: charm, manipulation, and a complete lack of empathy. He knew exactly how to prey on Robin's trust and her desire for stability. He used her unwavering belief in the perfect marriage as a shield, ensuring that even when the evidence of his lies was laid bare, she would rationalize it away.

For Joe, Robin was a means to an end—a prop in his carefully orchestrated facade. Her love and trust made his deception possible, allowing him to live two lives without consequence for far longer than anyone might have imagined.

After Joe's conviction, Robin was left to pick up the pieces of her shattered life. She replayed every moment, every red flag she had ignored, and wondered how she could have been so blind.

Chapter 9: Psychological Abuse and Its Impact

Friends and neighbors who had once envied her life now whispered behind her back, dissecting her failure to see the truth.

But Robin wasn't entirely to blame. Joe's manipulation was masterful, his lies seamless. Psychopaths like him thrive on their ability to distort reality, to bend the perceptions of those around them until their victims can no longer trust their own instincts. And in the quiet of the now empty house, Robin finally faced the most haunting question of all: *Had she really not seen it—or had she chosen not to?*

Robin often dismissed her initial feelings of unease. When red flags emerged—like the mysterious letter, the burner phone, or the neighbor's comment—she rationalized them away, preferring to believe in Joe's explanations.

Trusting her instincts would have been the first step toward facing reality. While it's natural to want to believe the best of a loved one, persistent doubt and recurring red flags shouldn't be ignored. Robin could have acknowledged her discomfort as valid and taken it seriously.

Sharing her suspicions with a trusted friend, family member, or counselor might have offered clarity. Outsiders are often better positioned to spot patterns of manipulation and dishonesty because they're less emotionally involved.

She could have taken photos of the messages, saved any questionable documents for future reference, and cross-checked his explanations. For example, she could have called "Lila" to confirm Joe's story about her being a travel agent, or used technology to verify his whereabouts, such as checking phone records or financial statements for inconsistencies.

Joe repeatedly dismissed Robin's questions with charm and vague reassurances, effectively shutting down her concerns.

Setting firm boundaries about transparency in their marriage could have forced Joe to be more forthcoming—or revealed more of his duplicity. For instance: Insisting on clearer communication about his work and travels. Asking for access to shared financial accounts to monitor transactions.

The frequent absences, often accompanied by vague explanations, should have raised red flags, but instead, they became part of the fabric of their everyday lives, accepted without question. Furthermore, Joe's lack of genuine emotional connection during conversations—his cold, calculated responses devoid of empathy—was another key indicator of his true nature, yet it went unnoticed or dismissed as normal. Perhaps most insidiously, Joe was able to turn Robin's suspicions back onto her, making her feel guilty for even questioning his actions, a common tactic among psychopaths to deflect blame and maintain control.

One of the most dangerous aspects of Joe's manipulation was his control over their financial resources. By tying Robin's financial stability to his own, he exploited her dependence and created a sense of vulnerability, then left her exposed when his schemes eventually unraveled. Maintaining some level of financial and emotional independence is crucial in any relationship, especially one where manipulation is at play. Robin could have taken simple yet effective steps to protect herself. Keeping a separate savings account would have given her a safety net, allowing her to maintain some control over her financial future. Consulting a financial advisor or lawyer about their shared assets, particularly when her doubts first began to emerge, could have provided clarity and a legal framework to safeguard her interests. Additionally, building a support system of friends or community members whom she could turn to for advice or emotional support would have helped Robin navigate the complexities of her relationship with Joe and may have offered the outside perspective necessary to see through his deceit. The failure to take these precautionary steps left Robin exposed to Joe's manipulations, but in retrospect, they were all actionable steps that could have mitigated the damage caused by his psychopathic behavior.

Robin avoided seeking outside help, likely due to denial and a fear of what she might uncover. Consulting professionals like a therapist, private investigator, or attorney could have helped Robin confirm her suspicions and prepare for potential fallout. A therapist could have guided her through the emotional challenges of facing the truth—that Joe's behavior was inconsistent with a loving partner, and that her version of their life might be a distortion.

While Joe's psychopathy and skillful deception made him difficult to uncover, Robin's denial and unwillingness to act on her instincts contributed to her prolonged vulnerability. By trusting herself, seeking help, and setting boundaries, she could have uncovered Joe's double life sooner and mitigated the fallout. The lesson here isn't just about vigilance but also about the courage to face uncomfortable truths and prioritize self-preservation over the illusion of stability.

The fight against psychopathy isn't just about identifying the monsters in our midst—it's about arming ourselves with knowledge, resilience, and the courage to see the truth. Because, in the end, the only way to defeat the devil is to stop pretending he doesn't exist.

Unresolved Trauma

Research suggests that those who have been in toxic relationships are at a higher risk of repeating the cycle: People are drawn to what they know, even if it's unhealthy. Without healing from past abuse, individuals may unconsciously seek out similar dynamics, believing they can "fix" the past through a new partner. They may also feel a misplaced sense of responsibility for the abuser's behavior, stemming from childhood experiences where they were conditioned to meet the needs of dysfunctional caregivers.

The Harlow's Monkeys experiment, an unsettling yet profoundly enlightening study by psychologist Harry Harlow, exposed the dark underbelly of attachment and dependency. In a stark laboratory setting, Harlow stripped infant rhesus monkeys from their biological mothers, replacing them with two surrogate "mothers": one constructed of cold, unyielding wire that provided milk and the other soft, cloth-covered, offering only tactile comfort. The infant monkeys gravitated overwhelmingly toward the cloth mother, clinging to her in moments of fear or stress, even when she offered no sustenance. This chilling observation underscored a truth that echoes through the lives of trauma survivors: the desperate human need for emotional connection often outweighs even the basic instinct for physical survival.

For victims of psychological abuse, Harlow's work implicates a devastating paradox. Much like his infant monkeys, these individuals may find themselves tethered to their abusers, drawn not by nourishment but by the fleeting comfort of familiarity and perceived security. Like Harlow's wire and cloth surrogates, abusers oscillate between cold detachment and moments of tenderness, creating a dependency rooted in intermittent reinforcement. The experiment, though conducted decades ago, reverberates in the lives of abuse survivors today, offering both a grim reflection of their pain and a starting point for understanding the intricate web of psychological dependency.

Bessel van der Kolk's trauma studies in *The Body Keeps the Score* reveal how psychological abuse reshapes the brain and body, leaving victims trapped in a cycle of fear and reactivity. For someone subjected to psychological manipulation, trauma doesn't fade with time—it persists, etched into the nervous system, dictating responses to even the most innocuous triggers. A raised voice, a disapproving glance, or the slightest confrontation can ignite a cascade of panic, as though the abuser's presence still looms. This is not accidental. By instilling fear and destabilizing the victim's sense of safety, the abuser renders their target-dependent, perpetually on edge, and easier to control.

The victim's mind and body, molded by trauma, enter a state of hypervigilance, an exhausting, self-reinforcing loop of scanning for threats. Victims may avoid intimacy altogether or cling desperately to anyone offering a semblance of safety; their behavior is driven not by logic but by the residue of their abuser's conditioning. Van der Kolk's work underscores a profound truth: psychological abuse isn't just a temporary disruption—it's a full-scale rewiring of the victim's inner world, a manipulation of their very essence. For the abuser, this is the ultimate power—the ability to dominate not just in the moment but to leave a lasting imprint, one that echoes long after the abuse has ended.

Surviving a psychopath isn't just about leaving; it's about never letting them back in!

CHAPTER ELEVEN
DAMAGE CONTROL

"The psychopath's greatest trick is convincing everyone that you're the problem. They don't just want to win the case— they want to annihilate your credibility." –Dr. Ramani Durvasula, Ph.D.

The Devil's Advocates

FOR TOO LONG, the justice system has turned a blind eye to psychological abuse, dismissing it as too subjective, too intangible, to warrant legal recognition. This loophole leaves victims vulnerable, and perpetrators empowered. Psychopaths thrive in this space. The courtroom becomes their stage, and the law, their playbook. For them, the legal system isn't a barrier; it's a tool of manipulation, a chessboard where they always aim to outplay you.

They are uniquely equipped to exploit the legal system and are adept at turning judges, attorneys, and even juries into unwitting allies. But here's the worst part: the system isn't just vulnerable to their tactics—it's built-in ways that often favor them. The burden of proof, the presumption of innocence, and the slow grind of justice all provide ample opportunities for psychopaths to wreak havoc.

And nowhere is a psychopath's manipulation of the legal system more evident than in custody disputes where the courtroom is a stage, the judge is an audience, and the stakes are not the children's welfare but their ability to win (at any cost) and defeat you.

Brooke, a nurse and mother of two, divorced her husband, Kyle, after discovering his double life. Kyle was everything she feared: manipulative, deceitful, and utterly devoid of empathy. When Brooke filed for full custody, Kyle transformed overnight. He portrayed himself as the perfect father, taking their children to school, attending every soccer game, and volunteering at church. Though he'd shown little interest in their children during the marriage, he suddenly became "Father of the Year," staging photo ops with their kids and even donating to their PTA to build his case as a loving, involved parent.

In court, he painted Brooke as unstable, fabricating stories about her "emotional outbursts" and "poor parenting." The judge, charmed by Kyle's polished demeanor, ruled in his favor. Brooke was left fighting for supervised visits with her own children.

For Brooke, this wasn't just a legal loss—it was a devastating reminder of how easily psychopaths can manipulate perception.

Family court judges sit in one of the most complex and emotionally charged arenas of the legal system. Every day, they make decisions that shape the lives of parents and children. But when one party in a custody battle is a psychopath, the stakes are even higher. These cases are not ordinary disputes—they are battlegrounds of manipulation, deceit, and psychological warfare.

It's easy to file a lawsuit. And psychopaths are undeterred by "facts" or "oaths." The *penalty of perjury* means nothing. In family court, judges rarely (if ever) penalize a party for "misrepresentations." If the psychopath retains counsel, his lawyer will (and should) zealously advocate for his client, advancing any number of positions, becoming, for all intents and purposes, the abuser's puppet. If the psychopath hires a "nice" attorney, a person easily manipulated and emotionally misled into becoming a staunch supporter of his "facts," this can be equally devastating for the victim. The psychopath will use all tools at his disposal, including child protective services, "check welfares," and other authority figures. Sadly, divorce for the psychopath is not the final frontier. All is a game to him; he will disregard court orders, find loopholes in the orders, look for inconsistencies or ambiguities to exploit in the court's language, quit jobs, file bankruptcy, forum shop for another judge or jurisdiction, concoct new allegations and, if exposed, will lie.

Be Honest to a Fault with Your Attorney

Sarah sat across from her attorney, Barbara, a seasoned family law specialist with a reputation for being both relentless and empathetic.

"Let's talk strategy," Barbara began, her voice low and steady. "No matter how ugly or uncomfortable the truth might be, I can't defend you against allegations I don't know about. So, tell me everything—the good, the bad, the downright awful. This is a no-judgment zone."

Sarah nodded, her hands twisting nervously in her lap. "I don't even know where to start."

"Start with what you think he might use against you," Barbara said. "Anything compromising—texts, photos, social media posts. People like your spouse often weaponize information."

Sarah's face paled. "There are... photos from when we were together. He'd always insist on taking them, even when I didn't want to. And social media... I've posted things when I was angry or upset."

Barbara's expression didn't change. "Okay, here's what we do. Lock down your social media accounts. Make them private, and don't accept new friend requests. Do not delete anything—that can be seen as an attempt to destroy evidence. Instead, take screenshots of anything you think could be used against you and send them to me. We'll be prepared to explain the context if it comes up."

Sarah's voice wavered. "And the photos?"

"If you suspect he might share them, we'll file a preemptive motion to prevent him from distributing or using them in court," Barbara said firmly. "Revenge porn laws are on your side. But you'll need to tell me exactly what's out there so I can prepare. We're not just fighting for a fair divorce; we're fighting to protect your reputation. That means we're going to take the sting out of anything negative he might say about you. If there's a text where you lost your temper, we'll own it. We'll show the judge the context—the months of manipulation and abuse that led to that moment."

"So, I have to be perfect?" Sarah asked, her voice tight.

"No. You have to be honest. Judges aren't looking for saints; they're looking for credibility. If you own your flaws, he can't use them to define you. We'll show the court who you really are—a human being trying to reclaim her life, not the caricature he'll try to paint."

Barbara opened a legal pad and began jotting notes. "Stop oversharing, especially with mutual friends or anyone who might report back to him. Stay off social media except for essential communication. And if he tries to bait you, don't respond. Silence is powerful."

"What about my friends?" Sarah asked. "He's already turned some of them against me."

"Stick to the people you trust implicitly, and don't engage with anyone who might be a conduit for him. This is about building a fortress around your life so he has fewer ways to get to you."

Communication

Effective communication during a divorce is critical to avoid becoming a target. Keeping interactions "neutral and factual" limits the emotional ammunition the other party can use. The goal is to starve the psychopath's need for control by setting clear boundaries. Strategies include sticking to written communication for documentation purposes, avoiding emotional language, and steering clear of blame or confrontation. Stay concise and focused on logistics—anything beyond that is fuel for manipulation. In cases where tempers flare, silence is often your best response. Each message should be crafted as though a judge might read it, ensuring it reflects rationality and calm, not reactive emotion. This is the foundation of preserving credibility and protecting oneself in the process. Lastly, agree on a method of collecting communication, such as through an app like Our Family Wizard, a subscription software that documents all exchanges.

1. **Stay Neutral:** Avoid engaging emotionally or defending yourself.
2. **Keep It Short:** Limit responses to one or two sentences.
3. **Focus on Logistics:** Redirect the conversation to practical, fact-based issues.
4. **Ignore Provocations:** Do not address insults or inflammatory remarks.
5. **Document Everything:** Always assume your communication could be presented in court.

1. When They Insult or Blame You

- **Their Message:** "You're the worst parent. You've ruined everything for our kids. This is all your fault!"
- **Effective Response:** "I disagree with your perspective. Let's focus on coordinating the parenting schedule."

2. When They Send Overwhelming Texts or Emails Full of Rants

- **Their Message:** *"You're so selfish and manipulative. No one can stand you. I don't even know why I put up with you!"*

- **Effective Response:** *"I'm only willing to discuss matters related to [topic]. Please stay focused."*

3. When They Make Baseless Accusations

- **Their Message:** *"You've always been a liar. I can't believe anything you say."*

- **Effective Response:** *"That's not true. I'm happy to discuss this further through our attorneys."*

4. When They Try to Provoke a Reaction

- **Their Message:** *"You're pathetic, and everyone knows it. You'll never get anywhere without me!"*

- **Effective Response:** *"Your opinion is noted. Let's move forward with addressing [specific topic]."*

5. When They Refuse to Stay on Topic

- Their Message: *"You always make everything about yourself. I've sacrificed so much, and this is the thanks I get?"*

- **Effective Response:** *"Let's stay on topic. I'm waiting for your response regarding [specific issue]."*

6. When They Make Threats

- Their Message: *"If you try to take me to court, you'll regret it. I have so much dirt on you."*

- Effective Response: "Threats are not constructive. Please have your attorney contact mine if needed."

7. **When They Demand an Immediate Reaction**
    - Their Message: "If you don't respond right now, I'll take that as an admission of guilt!"
    - Effective Response: "I will respond after I have had time to review this matter."

8. **When They Bring Up Past Arguments**
    - Their Message: "You've always been impossible. Remember when you did [specific incident]?"
    - Effective Response: "The past is not relevant to this discussion. Let's focus on resolving [specific issue]."

Financial Resources

Securing finances before initiating a divorce with a psychopath is critical for ensuring stability and avoiding financial manipulation. Strategies include gathering financial records, opening a separate bank account, securing passwords, and placing credit alerts to prevent unauthorized transactions. Avoid suspicious withdrawals or draining joint accounts, as these actions could backfire legally. Legal fees in divorces involving psychopaths often balloon due to the need for specialized professionals such as forensic evaluators, accountants, appraisers, and special masters. These experts are vital for uncovering hidden assets, evaluating property, and ensuring a fair division of resources. Psychopaths are notorious for financial sabotage—blocking access to funds, depleting joint accounts, or committing financial waste by frivolously spending marital assets. They aim to create chaos and wear down their opponent's resources. Effective preparation includes securing financial documents, creating a detailed inventory of assets, and working closely with legal and financial experts to track and protect resources. While expensive, these measures are essential for leveling the playing field and ensuring long-term financial security and a stronger position throughout the legal process.

Attorneys often require an up-front retainer so that their focus can remain on the litigation rather than worrying about compensation.

In high-conflict divorces, the balance between saving money and securing strong representation is delicate. *But a word to the wise*: while the mechanics of divorce may not be rocket science, the emotional toll can be leveling. If you choose to represent yourself, be prepared to be outmaneuvered by your opponent, face judicial bias, and manage your time. Legal systems are complex, and high-conflict cases often involve nuanced issues like custody battles, psychological abuse, and hidden assets. If you choose to hire a legal professional who is not an attorney, they can be financially cost-effective, but complex issues may exceed their expertise. They are most helpful in mediation, de-escalating conflicts, and facilitating agreements outside of court (all unlikely results when divorcing a psychopath).

What About Mediation?

Mediation with a psychopath is not only highly challenging but often futile, as their core traits— manipulation, lack of empathy, and disregard for the well-being of others—make genuine conflict resolution almost impossible. Psychopaths approach relationships and disputes through a lens of self-interest, viewing others primarily as tools to be used for their own gain. This means that any form of mediation is likely to be hijacked by their manipulative tactics. They might feign cooperation, but their end goal is rarely about finding a true resolution. Instead, they aim to bend the situation in their favor, often by exploiting the mediator's perception of fairness or moral integrity.

Furthermore, psychopaths lack the emotional depth necessary for authentic empathy, which is critical to understanding and resolving conflict. Without the ability to truly recognize the hurt or needs of others, the psychopath sees mediation as a game—one where their goal is to win, not to heal or compromise. The mediator, no matter how skilled, is often left in the dark, unable to pierce the thin veneer of charm and manipulation. Any progress made in the process is usually superficial, with the psychopath merely saying what they believe is required to get what they want, not because they are genuinely invested in a positive outcome.

In short, while mediation may work for individuals who have a capacity for empathy, self-reflection, and a genuine desire to resolve conflicts, with a psychopath, it often becomes little more than an exercise in futility. The true challenge lies in recognizing that they are not interested in resolution, but in furthering their own agenda, leaving the victim—and the mediator—at a severe disadvantage.

Beware Old Dynamics
Giving In—The Silent Cost of Relenting

The mediation room is eerily calm, the kind of stillness that lingers just before a storm. Sandra, the victim, sits across from Tom, the man who has tormented her for years. His smile is calculated, his eyes cold. It's a mask, carefully constructed to disarm, to manipulate. And it's working. Sandra can feel her heart rate accelerate, and the old, familiar dread settles in her stomach. She's been here before, many times. Only this time, the setting is different. The mediator—a well-intentioned professional who believes in the power of compromise—sits between them, offering that false hope of resolution.

Chapter 11: Damage Control

As the mediation started, Sandra felt that familiar knot in her chest. She's already doubting herself—wondering if she'll be able to keep her composure and if she'll be able to get through this without giving in. She knows that Tom will twist every word she says and that he'll use this session as a stage for his manipulations. And she's right.

The mediator begins by asking each person to outline their concerns. Sandra's voice trembles slightly as she starts speaking about Tom's manipulation, his emotional abuse, how he has undermined her confidence for years, how he's made every decision in their relationship, and even after their separation. As she speaks, she can feel Tom's eyes on her— he listens intently, but she knows he's not hearing her. He's just gathering ammunition.

He's already interjecting, his tone calm, smooth, almost too reasonable. He's making Sandra doubt her reality. He's saying things like, "I don't know why you're so upset; I've always been respectful," or "This is all in the past; can't we just move forward?" The language is designed to put the onus on Sandra, to make her feel irrational and emotional, as if She's the one causing the tension. The more he speaks, the more Sandra's frustration grows. But it's not just frustration—it's fear.

Sandra takes a deep breath, trying to steady herself. But the words are already slipping from her. She starts to feel small. She starts to wonder if maybe she's been too sensitive or too emotional. Maybe she's overreacting. Maybe Tom's right. Maybe it's all in the past, as he said. She feels the weight of his gaze, the way he's watching her, his lips curling into that smug, almost imperceptible smile. Her head spins, the familiar self-doubt creeping in. But she forces herself to keep going. She must. For her kids. For herself.

And this is where the damage is done. It's not in the words themselves but in the way Tom delivers them. He's stripping Sandra of her sense of reality, piece by piece. And with every comment, every deflection, he chips away at her confidence. In a mediation with a psychopath, the victim is always made to feel as if they are the one causing the problem, even when the evidence points to the psychopath's behavior.

The mediator tries to redirect the conversation, urging both parties to focus on the future and to consider what's best for the children. Sandra nods, but she can't shake the overwhelming feeling of dread. She knows the mediator is well-meaning, but she also knows that Tom will twist every suggestion, every solution, to his advantage. He will find a way to turn this into another victory for himself, to manipulate the system, to make her look like the irrational one.

As the mediation continued, Sandra felt the crushing weight of the past pressing on her shoulders. Every time she speaks, Tom finds a way to twist her words, to make her feel like the problem. By the end of the session, Sandra was exhausted, emotionally drained, and still no closer to a resolution. The mediator, unable to see through Tom's facade, believes the process is working. But Sandra knows better. She knows this was never about compromise. It was just another round in a long, exhausting battle for control.

For Sandra, this session is a reminder of how helpless and powerless she feels in Tom's presence. The mediator doesn't see the manipulation and doesn't recognize the psychological abuse. It's a crushing experience, and when she leaves, Sandra feels more defeated than when she walked in. The damage is invisible, but it's real. And it lingers long after the session ends.

Mediation with a psychopath isn't about resolution. It's about survival. And for victims like Sandra, the cost is high. The emotional toll of these sessions, these endless cycles of manipulation, gaslighting, and psychological warfare, is immense.

Sandra leaves the room feeling like she's just been through a battle—one she didn't win, but one she'll have to fight again and again until she finally breaks free from Tom's grip.

Chapter 11: Damage Control

The next week, she returns to the mediator's office, the air heavy with resignation. He sits across from her, a polished facade of charm and reason masking the predatory cunning beneath. His voice is calm and calculated, each word engineered to weave a narrative in which he is the victim, the hero, and the wronged party all at once. She sits slumped in her chair, hands clasped tightly in her lap, her eyes hollow from years of emotional attrition. She is no longer a person but a ghost of who she had been, conditioned to prioritize his needs, his truths, and his dominance.

Here, in this sterile room, her mind whispers the same refrain that has long since replaced her inner voice: It's not worth the fight. Let it go. You'll never win. And so, she nods in agreement to terms she neither wants nor deserves.

This was the genius of his strategy: the creation of "emotional false facts." He didn't need evidence. He just needed to make her doubt herself, to exploit her exhaustion until she relinquished her grasp on the truth. The mediator, eager to move things along, didn't challenge him. Why would she? His version of events was cohesive and believable—especially when her silence made it seem uncontested.

She didn't object when he insisted on primary custody, though the children cried for her every night. She didn't fight for the house she had poured her soul into, though he'd rarely set foot in it. She didn't demand the spousal support she was entitled to, though she knew she couldn't support herself on her current salary.

The dire consequences of her surrender are not immediate but insidious. Slowly, she lost more than property, custody, and support. She lost her sense of self. She had allowed his narrative to eclipse her own, had traded evidence-based truths for his emotionally charged fiction. And in doing so, she had ceded the last fragments of her power.

Perhaps that was his plan all along.

The cost of surrender may be too high a price when navigating "settlement" with a psychopath. What is your end game? And what are you willing to do to get there?

Sidebar: Insist on separate rooms so you are not forced to "negotiate" together.

What if the Mediator Brings in Reinforcements?

If a mediator refers a psychopath for a forensic evaluation, therapeutic intervention, or a meeting with a parenting coordinator, the outcome for both the victim and the psychopath is likely to be shaped by the core dynamics of psychopathy and the specific goals of the intervention.

For the psychopath, the referral might seem like an opportunity to further manipulate the system for personal gain. Psychopaths can often present themselves as cooperative and willing to undergo therapy or counseling, particularly if they believe it will help them achieve their goals, such as gaining access to children, reducing legal consequences, or gaining favor with others (like the mediator or a judge). They may participate in therapy superficially, giving just enough to appear compliant but without any real intention of change. Psychopaths lack the ability to genuinely reflect on their behavior or feel remorse, which is a foundational aspect of most therapeutic interventions. Their primary motivation is typically self-interest, not self-improvement. As a result, their participation may be strategic, designed to manipulate the situation, not to undergo meaningful personal growth. *Consider this: the goal of an "interventionist" is to reunite the psychopath with the child he has abused.*

A parenting coordinator, on the other hand, may be more effective if the focus is on practical, behavioral outcomes rather than emotional or therapeutic growth. Parenting coordinators work to ensure the child's well-being, often by enforcing boundaries, setting clear expectations, and limiting the psychopath's ability to manipulate situations. However, even in this context, the psychopath's manipulative tactics could still pose challenges. They may attempt to twist the coordinator's words, undermine authority, or use the child as a pawn. Over time, the victim may find themselves exhausted by the constant need to protect against these manipulations, with little to no support for their own emotional needs.

For the victim, the likely outcome is a continuation of emotional and psychological strain. If the psychopath participates in therapy or coordinates with a parenting coordinator, the victim may believe that some form of change is happening. This can provide a false sense of hope, which may ultimately lead to more frustration and despair when the psychopath's behavior remains unchanged or worsens. Even with interventions in place, the victim may still be caught in the cycle of emotional abuse, as the psychopath's manipulative behavior can continue under the guise of cooperation or compliance. The victim may also feel further isolated, as their concerns about the psychopath's true motives may be dismissed or minimized by those not fully understanding the nature of psychopathy.

In some cases, a well-intentioned therapeutic or parenting intervention could provide temporary relief, but it often doesn't break the underlying cycle of abuse. The victim may continue to feel marginalized, powerless, and blamed for not achieving the desired outcome, while the psychopath remains in control, using the intervention to further their own agenda. In the worst-case scenario, the victim might be retraumatized as the psychopath uses the process to deepen their control and continue their abuse under the guise of cooperation or reform.

Ultimately, while referrals to therapeutic interventionists or parenting coordinators can help manage the immediate situation, the real challenge is in understanding that psychopathy cannot be "cured" or mitigated through typical therapeutic means. The psychopath's behavior is deeply ingrained, and interventions may only serve to give them a platform to continue manipulating others. Without a clear and sustained recognition of the psychopath's tendencies, the victim may find that the process does little to protect them, and they could even be further victimized in the long run. Consider the goals of each participant:

ROLE/PRIMARY GOALS

Victim: Ensure the child's safety and emotional well-being. Prevent further abuse of manipulation by Psychopath. Advocate for legal measures to limit the abuser's influence (e.g. supervised visits); Rebuild stability and trust in their own and the child's life.

Psychopath: Regain control over victim and/or child. Manipulate legal and therapeutic system to appear as caring parent.

Mediator: Facilitate resolution between parties; emphasize compromise, encourage co-parenting.

Therapist: Provide emotional support and coping strategies for child/victims; address trauma and its long-term impact; encourage healthy boundaries and emotional resilience.

Forensic Evaluator: Assess fitness to care for child; investigate allegations of abuse or harmful behavior. Provide impartial recommendations.

Therapeutic Interventionist: Family reunification; foster communication between child and *both* parents.

Parenting Coordinator: Resolve conflicts between parents, improve co-parenting, implement court orders, reduce parental disputes rather than address dynamics of abuse or manipulation.

Systemic Blind Spots: Mediators, therapeutic interventionists, and parenting coordinators often prioritize neutrality or reunification, which can enable the psychopath's manipulation.

Redefining Parental Rights

Victims must meticulously document every interaction with the abuser, building an irrefutable case that highlights the psychopath's patterns of manipulation, deceit, and abuse. With the help of an experienced attorney, they can request court-mandated psychological evaluations of the abuser, arguing that the results should inform custody decisions. Protective orders, supervised visitation with trained professionals, or even virtual visits that can be monitored and recorded are critical tools for minimizing further harm. Courts must be made to understand that these measures are not about vindictiveness but about safeguarding the child's mental and physical well-being.

The courts themselves remain a significant hurdle. Many judges, clinging to outdated ideals of family unity, fail to grasp the unique dangers posed by psychopaths. *Parental rights are too often prioritized over a child's safety,* leading to rulings that facilitate abuse under the guise of reunification. Victims must counter this narrative by framing their arguments around the child's best interests—safety, stability, and the need for a nurturing environment free from the emotional chaos psychopaths create. By aligning their case with the child's developmental needs, victims can challenge the court's misguided belief that maintaining a connection with an abusive parent is inherently beneficial.

Take, for example, a mother battling for her child's safety against an abusive, psychopathic ex-partner. She compiles years of documentation: police reports of domestic violence, testimonies from therapists treating her traumatized child, and emails that reveal the ex-partner's manipulative tactics. She insists on a forensic psychological evaluation and introduces expert testimony to the court, painting a clear picture of the psychopath's inability to provide a safe and nurturing environment. When the court orders supervised visitation, she works closely with a professional trained in recognizing psychopathic behavior, ensuring any manipulative tactics are documented and reported. Reframe the focus so that the emphasis is on the child, not the abuser.

Ultimately, victims and their advocates must push for systemic change. Courts and therapeutic interventionists need specialized training in identifying psychopathy and understanding its implications in custody cases. Advocacy for policy reforms that prioritize child welfare over parental rights is essential. Public awareness campaigns can expose the inherent dangers of reunifying children with abusive psychopaths, challenging the narrative that family unity is always best.

If Mediation Is Unavoidable, Be Strategic

Psychopaths respond better to clear, unemotional logic. Keep discussions fact-based and avoid emotional appeals, as they may exploit vulnerability. Use evidence to support your position, making it difficult for them to manipulate the narrative. Save social media posts, text messages, and emails; keep a dated diary with times of noncompliance and be prepared to corroborate the facts.

Focus on *patterns of behavior*[11]: **Danger to the Children**—on June 12, he drove drunk with kids; on July 12, he put his fist through the wall in front of kids; **Disparaging Remarks in front of the Children**—on August 16, he raged at me in front of the kids, falsely accusing me

---

11 These should be based on the outcomes you are requesting.

of infidelity and telling the kids the divorce was my fault; **Abusing the System**—on October 30, he called police asking for a "check welfare" telling them I had left the kids home alone; on November 13, he reported to Child Protective Services that I was abusing the kids, an investigation ensued, after which the allegations were deemed "unsubstantiated." If there are no specific "acts" to record, note other patterns of behavior such as incidents of rage, threats, indifference to the children's welfare, interference with their medical treatment, falsehoods, etc.

Establish firm rules and boundaries for the mediation process. Psychopaths often push limits to gain control, so boundaries can reduce their ability to manipulate the situation. The mediator must be highly skilled, impartial, and assertive to manage manipulative behavior and keep discussions focused. Frame outcomes in terms of how the psychopath will benefit as they are more likely to cooperate if they perceive a personal gain.

When Mediation Fails....

Legal action might be the only way to ensure a fair resolution. While courts provide structure and enforceable judgments, reducing opportunities for manipulation and leverage is critical. Psychopaths are deterred more by the risk of tangible consequences (e.g., financial loss, legal repercussions) than moral or emotional arguments. Avoid showing anger, fear, or frustration. These emotions can encourage a psychopath to escalate manipulative behaviors. Instead, focus on what you need, not how you *feel*. *Save your emotional outbursts for a therapist.* Engage financial auditors, forensic psychologists, or legal experts as soon as possible to strengthen your case and expose manipulative tactics. *Always rebut the false allegations in writing. Written corrections protect you.*

CHAPTER TWELVE
CHILD'S PLAY

WHEN ONE PARENT is a master manipulator, and the legal system fails to account for psychological abuse, children become pawns in a game far more damaging than the courtroom drama that unfolds around them.

It isn't necessary for an ex-partner to be clinically declared a psychopath. Many people have one or more of the traits on the PCL-R, and they can also inflict devasting harm in a custody battle. The strategies that apply when dealing with genuine psychopaths will also be useful against non-psychopaths who are manipulative, prone to lying and lacking empathy.

Custody Wars

Grace had once lived a life most people envied. A successful career, a loving family, and two beautiful children. But when her marriage to a foreign businessman fell apart, it triggered a brutal custody battle that exposed how easily the legal system can be manipulated by a calculating party.

When Grace and her ex-husband separated, things escalated quickly. He argued the children should live with him overseas. In an unprecedented decision, the judge agreed—granting him primary custody and forcing Grace's children to relocate to Europe.

Chapter 12: Child's Play

Grace, an American citizen, was left to navigate a logistical and emotional nightmare, traveling thousands of miles just to see her children.

Grace's ex painted himself as the calm, rational parent, while Grace—emotionally exhausted from the fight—was depicted as unstable and uncooperative. His legal team framed her distress as evidence that she was emotionally unstable, while his own composed demeanor was presented as proof of his fitness as a parent. Judges, untrained in the nuances of psychological abuse, mistook Grace's visible anguish for irrationality—and his cold detachment for stability.

The court's ruling focused on logistics—the father's inability to live in the U.S.—while disregarding the psychological toll on the children and their mother. The children became collateral damage in the battle. Torn between two countries and two parents, they were forced to adapt to a new life in a foreign country dictated by legal rulings rather than their needs.

Abusers often use children as leverage, knowing that their victim's love for their children is a powerful weapon. The father's insistence on primary custody wasn't about the children's best interests—it was about winning, about control, about ensuring that Grace's life was forever tethered to his.

Grace was left to fight against a system that seemed designed to punish her for being a mother who dared to challenge her abuser.

By granting custody to the father, the court reinforced the message that abusers can use the system to punish their victims.

The toll was profound, "an unimaginable loss." Grace's case highlights the urgent need for courts to recognize and address the dynamics of psychological abuse and underscores the need for systemic change to protect children and ensure that the abused are not further victimized by the legal system.

Parental Alienation
The Puppet Master

"Alienating a child from a parent is a crime against the child, depriving them of their fundamental right to love and be loved by both parents." –Ludwig F. Lowenstein, Ph.D.

For a psychopath, the family is not a place of love or safety—it is a playground. And the child, like everyone else in their orbit, is just another pawn in the game.

Matthew is a 10-year-old boy caught between his divorced parents. His father, Cole, sits across from him at the kitchen table, speaking with the carefully calculated tone of someone planting a seed.

"Hey, buddy," his voice is soft and inviting. "How's school going? Did you talk to Mom about that science project you wanted to do?"

Matthew, shrugging, says, "Yeah. She said she didn't have time to help me this week."

Cole's smile falters just enough to convey disappointment. "That's a shame. I guess she's just really busy these days, huh? It's not like it used to be when we were all together. Remember how we used to build stuff in the garage? Those were the best, weren't they?"

Perking up, Matthew agrees. "Yeah, like the birdhouse! That was cool."

"Exactly! You're such a natural at that stuff," Cole says, grinning, leaning in conspiratorially. "It's too bad Mom doesn't see how talented you are. But hey, don't worry—I'll help you. You know I'll always make time for you, right?" Cole pauses, gauging Matthew's reaction. The boy fidgets with his hands, his young mind processing the subtle implication: Dad cares more. It's a small, seemingly innocuous comment, but for Cole, it's a calculated move in a larger game.

"You know, buddy, it's not really your mom's fault. She's got a lot on her plate. But sometimes, I just wish she could be a little more... I don't

Chapter 12: Child's Play

know... understanding? Like, when you told her about wanting to stay over here an extra night last week, she didn't seem too happy, did she?"

"She said I couldn't. She said it's her time with me."

Cole's voice is soft but insistent as he carefully positions himself as the "fun" parent, the one who prioritizes Matthew's feelings, while subtly painting Emily—his ex-wife—as rigid and dismissive. "Yeah, I know. And I get it. She loves you in her own way. But I just think it's important that you have choices, you know? You're old enough to decide what's best for you."

The message for Matthew is clear, even if unspoken: Dad cares. Mom doesn't. "I guess... I mean, Mom does stuff for me, too."

Cole, nodding, his tone neutral, says, "Of course she does. I'd never say otherwise. But it's okay if you feel like she doesn't always get it. You can tell me anything, you know that, right? I'll always listen."

The power of Cole's manipulation lies in its subtlety. He never outright criticizes Emily; that would be too obvious, too easy to challenge. Instead, he creates doubt, planting small but potent seeds that take root in Matthew's mind.

Over time, these interactions compound. The boy, yearning for approval and connection, begins to align more closely with his father. He starts to see his mother through the distorted lens Cole has carefully crafted.

Later that evening, Matthew returns to his mother's house, quieter than usual. At bedtime, Emily sits beside him, reading a book, but Matthew interrupts her.

"Mom, why didn't you help me with my science project?"

Emily, startled, says, "What? I said we'd work on it tomorrow, remember?" "Dad said he'd help me. He's always got time for me."

Emily feels the sting of the comment, but she doesn't yet realize the full extent of Cole's manipulation. The groundwork has been laid, and over time, it will grow into full-blown alienation—a wedge driven *deeper and deeper by Cole's calculated efforts to turn his son against her.*

Psychopaths excel at this kind of manipulation because they lack the emotional investment that typically comes with parenthood. To them, the child is a means to an end—whether that end is revenge against the other parent, a boost to their ego, or simply the pleasure of control. By framing themselves as the victim or the "better" parent, they weaponize the child's natural need for love and security.

But the damage doesn't end with the alienated parent. The child, caught in this psychological warfare, learns to doubt their own perceptions, to align their loyalty with the manipulator, and to suppress their natural affection for the alienated parent. The result is a fractured family dynamic that may take years, if not a lifetime, to repair.

Preventing or Mitigating Parental Alienation

Preventing or mitigating parental alienation caused by a psychopathic or manipulative co-parent is challenging but possible. Here are strategies that an alienated parent can employ to protect their relationship with their child:

STRATEGY	KEY ACTIONS	EXAMPLES/DETAILS
STAY EMOTIONALLY AVAILABLE	Be present and focus on positive, trust-building activities. Validate your child's feelings without defensiveness	"I love you very much, and I hope we can talk about how I show that love."
AVOID BADMOUTHING THE PARENT	Take the high road; avoid negative comments.	Instead of: "That's a lie," say, "Let me show you how much I care."
MAINTAIN COMMUNICATION	Keep in touch consistently via calls, texts, or letters.	Regular contact demonstrates involvement and counters alienation.
DOCUMENT INCIDENTS	Show interest in their life. Involvement counters alienation. Keep records of alienation attempts (dates, examples). Save evidence of your involvement (photos, cards).	Track refusals of visitation or negative comments involving the child.
STRENGTHEN LEGAL POSITION	Seek professional intervention (e.g., therapists, GALs). Present evidence of alienation to the court to enforce custody. Hire experts.	File legal motions if the alienating parent violates custody orders

Long-Term Support and Resilience Building

Convincing a judge that co-parenting with a psychopath is not just impractical but dangerous requires a strategic, evidence-based approach. A psychopath thrives on manipulation, control, and chaos— traits that make them fundamentally incompatible with the cooperation, empathy, and compromise necessary for successful co-parenting. Through her lawyer, the victim must craft a narrative that not only highlights these dangers but also offers practical, enforceable alternatives to protect the child's welfare and the victim's stability.

The key to educating the judge is to move beyond emotional appeals and ground the argument in observable behaviors, expert testimony, and potential scenarios. Judges may lack the psychological training to recognize psychopathy's nuances, so it is critical to frame the psychopath's behaviors in terms of their predictable impact on parenting dynamics and the child's well-being. This involves: (1) demonstrating the pattern of behavior, presenting concrete examples of the parent's manipulation, dishonesty, or disregard for boundaries, and tying these behaviors to potential harm to the child. (2) Highlighting likely scenarios: outlining realistic, evidence-backed scenarios that illustrate how the psychopath might use co-parenting to continue their pattern of control. For example: a) Undermining the victim's authority by disregarding agreed-upon parenting rules; b) using the child as a pawn to manipulate or punish the victim; c) exposing the child to inappropriate or harmful situations due to the psychopath's impulsivity or lack of accountability.

When presenting alternatives, the focus should be on enforceable solutions that minimize opportunities for manipulation. Sole custody, with the victim having primary decision-making authority, is often the safest option. The lawyer must argue that sole custody is not about excluding the other parent but about creating a stable, consistent environment for the child—something a psychopath cannot provide.

For cases where supervised parenting time is recommended, it's essential to stress the protective benefits of these arrangements. Supervision limits the psychopath's ability to manipulate or harm the child and ensures that interactions are safe and monitored. The victim's lawyer should propose specific, practical guidelines for supervised visits, such as neutral visitation centers or court-appointed supervisors, and emphasize how these measures prioritize the child's well-being.

A thorough custody evaluation conducted by a qualified forensic psychologist can provide the court with a comprehensive understanding of the psychopath's behavior. This process involves interviews, psychological testing, and assessments of both parents and the child. Evaluators can identify red flags—such as a parent's inability to prioritize the child's needs over their own—and recommend custody arrangements that minimize harm.

The victim's lawyer should emphasize that these evaluations are not about assigning blame but about ensuring the child's best interests. If the evaluation supports sole custody or supervised visitation, the lawyer can present this as an objective, professional endorsement of their argument.

Co-parenting with a manipulative individual often places the victim and child in a constant state of conflict and fear.

Custody Evaluations
The Good, the Bad and the Ugly

Court-appointed custody evaluators[12] play a critical role in shaping the outcomes of high-conflict custody cases. However, when they are unaware of the traits and tactics of psychopathy, they can inadvertently contribute to the victim's continued suffering and make decisions that may ultimately harm the child. Without a clear understanding of psychopathic tendencies, evaluators may misinterpret a psychopath's superficial charm as evidence of parental fitness or cooperation,

---

12 Most are **not** psychologists but family therapists or clinical social workers.

overlooking the deeper patterns of control, deceit, and emotional abuse that are at play.

Since psychopaths excel at creating a facade of normalcy, they can be articulate, composed, and appear genuinely concerned about the well-being of their children, which makes it difficult for evaluators to see beyond the surface. They may present a narrative that casts *them* as the victim of their partner, playing on the evaluator's desire for fairness and balance. In contrast, the victim—who is often emotionally drained, anxious, and possibly even gaslit into doubting their own perceptions—may struggle to present their case clearly or convincingly. The evaluator, lacking the ability to detect the subtle cues of manipulation or the emotional devastation that the victim is experiencing, might see this as a lack of credibility or emotional instability in the victim, further invalidating their concerns.

When evaluators miss these critical signs, they often make recommendations that place children in the care of a parent who may, on the surface, appear competent but whose emotional abuse and manipulative tendencies continue behind closed doors. This failure to recognize psychopathy can inadvertently place the victim in a position where their voice remains unheard, and the child remains in an environment where emotional neglect or psychological abuse is ongoing but hidden. The lack of awareness about psychopathy is not only a failure to protect the victim—it is a failure to protect the *child*, who may ultimately suffer more as a result.

The purpose of custody evaluations is to assess parental capacities, the psychological well-being of the children, and the impact of the family dynamics on custody and visitation recommendations. *In nearly all cases, the court adopts the custody evaluator's recommendations.* Therefore, **what** they report and **how** they frame the issues is vitally important to the outcome. They will need to understand the hidden dangers, why they should distrust the psychopath's statements about themselves and you, and why they will undoubtedly violate the court's orders.

Principles for Victims When Working with Court-Appointed Custody Evaluators

CATEGORY	BEST PRACTICES	KEY TIPS
INITIAL INTERACTION	Establish respect Cooperative tone	Be polite, professional Avoid confrontation
PRESENTING EVIDENCE	Share evidence directly supports your claims re: parenting	Focus on objective evidence, e.g. school and medical records, texts. Avoid hearsay
PRIORITIZE INFORMATION	Emphasize most relevant, avoid overwhelm	Select 3-5 examples No emotional facts
MAINTAIN CREDIBILITY	Just facts	Avoid accusations
PARENTING FOCUS	Actions/decisions prioritize child's best interest	Provide examples how you meet child's needs
ADDRESS CONCERNS	Calm, factual manner	Use specific examples Avoid personal attacks
RECORD	Organize all information	Present concise history Use binders, folders, labels
THE INTERVIEW	Honesty prevails	Admit Faults but be solution-oriented
CHILD'S NEEDS	Keep conversation child-focused	Avoid negative barbs about other parent

Retaining an expert on personality disorders or insisting that the psychopath be evaluated by a forensic psychologist is not only helpful for the custody evaluator and court but also validates your observations. In many high-conflict cases, courts may also appoint best interest counsel for the children. These advocates provide objective insight into the child's welfare, offering subtext to the evaluator's findings. They not only conduct interviews with the child, family members, teachers, and therapists but also review reports from custody evaluators, therapists, and Child Protective Services. These lawyers craft recommendations that may address custody arrangements, visitation schedules, and the allocation of parental responsibilities.

The following is an example of a skilled evaluator's likely observations when well-versed in psychopathy:

Parent A (*Melissa*):

Melissa presents as a thoughtful, composed individual who prioritizes the children's emotional and physical well-being. During the interview, she described the challenges of co-parenting with Adrian, detailing a pattern of manipulation and undermining behaviors. Her accounts were corroborated by documentation, including text messages and incident reports, which showed consistent boundary violations. Melissa exhibits insight into the children's needs and demonstrates a calm, nurturing demeanor. She is attuned to their emotional states and speaks of encouraging open communication, routine, and stability in their lives. Observations during a parent-child interaction session revealed a warm, supportive dynamic. The children appeared comfortable, engaged, and eager to interact with Melissa, further supporting her claims of being the primary emotional caregiver.

Parent B (*Adrian*):

Adrian presents as charming and articulate, often steering the conversation to highlight his perceived strengths as a parent. He spoke at length about his love for the children but frequently redirected discussions to grievances against Melissa, blaming her for the family's conflict. His responses lacked depth regarding the children's specific needs, focusing instead on how he felt unfairly treated in the custody proceedings.

During the interview, Adrian displayed a pattern of minimizing his concerning behaviors, including incidents of unauthorized contact with the children outside of agreed-upon times. He denied any wrongdoing and reframed these actions as "spontaneous acts of love." This aligns with documented manipulative behaviors, as Adrian consistently portrays himself as the victim while deflecting responsibility.

In a parent-child interaction session, the children exhibited mixed reactions. While they were initially excited to see Adrian, they grew visibly uneasy as he made disparaging comments about Melissa and asked probing questions about her activities. This created palpable tension, with the younger child withdrawing while the older child became visibly distressed.

Children's Interviews:

The evaluator conducted separate interviews with the two children, ages 9 and 12.

Older Child (Age 12): The older child expressed loyalty to both parents but shared concerns about Adrian's behavior. "Dad says things about Mom that make me feel bad," the child stated, adding that they often felt "caught in the middle." The child also described instances where Adrian pressured them to "choose sides" or report on Melissa's actions.

Younger Child (Age 9): The younger child appeared more reserved but indicated a preference for spending time with Melissa. "I feel safe at Mom's house," the child said, hesitating when asked about time with Adrian. The younger child mentioned that Adrian sometimes gets "angry out of nowhere," which makes them nervous.

Both children expressed a need for consistency and routine, voicing that disruptions to their schedule were stressful. They also shared a desire for reduced conflict between their parents.

Evaluator's Analysis and Recommendations

Adrian exhibits behaviors consistent with traits of psychopathy, including superficial charm, manipulation, and a lack of genuine empathy. His tendency to undermine Melissa and involve the children in parental conflict raises significant concerns about his ability to prioritize their well-being. While he demonstrates affection toward the children, this is overshadowed by his impulsivity and self-serving behavior, which has already begun to negatively impact their emotional stability.

Melissa, in contrast, provides a stable and nurturing environment. Her ability to set healthy boundaries and prioritize the children's needs suggests that she is better equipped to offer consistent care. However, Melissa's reluctance to confront Adrian more directly may hinder her ability to fully mitigate his influence, leaving the children vulnerable to continued emotional manipulation.

Recommendations:

1. **Sole Legal Custody to Melissa:** This arrangement would allow Melissa to make key decisions regarding the children's education, healthcare, and overall well-being without interference. Adrian's history of boundary violations and manipulative behavior demonstrates that shared decision-making would be detrimental.

2. **Supervised Visitation for Adrian:** Adrian's parenting time should be supervised at a neutral visitation center to ensure the children's safety and emotional stability. This arrangement limits his ability to manipulate or emotionally harm the children while allowing them to maintain a relationship with their father.

3. **Therapeutic Interventions:** Both children would benefit from therapy to address the stress and emotional conflict they have experienced. Melissa may also benefit from counseling to strengthen her ability to set firm boundaries and manage conflict effectively.

4. **Minimized Communication Between Parents:** All communication should be conducted through a court-monitored app to reduce conflict and provide documentation of interactions.

Limitations of Observations

While the evaluator's findings are based on interviews, documentation, and parent-child interactions, they are inherently limited by the controlled nature of these sessions. Adrian's charm and ability to mask his manipulative tendencies may obscure the full extent of his behavior, while the children's reluctance to share negative experiences candidly may reflect fear of reprisal or loyalty conflicts.

Additionally, while the recommendations prioritize the children's well-being, the success of these measures relies on strict enforcement. Without consistent supervision and therapeutic interventions, Adrian's ability to influence and manipulate the children may persist.

The evidence overwhelmingly supports granting Melissa sole custody and implementing safeguards around Adrian's visitation. These measures are necessary to shield the children from ongoing harm and to create a stable, supportive environment in which they can thrive. However, the long-term effectiveness of these arrangements will require vigilance, ongoing assessments, and a commitment to enforcing boundaries.

HOW CAN THE SYSTEM *HELP*?

Judges have the power to break the cycle of manipulation that psychopaths perpetuate. By focusing on evidence, utilizing expert assessments, and prioritizing the best interests of the children, they can navigate even the most complex custody battles.

In the end, the goal is simple but profound: to protect the innocent and ensure that justice, not deception, prevails.

Judges must learn to identify psychopathic behaviors in custody cases and make decisions that prioritize the best interests of the children.

PSYCHOPATH'S PLAYBOOK	HOW IT MANIFESTS IN FAMILY COURT	RED FLAGS
FEIGNING VICTIMHOOD	They are the aggrieved party, using charm to manipulate court perception.	Inconsistent statements.
WEAPONIZING EVIDENCE	Twisting facts, presenting selective evidence, or fabricating stories to build their narrative.	Evidence that seems overly rehearsed or inconsistent with the broader context.
EXPLOITING LOOPHOLES	Bend custody agreements, restraining orders, or court directives in their favor.	Discrediting the other parent rather than addressing children's needs.
LITIGATION ABUSE	Filing motions to intimidate, creating unnecessary conflicts, refusal to comply with orders.	Pattern of non-compliance with Court rulings or frequent legal challenges.

ACTIONABLE STEPS FOR JUDGES

- Focus on evidence, not emotional facts. Insist on verifiable claims like medical and police reports.

- Assign neutral, court-approved professionals to assess manipulative behavior.
- Involve third-party experts to oversee compliance with custody agreements.
- Specify details in all court orders, outlining custody exchange times, locations and methods to prevent ambiguity.
- Protect the children. Limit communication between parties, by insisting on monitored formats and apps like email, texts, or Our Family Wizard. Allow recordings.
- Enforce penalties for noncompliance, sanctions, fines, contempt, supervised or reduced parenting.

CHAPTER THIRTEEN
GLADIATORS

DIVORCE PREPARATION REQUIRES a meticulous, almost survivalist mindset—a calculated effort to secure your emotional and financial well-being before stepping onto the battlefield. Like "preppers" stockpiling supplies in anticipation of societal collapse, those planning for divorce must brace for potential fallout. This means copying vital records, safeguarding not only valuables but sentimental items, and ensuring critical documents—tax returns, medical records, passports—are stowed in a secure location, such as a fireproof safe. It means establishing control over your digital presence by changing passwords, setting up surveillance like a Ring camera, and photographing the current condition of furniture and personal property to document their state. Securing a private post office or UPS box for essential mail offers a layer of protection. Funds must be gathered, correspondence preserved, and access to important resources ensured. Divorce, much like survival, is not just about enduring the storm but emerging from it prepared, intact, and ready to rebuild.

Once the papers are served, the true fight begins, with the spouse transformed into a gladiator stepping into the arena. Like combatants circling each other in the Colosseum, every move—every word, every action—becomes a calculated strike or counterstrike. This is a fight for survival, where preparation and resilience are as critical as cunning, and the cost of losing can strip not only assets but a sense of security. The ring of the bell signals that the real battle is underway, and in this unforgiving arena, only the sharpest minds and steeliest resolve will prevail.

ASSEMBLING THE TEAM

Melissa knew she couldn't navigate this battle alone. The courtroom wasn't just a legal arena—it was a psychological battlefield, and she needed a lawyer who could fight with both strategy and heart. Someone who wouldn't just represent her but would understand her, stand with her, and bring clarity to the chaos Adrian had unleashed. This wasn't about finding just any attorney; it was about finding a gladiator with empathy.

Step 1: Vetting for Experience

Melissa began her search with precision, knowing the stakes were too high for a misstep. She sought out lawyers with a track record of handling cases involving domestic violence, psychological abuse, and high-conflict situations. These were the attorneys who understood not only the legal intricacies but also the psychological warfare that someone like Adrian wielded. She asked specific, targeted questions during consultations:

- *"How do you approach cases involving manipulative or coercive adversaries?"*
- *"What's your experience with psychological abuse in family or criminal courts?"*

- *"How do you counteract charm or deceit in a courtroom?"*

Melissa paid close attention to their responses, looking for depth and specificity. She wasn't interested in generic answers or platitudes. She needed someone who had seen cases like hers and won.

Step 2: Observing Their Demeanor

Melissa knew that charm alone wasn't enough. Adrian had taught her that. She needed someone who could blend compassion with confidence, someone who would listen actively without dismissing her fears or minimizing her experiences. During her consultations, she watched how the lawyers communicated:

- Did they explain strategies clearly without resorting to jargon?

- Were they genuinely engaged, or did they seem distracted or rushed?

- Did they acknowledge the emotional toll of her situation while focusing on the practical steps forward?

One attorney stood out. Diana's calm but fierce, her presence both reassuring and commanding. She didn't downplay Melissa's fears or dismiss Adrian's behavior as "overzealous." Instead, she dissected his actions with the precision of a surgeon. *"Adrian's behavior isn't about love or heartbreak,"* Diana had said. *"It's about control. And control is something we can dismantle."*

Step 3: Assessing Resources

Melissa knew that a good lawyer was only as strong as the team behind them. During her consultation with Diana, she asked about her network of professionals. Diana's answer sealed the deal:

"*I work with psychologists who specialize in psychopathy, forensic accountants who can trace financial manipulation, and private investigators who can gather the evidence we need. This isn't a solo fight—it's a team effort. And you're part of that team.*"

Melissa was impressed not just by Diana's connections but by her emphasis on collaboration. It wasn't about Diana taking over; it was about empowering Melissa to be an active participant in her own defense.

Step 4: Trusting Her Instincts

Ultimately, Melissa trusted her gut. She'd learned the hard way to listen to her instincts, and with Diana, she felt a sense of partnership. Diana didn't just see Melissa as a client; she saw her as a person—a person who had been through hell and deserved not just legal protection but justice.

Before signing the retainer agreement, Melissa asked one final question: "*What makes you different from other lawyers I've talked to?*"

Diana didn't hesitate. "*I fight hard, but I don't fight blind. I understand how people like Adrian think, and I know how to expose them for what they are. I'll advocate for you with everything I have, and I'll make sure your voice is heard. This isn't just your case—it's our fight.*"

In Diana, Melissa found more than an attorney—she found an ally. A gladiator armed not only with legal expertise but with empathy, strategy, and a clear vision for justice. Together, they would confront

Adrian, dismantling his facade piece by piece until the truth stood undeniable. And for the first time in months, Melissa felt a spark of hope. She wasn't alone anymore.

EXPERTS

Expert witnesses can be game changers in cases involving psychological abuse. Employing the **C.R.E.D.I.T.** framework—Choose, Review, Educate, Discuss, Integrate, Testify—can help structure the process of working with experts effectively. Each step ensures that their testimony strengthens your case and resonates with the court. Their testimony can lend credibility and provide a professional lens to interpret complex dynamics.

Psychologists or Psychiatrists: Experts in psychopathy can explain behaviors like gaslighting, coercive control, and lack of empathy in a way that judges and juries understand.

Forensic Accountants: If financial abuse is a factor, these professionals can trace hidden assets or demonstrate economic coercion.

Child Specialists: In custody battles, child psychologists can provide insights into how the abuser's behavior affects the children involved.

Special Masters: These are neutral third-party professionals, often an attorney or mental health expert, appointed by the court to assist in resolving specific disputes in family law cases. Their role is typically limited in scope, as defined by the court, and they work to expedite the resolution of contentious issues without requiring frequent judicial intervention.

Ensure your expert has access to all relevant documentation and understands the specifics of your case. Discuss potential challenges they might face on the stand, including cross-examination tactics designed to discredit them. Work with your attorney to weave expert insights seamlessly into your case narrative. Their testimony should complement your evidence and reinforce key points.

PRETRIAL PREPARATION

The methodical, psychological preparation necessary to face a manipulative adversary like Adrian requires **P.R.E.P.**: Prepare, Respond, Evidence, Poise.

This is how Melissa's attorney helped her **prepare**:

Attorney: Adrian thrives on control and manipulation. He'll try to rattle you, provoke you, make you question your own narrative. But he doesn't know we've dissected his every move. By the time we're done here, you'll be unshakable. Stick to the facts. Clear, concise, no speculation. The opposing counsel will try to frame those early behaviors as harmless—"just a man in love." But we'll counter that with patterns and escalation. When they ask why you didn't act sooner, what will you say?

Melissa: I thought I could handle it, that he'd stop if I made it clear I wasn't interested anymore?

Attorney: We want to show the court that you acted reasonably under the circumstances. **Respond** like this: *"I didn't act immediately because I didn't yet recognize the danger. But as soon as I realized his behavior was escalating, I took steps to protect myself."* Every answer you give should anchor itself to the facts and **evidence**. When they ask about the note he left on your windshield, how will you respond?

Melissa: It said, *"I'll always find you."* I took a photo of it and reported it to the police.

Attorney: Perfect. Short, direct, tied to evidence. If they press you—asking how you *felt* when you found the note—what will you say?

Melissa: I felt scared… can I say that?

Attorney: You're allowed to feel. That's human. But don't let fear dominate your testimony. Stick to the impact: *"I felt unsafe in my own home and realized I needed legal protection."* Turn emotion into action. Now, the final piece: **poise**. Adrian's attorney may try to provoke you. They'll use his charm, his lies, to paint a different picture. How will you handle that?

Melissa: I'll stay calm. I'll pause before I answer.

Attorney: It will help you reclaim control. When you stick to facts, you strip him of his power. Adrian's strategy is to manipulate; ours is to dismantle. Let's role-play: *Ms. Cooper, isn't it true that you continued to post on social media even after you claimed Adrian's behavior made you feel unsafe?*

Melissa: Yes, but I adjusted my privacy settings and limited what I shared publicly.

Attorney (as Opposing Counsel): *But don't you think those posts encouraged Adrian? You were essentially inviting him to find you, weren't you?*

Melissa: No. Adrian's actions were his choice. My posts were not an invitation for harassment. His behavior violated the boundaries I clearly set.

Attorney: Perfect. You stayed calm, answered directly, and shifted the responsibility back where it belonged—to Adrian. That's how you win this, Melissa. You've already survived him. This is about reclaiming your narrative.

Managing Expectations

Family court is not a place of resolution; it's a fast-paced, high-stakes arena where decisions that alter lives are made in the blink of an eye. Trials are astonishingly brief—often just one to two hours, with time split between parties, leaving mere minutes to present evidence and address critical issues. The disputes are frequently reduced to "he said/she said" narratives, making detailed, easily accessible evidence the linchpin of a successful argument. Judges, tasked with making life-altering decisions, sometimes have less than ninety minutes to sift through the noise and uncover the truth.

The cost? More than you can imagine—especially when protective or temporary orders turn into costly mini-trials within trials. Ironically, little law is actually decided; the focus is on resolving facts, and in an adversarial system, the loudest, most aggressive voices often prevail. There are no "fact-checkers," no filters for truth—parties can make accusations without accountability and return to court repeatedly without consequence. Parenting and child support rulings remain perpetually modifiable, leaving families in a state of endless flux, devoid of the closure they so desperately seek. This is not justice; it's survival in a fractured system.

In most states, "no-fault" divorce laws strip the process of its moral reckoning, reducing the once dramatic allegations of adultery, abandonment, and even domestic violence to irrelevance in the eyes of the court. These laws aim to diffuse the emotional landmines of blame and fault, redirecting the parties' attention to pragmatic concerns: parenting plans, financial support, and the division of assets. The intention is to create a streamlined, less combative process, but in doing so, the system often leaves victims of egregious behavior without a voice, their experiences rendered legally insignificant. Instead, the focus shifts to the utilitarian tasks of assigning property, calculating support, and shaping co-parenting frameworks, where even deeply personal betrayals become irrelevant footnotes. The result is a process designed to minimize conflict on paper while often leaving raw emotional wounds festering beneath the surface.

How to Present Your Case
Think Like a Judge

Frame Your Arguments Around the Child's Best Interests: The family court is fundamentally concerned with what will benefit the child. Focus your case on how the psychopath's behavior impacts the child's well-being. Avoid framing your arguments as a personal vendetta; instead, present the psychopath's behavior as a risk to the child's emotional, psychological, or physical health. Judges are looking for evidence of the child's stability, safety, and overall welfare.

Evidence is Your Lifeline: Emails, texts, voicemails, financial records, and any documented patterns of manipulation, dishonesty, or neglect. Present facts, not feelings.

Stay Calm and Controlled: Maintain composure at all costs. Present your case methodically and avoid engaging in reactive behavior, which can undermine your credibility.

Anticipate Manipulative Courtroom Tactics: Expect psychopaths to present themselves as the victim and twist narratives to make you appear vindictive or irrational. Judges favor shared custody unless presented with compelling evidence otherwise. They see a snapshot of your lives, not the full picture. What image will you show them?

Anticipate Your Opponent's Arguments

- **"Parental Alienation"**: Psychopaths frequently accuse their victims of alienating the child. They may paint you as controlling or emotionally abusive for setting necessary boundaries.

- **"I'm the Stable Parent"**: Expect them to fabricate stories of their own "calm and reasoned" parenting while portraying you as volatile and uncooperative.

- **"False Allegations"**: Psychopaths may file false claims of abuse or neglect against you to shift the court's focus and put you on the defensive.

Rebut with....

1. **Evidence:** Keep detailed records of all interactions with the psychopath. This includes text messages, emails, and incidents where their behavior directly impacts the child.

2. **Experts:** If possible, involve a custody evaluator, therapist, or other professionals who can attest to the psychopath's behavior and its impact on the child. Their clinical perspective can carry significant weight in court.

3. **Patterns:** Emphasize patterns of behavior that demonstrate the psychopath's inability to act in the child's best interests.

4. **Clothing Tells a Narrative:** Attire persuades without words by bypassing rational analysis and appealing directly to emotions. Research in impression formation reveals that clothing triggers automatic judgments about trustworthiness, vulnerability, and character. Clothes that fit well convey confidence and composure. Neutral tones reflect seriousness and professionalism. Keep jewelry to a minimum and make-up light. For men with facial hair, be well-groomed. Shoes, close-toed pumps, or flats in neutral colors for women; for men, dress shoes in black or brown with matching belts.

POST-DIVORCE REALITIES WITH A PSYCHOPATH

Divorcing a psychopath doesn't end the nightmare—it opens a new front. Their need for control doesn't vanish; it adapts. What follows is a calculated assault on court orders, finances, and custody agreements, all while they present a facade of reason and victimhood to the legal system.

Psychopaths don't respect court rulings. To them, child support, alimony, and settlements aren't obligations but weapons. They evade, stall, and defy, forcing victims into a relentless cycle of legal battles. Compliance is never the goal—domination is.

- **Child Support:** A psychopath may skip payments, knowing that the burden falls on the victim to pursue legal action. They might also use child support as leverage, threatening to withhold funds unless their demands are met.

- **Spousal Support:** Psychopaths are notorious for contesting spousal support orders, often arguing that the victim doesn't "deserve" it. They may file motions to reduce payments or falsely claim changes in income.

- **Real Estate Liens:** Even if a court orders the sale or division of property, a psychopath may refuse to cooperate, delay proceedings, or damage the property out of spite.

Restraining Orders – Pros and Cons — Restraining orders provide legal protection on paper but are often insufficient when dealing with a psychopath. To them, a restraining order is not a boundary but a challenge. They may comply initially to avoid legal repercussions, but violations are common. While restraining orders can help establish a legal record, they are only as effective as the victim's ability to enforce them, and enforcement is often reactive, not preventative. Psychopaths may escalate covert harassment to avoid detection, such as using third parties or exploiting loopholes.

When filling out protective orders, focus on patterns of abuse, choosing three specific instances that illustrate each: violence, reckless conduct, substance abuse, threats.

Parenting Time Orders — Psychopaths often weaponize their children, using custody arrangements to maintain control over their ex-spouse. They may violate parenting time orders by refusing exchanges, returning children late, or engaging in alienation tactics. The result is a toxic dynamic where the victim must pick up the emotional and practical slack, further exhausting their resources.

Courts can impose penalties, fines, reduced parenting time, or even contempt charges—but the psychopath's disregard for authority often renders these measures ineffective.

Contempt proceedings are one of the few tools available to enforce compliance with court orders, such as child support payments, spousal support, property division, or parenting time agreements. However, when dealing with a psychopath, they can feel more like an uphill battle than a resolution.

Sanctions and Penalties Courts Can Impose Courts have a range of sanctions for contempt, which vary in severity based on the violation:

- **Monetary Fines:** Courts may impose fines for violations like nonpayment of child or spousal support.
- **Wage Garnishment:** For unpaid financial obligations, the court can order direct garnishment of wages.
- **Asset Seizure:** The court may seize bank accounts or other assets to satisfy financial orders.
- **Compensatory Sanctions:** The victim can be reimbursed for attorney fees or other costs incurred due to the violation.
- **Reduction of Parenting Time:** Courts may reduce or suspend parenting time if the psychopath's actions are harmful to the child or violate custody agreements.
- **Incarceration:** In severe cases, such as chronic refusal to comply with support payments, the court can impose jail time.
- **Community Service:** Courts may order community service as a penalty for contempt.
- **Court-Mandated Therapy:** In cases involving children, the court might require a parent to attend therapy or parenting classes.

Sidebar: Court-imposed sanctions are rarely a deterrent to the psychopath. Instead, they view them as temporary setbacks. Jail time, fines, or reduced parenting time might inconvenience them in the short term, but they often interpret these consequences as further opportunities to play the victim, blame the system, or manipulate their way back into control.

Post-divorce hearings are inevitable, surfacing sometimes weeks, sometimes years later— especially if the psychopath didn't get their way. Their motives aren't rooted in genuine change or new circumstances; often, the "change" is their own erratic behavior or simply a refusal to accept the court's decisions. They thrive on chaos and use the legal system as a weapon to perpetuate conflict, pulling their ex-partner back into a vortex of hearings, disputes, and endless modifications.

CHAPTER FOURTEEN
THE RIPPLE EFFECT

"Psychological abuse is not just about what abusers do—it's about the world they create for their victims, one where fear and dependency replace autonomy and safety." –Dr. Evan Stark, author of Coercive Control: How Men Entrap Women in Personal Life

VICTIMS DESCRIBE LITIGATION with a psychopath as retraumatizing, forcing them to relive the abuse in a setting where their abuser often appears calm, composed, and credible. Jenna, whose husband Mark dragged her through a three-year divorce, described it as "a nightmare I couldn't wake up from. He smiled at me in court like we were still married, like none of it was real. Meanwhile, I was crumbling inside."

And it isn't just the judges who are played, it's also the psychopath's lawyers.

Marci's Story

Peter adjusted the cuffs of his tailored shirt and glanced around the dimly lit conference room. He wasn't in a courtroom yet, but this was just as important. His lawyer, Marci, was meticulously reviewing the

Chapter 14: The Ripple Effect

documents spread before her. She was sharp, her reputation legendary in criminal defense circles. But Peter had always enjoyed a challenge.

He wasn't guilty, at least not in the sense that mattered to him. Sure, he had done what they said— embezzled money, defrauded a few clients, fabricated documents—but he didn't feel guilty. And feelings, as far as he was concerned, were for fools. What mattered was avoiding consequences, and that meant Marci needed to believe him.

"Thank you for meeting me," Peter began, leaning forward with just the right mix of vulnerability and composure. "This whole situation has been... devastating."

Marci glanced up, her expression professional and unreadable. "Let's cut to the chase. They've got you on wire fraud, falsifying contracts, and conspiracy. That's a lot to explain."

Peter exhaled sharply, running a hand through his perfectly combed hair. "I know it looks bad. But you must understand, this isn't who I am. I got in over my head. A few bad decisions snowballed, and now here we are." He paused, letting the weight of his words settle. "I trusted the wrong people. If I could go back and fix it, I would."

His voice cracked slightly on the last word, a subtle touch of practiced emotion. He noticed Marci's brow furrow slightly. *Good*, he thought. *She's buying it.*

Over the next hour, Peter laid out his story—a carefully curated version of events that painted him as a victim of circumstance. He talked about the pressure he was under, the manipulative business partner who had "led him astray," and his desire to provide for his ailing mother (a complete fabrication, as his mother was alive, healthy, and living in Florida).

He knew exactly when to inject emotion, when to pause for dramatic effect, and when to let his voice quaver just enough to seem genuine. By the end, Marci was nodding, her demeanor softening.

"You're saying you were a pawn in someone else's scheme?" she asked.

"Exactly," Peter said, leaning back with a sigh. "I was naive. I thought I was helping the company. I didn't realize what was happening until it was too late."

Peter's strategy was a calculated and multifaceted manipulation designed to exploit every vulnerability in the system. At the core of his approach was a careful cultivation of pity and empathy. He painted himself as a good man who had simply made a series of unfortunate, but understandable, decisions under duress. With practiced sincerity, he conveyed the emotional toll the situation had taken on him, using phrases like "I haven't slept in weeks" and "I just want to make things right." This framing was intended to elicit sympathy and diminish any sense of personal accountability.

Simultaneously, Peter masterfully redirected blame, subtly shifting the narrative to implicate others as the true culprits. By suggesting, "Check the emails—you'll see the pressure they were putting on me. They knew I didn't have the experience to question them," he deflected responsibility, framing himself as a victim of circumstances beyond his control. This tactic served to obscure his role and keep the focus away from his own actions.

Peter's manipulation was further refined by his use of selective truth-telling. He provided just enough verifiable facts to make his story appear credible, carefully omitting any incriminating details that would have undermined his narrative. For instance, he admitted to signing documents but claimed he had been misled about their contents, a half-truth that further clouded the issue and reinforced his victimhood.

Finally, Peter appealed to his attorney's ego, positioning Marci as his savior. "I know I don't deserve a second chance," he said, his voice low and filled with feigned humility, "but if anyone can help me show the court the truth, it's you." This appeal not only flattered her but also cast her as the key to his redemption, further manipulating her into aligning herself with his narrative. Each element of Peter's strategy was designed to manipulate emotions, redirect attention, and obscure the truth, all while maintaining a carefully crafted image of innocence and victimization.

When the trial began, Peter continued his performance. On the stand, he was composed but contrite, striking a careful balance between confidence and humility. He spoke about his supposed remorse and his commitment to "rebuilding his life." He even produced character witnesses—former colleagues and acquaintances he had manipulated into vouching for him.

"I trusted the wrong people," Peter told the jury, his voice steady but tinged with regret. "I made mistakes, and I take responsibility for them. But I'm not the monster the prosecution wants you to believe I am."

The prosecution pushed hard, presenting emails and financial records that painted Peter in a damning light. But Peter was prepared. He deflected questions with precision, acknowledging minor faults while denying major accusations.

"That email was taken out of context," he said calmly. "I was following instructions from my superiors."

When pressed, he used his favorite tactic: turning the focus back on his accuser. "Why don't you ask my former business partner? Oh, that's right—he's conveniently disappeared."

The jury was divided. Some believed Peter's story, moved by his apparent sincerity. Others were skeptical but couldn't ignore the reasonable doubt he had planted. In the end, Peter was convicted on lesser charges, avoiding the harshest penalties. His sentence was reduced to two years, with eligibility for parole after eighteen months.

As the judge read the verdict, Peter's face remained impassive, but inside, he was triumphant. He had played the system and won—just as he knew he would.

Peter's articulate and engaging demeanor had disarmed his lawyer, making her overlook inconsistencies in his story. His narrative focused on scapegoating others, but Marci failed to question why he took no true responsibility. His emotional outbursts were convincing, but upon reflection, they always seemed conveniently timed. Peter provided just enough plausible details to misdirect her, but she hadn't pushed him hard enough for verifiable facts.

Peter's manipulation of his defense attorney and the legal system was a master class in psychopathy. He used charm, deceit, and emotional manipulation to create a narrative that minimized his culpability and maximized his chances of leniency.

The Psychological Toll on Defense Teams

Defending clients with psychopathic traits, especially in high-profile cases, exacts a profound psychological and emotional toll on defense attorneys. The cases of Jodi Arias and James Holmes illustrate the unique challenges and ripple effects of representing individuals whose crimes, personalities, and public scrutiny push attorneys to their limits.

Kirk Nurmi, lead defense attorney for Jodi Arias, experienced firsthand the emotional strain of representing a client he later described as manipulative and deceitful. Arias's shifting narratives, lack of remorse, and attempts to control her defense made the case a moral and professional minefield. Nurmi later revealed that defending Arias was a career-defining burden that left him emotionally drained and physically unwell.

> *You can't turn it off. Your family, your friends—they see the toll, even when you try to hide it. I'd sit down for dinner and realize I hadn't eaten all day, not because I wasn't hungry, but because my mind was so consumed with trial prep or a new piece of evidence. Relationships strain under the weight of your absence—physically and emotionally. I'd miss birthdays or vacations because I couldn't escape the courtroom or the deadlines. My spouse, at one point, told me they felt like a widow.*
>
> *It's like living in a state of constant hyper-vigilance. You worry about everything—did you file the right motions? Did you miss something in the discovery? Did you fail to connect with the jury in closing arguments? And if you lose? The guilt is crushing. I've spent hours replaying cases in my mind, wondering if I could've done something differently. It doesn't help that society often sees you as the villain, defending someone accused of heinous crimes. That isolation only deepens the depression.*
>
> *It's not about excusing what they've done—it's about believing that no one deserves to be thrown away. That belief, however bruised, is what keeps me going. But the scars—emotional and physical—don't disappear.*

In his memoir *Trapped with Ms. Arias*, Nurmi recounts how the weight of defending someone so reviled by the public became a personal and professional nightmare. The media labeled him a villain for doing his job—zealously defending his client. In one instance, Nurmi recalls being publicly mocked for his appearance, with one commentator cruelly labeling him as "fat" and "unfit" for the job. His physicality became the subject of ridicule, detracting from his legal abilities and amplifying the personal attacks.

The stress, compounded by the media's savaging, led to severe health problems, including cancer. He ultimately left the legal profession, citing the experience as one that made him question not just the value of his work, but the entire purpose of engaging in a profession that could lead to such destructive personal consequences.

Reflecting on the toll that high-profile cases like his have on lawyers, Nurmi has become a vocal proponent of self-care for those in the legal field. He speaks candidly about the need for lawyers to recognize the emotional and psychological challenges they face, particularly when defending clients in highly charged, emotionally draining cases. His advocacy underscores the importance of prioritizing mental well-being, especially for those navigating the morally complex terrain of criminal defense.

James Holmes
The Cost of Defending a Mass Murderer

In the case of James Holmes, the perpetrator of the Aurora, Colorado, movie theater shooting that left 12 people dead and 70 injured, his defense attorneys faced extraordinary emotional and physical tolls. Their job was to present Holmes, who displayed psychopathic traits and severe mental illness, as not guilty by reason of insanity—a defense that sparked intense public outrage.

The emotional fatigue endured by attorneys like Tamara Brady and Daniel King during their defense of James Holmes was not just a result of the sheer complexity of the case but also the relentless public scrutiny that came with representing someone responsible for such immense suffering. From the outset, both Brady and King were labeled as complicit in Holmes's atrocities by the public, and media outlets were quick to paint them as enablers of evil. For example, in one of the more venomous moments of the trial's coverage, media commentators accused them of defending a monster, questioning their moral integrity and suggesting that by simply doing their jobs, they were tacitly supporting Holmes's actions. As the trial unfolded,

Brady and King were forced to confront the most harrowing aspect of their work: the constant reminder of the victims' grief.

The physical strain on the defense team was equally profound. Reports from within the team revealed that many attorneys were dealing with sleepless nights, deteriorating health, and mental exhaustion.

They were tasked with finding a way to present Holmes not as a monster but as a human being with a history and a psyche that could be understood—no matter how painful or unsettling that might be. This moral conflict permeated every decision, every statement, and every argument they made. They were forced to balance the dissonance between their own personal distaste for Holmes's actions and their professional responsibility to provide him with a robust defense.

For Brady, King, and the rest of the defense team, the consequences of their work extended far beyond the courtroom. The personal cost of defending James Holmes would be felt long after the verdict was delivered.

Advocating for the Psychopath in Family Court

Representing a psychopath in family court is like enabling an addict. It starts with a hook—as the psychopath draws their lawyer in with a compelling narrative, painting themselves as the misunderstood party, the victim of a vindictive ex-spouse. It's seductive, this illusion of being their ally, their savior. But like an addict, the psychopath is never satisfied. They need more—more control, more power, more validation—and their lawyer becomes an unwitting enabler.

At first, the lies are subtle, even plausible. The psychopath spins stories of betrayal and injustice, and the lawyer, eager to advocate zealously, accepts their version of reality. Over time, the lies grow bolder, the fabrications more elaborate. Yet, by this point, the lawyer is emotionally hooked, invested in their client's success. They start rationalizing the red flags—"Maybe they're just passionate," or "The other side must be exaggerating." The lawyer becomes complicit in perpetuating the psychopath's narrative, just as an enabler excuses the addict's destructive behavior.

Psychopaths have a knack for reading people, for identifying vulnerabilities and exploiting them. They know how to make their lawyer feel indispensable, valued. They might praise the lawyer's skill and confide personal details to foster a false sense of intimacy or frame their demands as urgent and justified. This emotional manipulation traps the lawyer in a cycle of validation and dependency, much like an enabler who feels needed by the addict but can't see they're being used.

The lawyer starts losing their objectivity and their ability to step back and assess the situation critically. They become entangled in the psychopath's agenda, prioritizing the client's whims over their professional boundaries. Every interaction feels high-stakes, fraught with the urgency and drama the psychopath thrives on. The lawyer's own identity begins to blur as they are consumed by their client's narrative, much like an enabler who sacrifices their well-being for the addict's chaos.

Ultimately, the lawyer risks becoming an extension of the psychopath—a tool in their arsenal, a puppet in their game. The lawyer finds themselves arguing outrageous positions in court, making demands that defy reason, and battling not for justice but for the psychopath's sense of victory. They may lose credibility with judges and opposing counsel, their professional reputation tainted by association.

This transformation is eerily like an enabler who loses themselves in the addict's world, unable to distinguish their own needs and values from the addict's insatiable cravings. The lawyer starts experiencing the same volatility as their client—moments of triumph when the psychopath succeeds in manipulating the system, followed by crushing lows when the lies unravel, or the manipulation backfires.

The emotional toll on the lawyer can be devastating. They may feel used, betrayed, and disillusioned when they realize the extent of their client's deceit. Worse, they may struggle with guilt—guilt for enabling the psychopath's harm, guilt for failing to protect the victim, or their own ethical boundaries. Like an enabler waking up to the destruction wrought by an addict, the lawyer is left to pick up the pieces, often at great personal and professional cost.

To break free from this dynamic, lawyers must recognize the patterns of manipulation and enforce strict boundaries. They must remind themselves of their ethical duties—not just to their client, but to the court, the opposing party, and themselves. Walking away from a toxic client may feel like defeat, but it's often the only way to regain clarity and integrity. Much like the enabler who steps back from the addict, choosing to protect themselves is the first step toward healing.

The Puppet and the Puppet Master

Taylor prided herself on being a fighter in family court. She'd built her reputation on taking tough cases and winning, her relentless drive earning her the nickname "The Bulldog." But when James walked into her office one humid September afternoon, Taylor had no idea she was about to become someone's puppet.

James had everything—movie-star looks, a disarming smile, and the charm of a late-night talk show host. He sat in her office, recounting how his wife, Rachel, had ruined his life. She'd left him with nothing but a pile of unpaid bills, poisoned their daughter against him, and smeared his name to anyone who would listen. His voice trembled just enough to suggest vulnerability; his anger kept in check like a man who had mastered the art of self-restraint.

Taylor leaned forward. *Another victim in need of justice*, she thought. She accepted the case without hesitation.

In the early days, James was the ideal client. He responded to emails promptly, brought detailed documentation, and praised Taylor at every turn. "You're the only one who believes me," he'd say, his voice heavy with gratitude. Taylor couldn't help but feel protective of him. She stayed up late drafting motions, combing through financial records, and crafting arguments to expose Rachel as the manipulative liar James claimed her to be.

The first red flag came when James insisted on filing an emergency motion to modify custody. "Rachel's boyfriend is dangerous," he told Taylor, his eyes wide with fear. "I overheard my daughter say he yells at her." Taylor, concerned for the child's safety, agreed. But when they arrived in court, James's testimony was shaky. The judge denied the motion, citing a lack of evidence.

Afterward, James exploded. "How could you let this happen?" he hissed, his voice low but sharp. Taylor apologized, feeling an unfamiliar pang of inadequacy. *Maybe I should've pushed harder*, she thought. She doubled down, determined not to let him down again.

As the case dragged on, James's demands grew more erratic. He wanted Taylor to subpoena Rachel's employer, claiming she was hiding income. He insisted on filing contempt motions over missed custody exchanges, even when they seemed trivial. He'd call Taylor at odd hours, his tone oscillating between desperate and accusatory.

"You don't understand how she's ruined me!" he yelled during one late-night call. Taylor found herself soothing him, offering reassurances she didn't entirely believe. She told herself it was part of the job, that James was just under immense stress. But privately, she started to dread his calls.

Chapter 14: The Ripple Effect

One morning, Taylor walked into the courtroom clutching a file filled with James's latest accusations. She felt uneasy, but Zach had insisted. "Rachel is a liar," he said, leaning across her desk with an intensity that made her stomach churn. "You need to expose her."

As Taylor stood before the judge, she felt the weight of the courtroom's skepticism. Rachel's lawyer was calm and methodical, dismantling James's claims with precision. By the time Rachel herself took the stand, she came across as a weary but devoted mother, far from the monster James had described.

Taylor glanced at James, seated beside her. His jaw was tight, his knuckles white as he gripped the table. He shot her a glare that made her chest tighten. She turned back to the judge, her voice faltering as she tried to salvage what she knew, deep down, was a losing argument. When the judge ruled in Rachel's favor, James stormed out of the courtroom without a word. Taylor sat alone at the defense table, feeling like she'd been stripped of her armor.

It wasn't until Taylor ran into Rachel's lawyer a few weeks later that the full picture emerged. "James?" the lawyer said, raising an eyebrow. "You know he filed a restraining order against his first ex-wife too, right? The same story—she was 'crazy,' 'unstable.'" Taylor felt the blood drain from her face. She'd been played.

The realization hit like a punch to the gut. James had used her—weaponized her expertise and her instincts to fight for justice. She'd been his tool, his puppet, in a vendetta that had nothing to do with his daughter's well-being and everything to do with his need to win.

Taylor dropped James as a client the next day, but the damage was done. She spent weeks replaying every decision, every motion she'd filed on his behalf. She questioned her judgment, her ability to see people for who they truly were. The sleepless nights turned into migraines; her appetite disappeared. She started to resent her job, the very work she'd once loved.

It took time for Taylor to rebuild her confidence, to trust her instincts again. But the experience left scars—a constant reminder of how easily even the most seasoned advocate can become entangled in a psychopath's web.

And every now and then, when she sits in court and sees that flash of charm on a client's face, she wonders: Is this another James?

CHAPTER FIFTEEN
HEALING FROM HELL

"After years of walking on eggshells, you'll be tempted to make yourself small, invisible, safe. Resist that urge. Find your voice. Use it. It's the only way to reclaim your life.... you're not crazy—you're just surviving crazy." –Dr. Ramani Durvasula

Kristin's Story

It wasn't the broken vase or the bruised arm that finally made Kristin question her marriage. Those were surface wounds, visible and fleeting. It was the way her eight-year-old daughter, Emma, flinched when her father raised his voice at dinner. It was the hollow, detached way her ten-year-old son, Luke, stared at the floor as if willing himself to disappear.

For years, Kristin had told herself she could manage her husband, Ken. His charm had once enchanted her, but over time, it became a weapon he wielded against her and everyone around them. He would gaslight her until she doubted her own memories, isolate her from her friends and family, and undermine her confidence so completely that she felt like a ghost in her own home.

But Kristin stayed. For the kids, she told herself. For the stability. For the hope that he might change. But in the quiet of her mind, she knew the truth: she stayed because she didn't believe she deserved better. Ken had seen to that.

Kristin's body bore the brunt of her marriage long before she realized it. The constant stress left her with migraines that felt like thunder in her skull. She developed an ulcer from the anxiety of trying to anticipate Ken's next mood swing. Sleep became a distant memory; every noise in the night made her sit bolt upright, her heart pounding as she waited for his footsteps.

Her hair thinned. Her weight fluctuated as she alternated between stress-induced starvation and binge eating for comfort. Even her posture changed—she walked hunched, shoulders drawn inward as if trying to make herself smaller, less noticeable, less of a target.

But it wasn't just the physical symptoms. It was the shame she felt when doctors asked about the bruises on her arms or the stress that seemed to radiate from her. "Just clumsy," she'd say with a nervous laugh. "You know how it is."

Her children noticed. Emma started biting her nails until they bled, mirroring her mother's nervous habits. Luke developed asthma, his shallow breaths echoing the suffocating tension in their home. Kristin saw it all but felt powerless to stop it.

Kristin's emotional world was a barren landscape. Ken had stripped her of joy, of hope, of any sense of self. He ridiculed her dreams, calling her writing "a hobby for bored housewives." He controlled every aspect of her life, from what she wore to how she spent money, and any attempt to assert herself was met with ridicule or rage.

"You're so dramatic," he'd sneer when she tried to address his behavior. "This is why no one takes you seriously."

Over time, Kristin internalized his voice. She second-guessed every decision, convinced she was as incompetent and unworthy as he made her feel. She stopped confiding in friends, ashamed to admit the reality of her life. Isolation became her default state, and loneliness was her *constant companion. Her children absorbed this emotional chaos like sponges. Emma, once bubbly and outgoing, became withdrawn and overly eager to please. She learned early that keeping quiet and agreeing with her father was the safest route. Luke, on the other hand, became defiant, challenging his father in ways that left Kristin terrified for him.*

"You're just like your mother," Ken would spit at him, turning the boy's anger into another weapon against her.

As the years passed, the toll on Kristin and her children became more pronounced. Emma grew into a young woman who struggled to set boundaries, constantly seeking validation from others but terrified of rejection. She entered a string of unhealthy relationships, drawn to men who mirrored her father's controlling tendencies. "I just want someone who loves me," she'd say, unable to see how her past had shaped her choices.

Luke's rebellion turned into outright self-destruction. He started skipping school, getting into fights, and experimenting with drugs. The anger he'd carried for years spilled out in dangerous ways, and though he loved his mother, he couldn't forgive her for staying. "You let him do this to us," he told her once, his voice cracking with hurt. Kristin had no response. She carried that guilt like a stone around her neck.

For Kristin, the scars were both visible and invisible. She eventually left Ken, but the years of abuse had eroded her health and her spirit. She struggled with PTSD, her mind replaying his harsh words and cruel actions like a broken record. She feared intimacy, certain that any new relationship would end the same way. Therapy helped, but the healing was slow and incomplete.

Kristin's story isn't one of total defeat, but it is a cautionary tale. The physical and emotional toll of staying with a psychopath ripple outward, affecting not just the victim but everyone in their orbit. For her children, the scars of their childhood became hurdles they would spend their adult lives trying to overcome.

Leaving a psychopath isn't freedom—it's only the first step. True freedom comes from rebuilding the identity they tried to erase. They convinced you that you were weak, dependent, less without them. That was never true. Rebuilding isn't just healing—it's defiance. Their control ends the moment you decide it does.

But leaving requires strategy, secrecy, and precision. Secure your finances by opening a separate bank account, stashing cash, and gathering important documents, including birth certificates, passports, and financial statements. Have a safe place to go when the time comes. Whether it's a trusted friend's home, a shelter, or even a new apartment, ensure your escape route is secure and that you have a place to turn to for refuge when the exit is made.

Once you leave, the psychopath will likely escalate their tactics. They'll beg, threaten, manipulate, and lie—all to regain control. They'll say whatever they think you want to hear: that they've changed, that they love you, that they're nothing without you. It's not love—it's desperation. Don't fall for it. The only way to protect yourself is through clear and firm boundaries. Block all contact, refuse to engage, and if necessary, pursue a restraining order.

When it comes to future relationships, be explicit about what you will and won't tolerate. You don't owe anyone access to your life if they can't honor your needs. Equally important is protecting yourself internally. Give yourself permission to walk away from situations, places, or people that bring up old wounds or triggers. It's not selfish to prioritize your mental health; it's a necessary act of survival.

If you share children, expect your ex to weaponize custody. Stick to court orders—deviating gives them ammunition. Parental alienation accusations are their favorite tool. Protect your children by getting them into therapy before the damage becomes permanent.

Psychopaths don't just steal your resources—they steal your sense of self. Rebuilding after the escape is about rediscovering who you are outside of their influence.

Trauma-informed therapy—especially CBT (Cognitive Behavioral Therapy)—helps survivors separate the psychopath's voice from their own. They never told the truth. They used words as weapons.

EMDR (Eye Movement Desensitization and Reprocessing) therapy can be particularly effective for reprocessing trauma and loosening its grip. But healing isn't just mental—it's physical and emotional. Journaling, rediscovering passions, reconnecting with trusted friends—these are acts of defiance. Rebuilding joy is the final victory.

Forgiveness is not for them—it's for you. Survivors blame themselves—for not seeing the signs, for staying too long, for believing the lies. But as Dr. Bessel van der Kolk wrote in The Body Keeps the Score: "Trauma survivors are not responsible for what happened to them, but they are responsible for their recovery."

Healing often requires rituals of release. Some survivors write letters they never send—declaring their freedom and burning them as a symbolic act. Others use visualization techniques—imagining themselves cutting the invisible cord that ties them to their abuser. Every act of reclamation weakens their hold.

Psychopaths leave you hypervigilant, wary, afraid to open your heart. Trust isn't blind faith—it's self- awareness. It's recognizing red flags, honoring instincts, and giving yourself permission to walk away.

Healing isn't linear—it's a labyrinth. Some days, the past feels closer than the future. But every step forward is a step away from their shadow—and back into your own light.

STRATEGY	WHY IT WORKS	HOW TO DO IT	EXAMPLE
SET AND ENFORCE CLEAR BOUNDARIES	Psychopaths thrive on violating personal boundaries. Clear limits disrupt their ability to manipulate and control.	- Communicate boundaries assertively (e.g., "I will not discuss this topic further" or "I need space right now").	"I said no, and I'm not changing my mind."
MANAGE EMOTIONAL REACTIONS	Psychopaths feed off emotional responses. Remaining calm denies them the reaction they seek	Enforce consequences consistently Practice mindfulness (deep breathing, counting to 10, taking a sip of water).	"That's interesting," and move on.
DOCUMENT EVERYTHING	Psychopaths rely on lies and distortions of reality. Documenting creates an objective account that can counter their manipulation.	Write down details of interactions, including dates and times. Save texts, emails, and other written communication.	"On [date], you said X. I have it in writing."
LEVERAGE THEIR WEAKNESS	Psychopaths crave power, making them susceptible to subtle manipulations.	Offer something that appears to enhance their power or image (only if it aligns with your goals). Use flattery strategically.	"I know you're the best person to handle this situation, so I trust you'll manage it perfectly."
SEEK SUPPORT AND STAY CONNECTED	Psychopaths aim to isolate their victims. A strong support system makes it harder for them to succeed.	Maintain contact with trusted friends, family, or colleagues. Share experiences with someone who can offer insight.	If the psychopath tries to alienate you, involve your support network in decisions to counteract their narrative.
TIP:	Psychopaths relentlessly pursue control.	Cut ties and limit contact if possible.	

Chapter 15: *Healing from Hell*

Know When to Walk Away
Olivia's Story

For years, Olivia lived in a haze of confusion and fear. What had begun as a whirlwind romance with Greg—an investment banker with charisma to spare—had descended into a labyrinth of control and psychological torment. Greg was a master manipulator. He isolated Olivia from her friends and family, convinced her to quit her job to "focus on us," and dismantled her self-esteem piece by piece. By the time Olivia realized she was being abused, she was financially dependent on Greg and trapped in a cycle of gaslighting and blame.

The breaking point came on a stormy autumn evening. Greg had accused Olivia of sabotaging his career after she asked a seemingly innocuous question about a late-night phone call. His rage was volcanic—shouting, breaking dishes, and then the chilling quiet. That night, as she huddled in their bedroom, Olivia resolved to leave. She didn't know how she would do it, but she knew staying meant losing herself entirely.

Olivia's first step was to contact a domestic violence advocate, who helped her understand her legal rights. The advocate guided Olivia through the process of filing a restraining order. It wasn't easy; Greg, true to his manipulative nature, presented himself as a victim in court, charming the judge and casting doubt on Olivia's claims.

Greg's legal tactics were classic psychopathy: using the system as a weapon to maintain control. He delayed proceedings, filed counterclaims, and even spread false rumors about Olivia to their mutual acquaintances. *"The legal system wasn't designed to deal with someone like him,"* Olivia later reflected. *"He turned every hearing into a theater, and for a while, it felt like I was the one on trial."*

What worked was meticulous preparation. Olivia began documenting everything: text messages, emails, financial transactions, and even voice recordings of Greg's outbursts. With the help of her advocate and a trauma-informed attorney, she built a case that painted a clear picture of Greg's abusive behavior.

Still, the process took its toll. Olivia described court appearances as *"a minefield of humiliation,"* where Greg would smirk at her from across the room as if daring her to continue. But each small victory—a motion granted, a lie exposed—strengthened her resolve.

Even after securing a protective order and beginning divorce proceedings, Olivia's battle was far from over. The psychological scars Greg had inflicted ran deep. She struggled with self-doubt, nightmares, and an overwhelming sense of guilt. *"Why didn't I see it sooner? Why did I let it go on for so long?"* were questions that haunted her.

What didn't work initially was traditional talk therapy. *"I wasn't ready to talk about my feelings because I couldn't even name them,"* Olivia explained. *"I felt like I was drowning, and I needed someone to throw me a life raft—not ask me how the water felt."*

It was a trauma-focused therapist who finally helped her turn a corner. The therapist introduced Olivia to Eye Movement Desensitization and Reprocessing (EMDR), a technique designed to help process and reframe traumatic memories. Through EMDR, Olivia began to untangle the web of Greg's manipulation and see his behavior for what it truly was: calculated, pathological, and not her fault.

Meditation and mindfulness practices also became part of Olivia's healing toolkit. At first, the idea of sitting alone with her thoughts was terrifying. *"I'd been conditioned to second-guess everything, so silence felt like an enemy,"* she said. But over time, guided meditations helped her reconnect with her body and learn to trust her instincts again.

Rebuilding her life meant reclaiming the independence Greg had systematically stripped away. Olivia started with small, symbolic acts: opening a bank account in her name, redecorating her apartment to reflect her tastes, and even adopting a rescue dog—a German shepherd mix she named Hope.

But the most transformative step was returning to work. Olivia had been a project manager before Greg convinced her to leave her job, and reentering the professional world was daunting. "I *felt like a fraud*," she admitted. "*Like everyone could see how broken I was.*"

Her first job interview was a disaster. When the hiring manager asked about the gap in her resume, Olivia stammered and froze. But instead of giving up, she sought out a career coach who specialized in working with survivors of domestic abuse. Together, they crafted a narrative that highlighted Olivia's resilience and transferable skills without delving into her personal history.

Eventually, Olivia landed a position at a nonprofit organization dedicated to supporting survivors of abuse. The work was challenging but deeply fulfilling. "*Helping others gave me a sense of purpose,*" Olivia said. "*It reminded me that I wasn't defined by what happened to me—I was defined by how I chose to move forward.*"

CHAPTER SIXTEEN
WARRIORS

SURVIVORS OF PSYCHOPATHY are modern-day warriors who fight an invisible battle against an enemy few understand. Their battlefield is psychological, their weapon is truth, and their armor is resilience. By embracing the warrior's creeds, survivors not only protect themselves from further harm but also transform their lives, reclaiming their power and purpose with dignity and strength. In doing so, they embody the essence of a warrior: unyielding in the face of adversity and unshakable in their pursuit of freedom and peace.

HONOR TRUTH	Uphold honesty with self and others.	Recognize the reality of their experiences and reject the lies imposed by the psychopath. Use truth as a shield against manipulation.
FACE FEAR WITH COURAGE	Confront fear head-on with bravery.	Break free from the abuser's control, challenge societal ignorance about psychopathy, and face the healing process with determination.
SET BOUNDARIES AND PROTECT SEEK	Defend what matters most. Transform struggles into growth.	Establish firm boundaries, protect their children, and prioritize safety and well-being.
WISDOM AND LEARN	Stay true to values, even under pressure.	Use experiences as lessons to gain insight into human behavior, resilience, and personal strength.

ACT WITH INTEGRITY	Rely on trusted allies for strength and support.	Avoid stooping to the psychopath's level. Choose justice over revenge and lead a life of authenticity.
BUILD A COMMUNITY	Persist even when the battle grows difficult.	Surround themselves with supportive friends, family, therapists, or survivor groups that empower and uplift them.
ENDURE WITH RESILIENCE	Use hardship as a catalyst for growth.	Take small steps forward in healing, recognizing that recovery is a journey that requires perseverance and patience.

It Isn't Personal

Taking back your power after enduring a relationship with a psychopath requires strength, strategy, and unwavering self-compassion. It's essential to understand that their actions were never about you but about satisfying their insatiable hunger for power, control, and validation. Their cruelty, lies, and betrayals are not reflections of your worth but symptoms of their disorder. The key to liberation lies in learning how to protect yourself, rebuild your identity, and move forward with a clear-eyed view of the world and your own inner strength.

Practice detachment. Visualize yourself as an observer in the situation, analyzing their behavior with clinical curiosity rather than emotional investment. Remind yourself daily: *I am not their victim; I am their survivor.* And make a "Reality Checklist" for moving forward:

- **Acknowledge Reality**: The relationship was built on manipulation, not mutual respect or love. Accepting this truth is painful but necessary for healing. Carry a paperweight or rock around with you until you no longer blame yourself or feel guilty.

- **Protect Your Energy:** Evaluate relationships and interactions carefully. Ask yourself: *Does this person make me feel safe, respected, and valued?*

- **Trust Patterns, Not Promises:** People reveal their true selves through repeated actions, not words. Pay attention to consistency.

- **Rebuild Trust in Yourself:** Your intuition was likely suppressed or dismissed by the psychopath. Start small, listening to your gut in low-stakes situations to rebuild confidence in your instincts.

- **Celebrate Progress:** Healing takes time, but every step forward is a victory. Acknowledge milestones, no matter how small, to reinforce your strength. Reward yourself.

- **Stay Grounded:** Practice mindfulness or journaling to stay present. Try "Here and Now" prompts—write where you are physically and emotionally. Write affirmations and repeat them daily until they are memorized. Examples: *I am safe. I am strong. I am worthy. I am loved, loveable, and loving.* Grounding exercises can help you avoid being pulled back into the past or overwhelmed by fear of the future. Try a silent hike, no music, no talking, just whispers of the trees.

- **Seek Justice, Not Revenge:** If legal proceedings are necessary, focus on protecting yourself and your family, **not** punishing the psychopath. Their lack of conscience means revenge will have no impact on them but could derail their own healing.

Chapter 16: Warriors

Psychological Abuse, a Crime Without a Crime Scene

Other nations have led the charge in broadening the definition of domestic abuse to include coercive control and emotional manipulation. The United Kingdom, with its 2015 *Serious Crime Act*, introduced the offense of "coercive and controlling behavior." This legislation explicitly criminalized non-physical abuse, such as gaslighting, financial control, and emotional manipulation. By focusing on the cumulative impact of these behaviors rather than requiring a single incident, the law placed the victim's lived experience at the forefront. Alongside legal measures, the UK has invested in comprehensive training for police and judicial officers, ensuring they are equipped to recognize and prosecute these cases effectively. This approach has proven successful, with thousands of convictions demonstrating that psychological abuse can be identified, addressed, and deterred within a legal framework.

France has similarly recognized the importance of addressing psychological abuse, enacting laws against "psychological violence" in 2010. These laws encompass verbal abuse, coercive control, and emotional manipulation, broadening the definition of domestic violence. Public awareness campaigns and holistic victim support, including psychological services and legal aid, further bolster the law's effectiveness, emphasizing not just punishment but also rehabilitation and recovery.

Australia has taken a similar approach, with states like Tasmania integrating emotional abuse and intimidation into their domestic violence laws. By defining abuse broadly and fostering collaboration between law enforcement, social services, and healthcare providers, Australia has built a system that not only prosecutes abusers but also supports victims in meaningful ways.

In the United States, some states are beginning to follow suit with innovative legislative proposals. California has explored formal recognition of coercive control within its domestic violence statutes, emphasizing the need for judicial education on non-physical abuse. Proposed reforms include incorporating evidence of psychological abuse into child custody decisions and mandating training for legal and family court professionals to ensure they understand the nuances of coercive control. Similarly, New York introduced legislation in 2021 to address patterns of behavior that isolate, intimidate, or dominate victims, with provisions for public awareness campaigns and recognition of the heightened vulnerabilities of marginalized communities, such as immigrants and LGBTQ+ individuals.

Globally, other innovations have been proposed to address psychological abuse more effectively. Restorative justice models, such as those trialed in New Zealand, focus on empowering victims and holding abusers accountable through mediated dialogues, reparations, and therapy. Technology-driven solutions also show promise—apps like Bright Sky in the UK and Daisy in Australia help victims document abuse, access legal information, and connect with resources. Proposals in Europe have even suggested real-time digital platforms to track and report coercive control, enabling victims to gather evidence and seek support without fear of reprisal. Additionally, mandatory screening for domestic violence in healthcare settings, proposed in countries like Canada and Denmark, includes a focus on identifying psychological abuse. Paired with training for law enforcement, therapists, and legal professionals, these initiatives aim to create a unified understanding of the dynamics of coercive control.

Despite these advances, challenges persist. Psychological abuse is often dismissed as too subjective or intangible, making it difficult to prove in court. Cultural stigma also plays a role, as emotional abuse is frequently normalized or minimized, preventing victims from seeking help. Furthermore, resource gaps, particularly in victim support services, risk making legal reforms symbolic rather than substantive. To address these barriers, legislation must balance the complexities of psychological abuse with actionable, enforceable measures. Drawing from successful models in the UK, France, and Australia, lawmakers in the United States and elsewhere can craft robust, victim-centered approaches to a pervasive form of violence that has long been ignored. By combining public awareness, judicial training, and comprehensive victim support, society can take meaningful steps toward recognizing and addressing the profound harm caused by psychological abuse.

Stalking, The First Breakthrough

The Watcher

Maria first noticed the drone when she was watering her backyard plants. It hovered just above the treetops, its soft buzz blending with the chirping of birds. She dismissed it as a neighbor's toy, but as the days passed, it returned—always lingering just outside her reach. By the third time, her chest tightened with unease. Something about its deliberate movements felt unnatural like it was watching her.

Her phone vibrated. Another anonymous message. "Nice sundress. Red suits you." Maria froze. She was wearing a red sundress. Her gaze darted toward the drone, which zipped away as if on cue.

She'd been receiving messages like this for months—cryptic, invasive, and always unnervingly accurate about her whereabouts or appearance. At first, she blocked the numbers, then switched phones, but the texts continued. She deleted her social media accounts, only to find new ones created in her name. Fake profiles tagged her friends in photos she'd never taken, accompanied by captions that made her sound unhinged. "Feeling watched? You should."

One night, the messages escalated. A photo of her bedroom window, taken from the street, arrived with the caption: "Close the curtains. Or don't. I like the view." Maria called the police, but without evidence of direct harm, they shrugged it off as a prank. Her words, they suggested, weren't enough to track down whoever was behind this.

Then came the package. Inside was a flash drive labeled "Your Life." Her stomach churned as she opened it on her laptop. It contained screenshots of her texts, emails, and private conversations with friends—conversations no one else could have seen. There were videos, too: grainy footage of her walking to her car, shopping at the grocery store, and sitting in her living room. A chilling realization settled over her: the stalker wasn't just online. He was everywhere.

Maria noticed small changes around her home. The gate to her backyard, usually locked, was ajar. Her Wi-Fi router blinked erratically, and a sign, the tech expert later explained, was that someone might be intercepting her connection. When she hired a private investigator, they discovered a GPS tracker tucked beneath her car and spyware installed on her phone.

But the worst was yet to come. One evening, as she sat on the couch, she heard the familiar buzz of the drone outside her window. This time, it wasn't retreating. It hovered just feet away, its tiny camera lens fixed squarely on her. Gathering her courage, she grabbed a broom and swung at it through the open window, knocking it to the ground. She stomped it to pieces, but the victory was short-lived. Her phone pinged with a new message: "That was expensive. Don't worry—I have backups."

The police, finally recognizing the escalation, traced the drone's registration to a man Maria had never met but whose name was disturbingly familiar from her inbox: Andrew K. He'd been following her for over a year, using social media posts to track her movements, hacking her devices to steal personal information, and deploying drones for physical surveillance.

Chapter 16: Warriors

The arrest brought temporary relief, but the damage lingered. Maria couldn't shake the feeling of being watched. Every time she passed a reflective surface, she half-expected to see Andrew's shadow behind her. Though he was gone, the scars of his intrusion remained—a constant reminder of how easily technology could turn someone's life into a nightmare.

Victims like Maria can take several proactive steps to combat their stalkers and protect themselves, especially in cases involving cyberstalking and drone surveillance.

Document the Harassment. Stalkers thrive on deniability, but documentation removes doubt. Every text, email, drone sighting, and unwanted encounter must be recorded. Screenshots saved messages, and written logs—complete with dates, times, and locations—build a timeline of harassment. Evidence is power.

Fortify Physical & Digital Security. Your home should be your sanctuary. That means security cameras, motion detectors, reinforced locks, and blackout curtains to block surveillance. Digital security is just as crucial. Change all passwords, enable two-factor authentication, scan for spyware, and shut down location-sharing. Refrain from posting location-based updates or personal information. Disconnect Wi-Fi when not in use. Every piece of online information is a breadcrumb a stalker can follow.

Leverage the Law—Take Action, Not Chances. Police reports aren't just paperwork—they create legal accountability. Maria must file a report, provide evidence, and follow up regularly. Restraining orders matter. While they don't stop every stalker, they provide legal leverage for prosecution if violated. In cases of drone surveillance, reporting to the FAA (Federal Aviation Administration) and law enforcement is essential.

Bring in Professionals. A private investigator can track the stalker's movements and uncover evidence beyond Maria's reach. A cybersecurity expert can identify weaknesses, lock down digital access, and trace electronic footprints. Self-defense training isn't just about combat—it's about confidence. Preparedness shifts fear into control.

Strengthen Psychological Resilience. Stalking isn't just a threat to safety—it's a slow erosion of mental and emotional stability. Therapy provides tools for coping. Support groups reinforce that you are not alone. Both are essential to combat the isolation and fear stalkers rely on.

A Safety Plan Is Not Paranoia—It's Survival. Vary your routines, use a safe mailing address, install personal safety apps, and keep emergency contacts ready. Predictability is a stalker's greatest weapon— unpredictability is a victim's greatest defense.

Advocacy Turns Fear into Power. Reaching out to victim advocacy groups, legal organizations, and awareness campaigns can provide resources while helping others navigate similar threats.

Refuse to Engage

Stalkers, particularly those who thrive on terror, often feed off the emotional reactions of their victims, seeking to instill fear, control, and a sense of helplessness. To strip them of this power, victims must adopt behaviors that deny stalkers the psychological "reward" they seek. First and foremost, refusing to engage is critical. Stalkers thrive on attention and emotional responses—anger, fear, or even acknowledgment fuels their obsession. By maintaining a strict no-contact policy and refusing to react to provocation, the victim begins to starve the stalker of the emotional sustenance they crave.

A key tactic is to make oneself "boring" to the stalker by limiting the flow of personal information, such as halting social media posts or maintaining strict privacy. Coupled with unpredictability—frequent changes to routines, habits, and even social circles—the victim disrupts the stalker's sense of control, making it harder for them to anticipate movements or maintain their psychological grip.

Projection of confidence is another vital strategy. Stalkers are drawn to vulnerability, and while the victim may feel anything but secure, outwardly displaying resilience and self-assuredness can deter their tormentor. This confidence is bolstered by preparedness: enrolling in self-defense courses, creating a safety plan, and involving a trusted support network provide not only practical protection but also diminish visible signs of fear, robbing the stalker of their perceived dominance.

Deterrence is further enhanced through strategic actions. Filing restraining orders, documenting every instance of stalking, and involving law enforcement signal to the stalker that their actions are neither unnoticed nor unchallenged. Public exposure of the stalker's behavior—where it is safe to do so—can often undermine their anonymity and embolden the victim's position, diminishing the stalker's control over the narrative.

Confrontation can provoke escalation, feeding the very dynamics the stalker seeks. Instead, leveraging expert assistance, such as behavioral specialists and security professionals, can tailor deterrence strategies to the specific psychology of the stalker. By removing the emotional rewards, increasing practical and psychological resilience, and seeking legal and community support, victims can shift the power dynamics in their favor, diminishing the stalker's hold and reducing their interest. As with all manipulative predators, denying them control is the most potent weapon.

Support of Allies

The support of allies is not only invaluable but transformative, creating ripples of change that empower victims and challenge systems of control.

Allies must begin by listening without judgment. Often, victims feel isolated and disbelieved, especially when their abuse doesn't leave visible scars. Allies can counteract this by believing victims, validating their experiences, and supporting their efforts to seek justice. Listening isn't passive—it's an active choice to stand alongside someone and help them find their voice when it's been suppressed.

Advocacy in the community is another powerful tool. Allies can use their platforms, however large or small, to amplify victims' voices. Whether it's speaking at public events, sharing resources online, or simply starting conversations, advocacy raises awareness and reduces stigma. Allies can also support legislative reform, which is vital to closing the gaps in legal protections. Writing letters to lawmakers, attending rallies, donating to organizations, and urging policymakers to recognize the impact of psychological abuse and prioritize legislation regarding psychological abuse are tangible actions that can shift the needle toward justice.

The Changing Legal Landscape

Stalking has emerged as one of the most visible forms of domestic violence, and for good reason— it's tangible, relentless, and terrifying in ways that are hard to ignore. Unlike other forms of psychological abuse that can be subtle or invisible, stalking leaves behind a trail: the late-night phone calls, the ominous texts, the car parked down the street. These behaviors make it easier for the public—and the legal system—to recognize the danger. In the United States alone, over 1 in 6 women and 1 in 17 men have experienced stalking in their lifetime, with most victims knowing their stalker intimately. That's more than 7.5 million people a year living with the constant fear of being watched or followed. This recognition has shown us the power of naming abuse and demanding systemic accountability. If we can shine this same spotlight on other forms of psychological abuse—like coercive control and gaslighting—we can start breaking the silence on the damage they cause and create the same momentum for change.

Several states have begun addressing stalking through targeted legislation, recognizing its unique dynamics, the psychological toll it exacts on victims, and the patterns of control often exhibited by individuals with psychopathic traits.

California has been at the forefront of legislative reform addressing stalking, particularly where it intersects with the potential for escalating violence. In 2023, California Governor Gavin Newsom signed expanded gun control measures into law, broadening the criteria for firearm restrictions. For the first time, stalking and animal cruelty were included as grounds for courts to prohibit individuals from accessing firearms. These reforms were driven by growing awareness of how stalking behaviors often precede acts of physical violence. This recognition aligns with research showing that individuals with psychopathic tendencies often escalate their actions from psychological intimidation to more overt aggression, particularly when denied access to their victims. California's reforms reflect an acknowledgment of the connection between stalking, coercive control, and lethal outcomes.

While these changes are a critical step forward in protecting victims, enforcement remains a challenge, and victims often feel the burden of ensuring the laws are applied in their specific cases. By recognizing stalking as a warning sign and tying it to proactive gun control measures, California is setting a precedent that could save countless lives—but only if we ensure these laws are consistently upheld and expanded nationwide.

Connecticut's 2021 enactment of *Jennifers' Law* marked a significant shift in how domestic violence is defined. The law expanded the definition to include "coercive control," explicitly encompassing behaviors such as stalking, isolation, and emotional manipulation. Named in honor of Jennifer Dulos and Jennifer Magnano, both victims of domestic violence and coercive control, the law was catalyzed by public outrage over these high-profile cases. It empowers victims to seek restraining orders for non-physical abuse, offering legal protection for behaviors that were previously dismissed as "minor" or "subjective." The inclusion of stalking as part of coercive control highlights how it is used to instill fear, undermine autonomy, and maintain dominance—core characteristics of psychopathic behavior.

Jennifers' Law provides a framework for recognizing and addressing the psychological harm inflicted by abusers who manipulate and intimidate from the shadows.

Chapter 16: Warriors

Jennifer Dulos vanished after dropping her children off at school. Despite an extensive investigation, her body has never been found, making her case particularly haunting and unresolved. She came from an affluent background, living in an upscale community, which challenged stereotypes about domestic violence being confined to lower socioeconomic classes. Jennifer alleged in court filings that her estranged husband, subjected her to years of coercive control and psychological abuse, including financial manipulation and threats. Her husband used the family court system to continue his control over Jennifer during their contentious divorce proceedings, exemplifying how abusers exploit legal avenues. The case attracted national attention due to its sensational elements, including her husband's arrest, his later suicide, and his girlfriend Michelle's involvement.

Jennifer Magnano fled with her children to a domestic violence shelter, seeking safety after years of emotional, physical, and psychological abuse. Despite her efforts, she was forced by legal pressure to return home, where her husband, Scott Magnano, murdered her. He violated restraining orders, yet the legal system failed to enforce protections effectively, exposing how such orders often lack real teeth. Scott was described as outwardly charming and respected in the community, masking his abusive nature and making Jennifer's plight harder for outsiders to believe. Scott used the family court system to force Jennifer into untenable positions, including the court-mandated reunification that led directly to her murder. Jennifer's family became vocal advocates for legal reform after her death, highlighting the critical need for laws addressing coercive control and ensuring victim safety

New York has also taken significant steps to address stalking through its recognition of coercive control within the context of domestic violence. Proposed legislation in recent years has sought to explicitly incorporate stalking behaviors, such as persistent following and intrusive monitoring, into the legal framework governing coercive control. These proposals emphasize education for law enforcement and judicial officials to recognize the patterns of psychological abuse that underlie stalking behaviors. While these laws have yet to achieve the comprehensive reach of Connecticut's reforms, they represent an important step toward recognizing stalking as a key tactic in the arsenal of psychological abusers.

Florida has taken a punitive approach to stalking, introducing enhanced penalties for repeat offenders. Recent reforms include longer sentences and the designation of certain stalking cases as felonies, particularly when they involve repeated violations of restraining orders or acts intended to intimidate victims further. These changes stem from a series of high-profile cases in which victims were murdered after repeated incidents of stalking went unaddressed. The reforms aim to prevent escalation by treating stalking as a serious and immediate threat rather than a precursor to physical violence.

In 2024, Pennsylvania became one of the first states to directly tackle the misuse of technology for stalking purposes. The state passed legislation criminalizing the unauthorized use of Bluetooth tracking devices, such as Apple's AirTags, to monitor victims without their consent. The law arose from a surge in cases where perpetrators, often domestic partners or former intimate connections, exploited these devices to track their victims' locations covertly. By recognizing this new avenue of psychological abuse, Pennsylvania's reform underscores the evolving nature of stalking as a crime and the need to address it comprehensively in a digital age. This legislation is particularly significant as it.

Preemptively closes a gap in the legal system that could be exploited by individuals with psychopathic tendencies who are adept at using technology to sustain their patterns of control and surveillance.

Arizona's 2022 amendment to its stalking laws demonstrates a growing awareness of the diverse tactics used by stalkers. The updated legislation expanded the definition of stalking to include digital communications, such as persistent emails, text messages, and social media interactions. The change was precipitated by the increasing prevalence of cyberstalking and its devastating psychological impact on victims. Traditional stalking behaviors, like following someone in person, have now evolved into high-tech harassment. Stalkers have exploited GPS tracking devices planted on cars or in personal belongings to monitor victims' every move. Others have turned to digital tools, using spyware apps to hack into phones or sending a relentless barrage of harassing messages across social media platforms.

This reform makes it easier to prosecute individuals who engage in digital harassment, offering broader protections for victims. Arizona's laws reflect an understanding that stalking, particularly when paired with digital harassment, serves as a form of psychological abuse, leaving victims feeling constantly monitored, trapped, and isolated, hallmarks of coercive control often seen in psychopathic offenders.

These legislative reforms reflect a growing recognition of stalking as a profound form of psychological abuse, often wielded by individuals with psychopathic tendencies who exploit the inadequacies of legal systems. Stalking is not a crime of passion; it is a crime of control, executed with precision to dismantle a victim's sense of safety, autonomy, and reality. Despite progress in states like California, Connecticut, and Pennsylvania, gaps remain in how stalking is prosecuted and understood. Laws must continue to evolve to address the digital tools, psychological strategies, and persistent tactics that stalkers employ. Without such reforms, victims will remain trapped in a cycle of fear, gaslighting, and isolation, and abusers will continue to operate unchecked. Recognizing stalking as a form of domestic violence and psychological abuse is not just a legal imperative—it is a moral one.

Survivors of psychological abuse and stalking hold a unique and powerful position to drive awareness and reform. Their voices can illuminate the insidious nature of these crimes, inspiring others to recognize the signs and demand change in both societal attitudes and legal systems. By sharing their stories, survivors can break the silence that abusers rely upon, giving a name to the fear, confusion, and isolation that many victims endure in silence. These personal accounts not only validate the experiences of other victims but also help lawmakers, law enforcement, and the public understand the profound psychological impact of coercive control, gaslighting, and stalking. Survivors can play a critical role in educating communities by working with advocacy groups to organize workshops, campaigns, and public discussions to dismantle the stigma surrounding non-physical abuse.

To empower others, survivors can also push for systemic reform by collaborating with domestic violence organizations, testifying in legislative hearings, and advocating for enhanced protections, such as the criminalization of coercive control and improved support for victims. Grassroots efforts, like forming survivor-led support groups, can provide a lifeline for individuals currently trapped in abusive relationships, offering them validation, resources, and strategies to regain control of their lives. Survivors can emphasize the importance of maintaining documentation—keeping records of abusive messages, stalking incidents, or financial control tactics—as these often serve as critical evidence in both legal proceedings and public awareness campaigns.

Furthermore, survivors can champion the integration of

psychological abuse education into schools, workplaces, and law enforcement training programs, ensuring that future generations recognize and respond to red flags before they escalate. They can advocate for increased funding for shelters, legal aid, and mental health services that specifically address the unique needs of those recovering from psychological trauma. By standing together and speaking out, survivors send a clear message: that psychological abuse is not invisible, and its survivors will not remain silent. Through collective action and unwavering courage, they not only empower themselves but also pave the way for a society where no victim is left to navigate the shadows of abuse alone.

ACKNOWLEDGMENTS

To the survivors of psychological abuse: Your strength, resilience, and courage have been my greatest teachers. Thank you for sharing your stories, your pain, and your triumphs. You have shown me the depth of the human spirit and the power of healing, even in the face of darkness. Your voices have inspired me, guided me, and reminded me why this work matters.

To my dear friends who walked with me through this journey. Your unwavering support, love, and patience were my anchor. Thank you for lifting me when I faltered, for believing in me when I struggled to believe in myself, and for reminding me that I was never alone.

To those who shared their insights, stories of survival, and courageous souls with me: You are the lifeblood of this work. Your willingness to open up and share your truths has enriched my understanding and shaped my approach to navigating the complexities of family and criminal court.

And to those who encouraged me to step into the courtroom, to fight for justice, and to help others navigate the legal landmines of the just(us) system: You saw something in me that I couldn't yet see in myself. Your faith pushed me to litigate with purpose, compassion, and determination.

This book is a testament to all of you—to your bravery, your wisdom, and your unyielding spirit. Thank you for being my guides and my inspiration. This is as much yours as it is mine.

With deepest gratitude,

Kerrie

APPENDIX A

Twenty Questions, One Answer

"The Subtle Sociopath: Is Someone in Your Life Exhibiting Harmful Traits?"

Use this quiz to assess whether someone you know may exhibit traits of mild sociopathy—not to the extreme of criminal behavior like murder, but still capable of causing harm and emotional suffering. Answer "**Yes**" or "**No**" to each question based on your experiences with this person.

- Does this person disregard rules, boundaries, or social norms when it suits them?
- Do they lack genuine remorse or guilt when they hurt or inconvenience others?
- Do they manipulate others to get what they want even if it causes harm?
- Have you noticed they often lie or distort the truth to serve their own agenda?
- Do they have a pattern of making excuses for their harmful behavior, shifting blame onto others?
- Does this person struggle to maintain long-term relationships due to conflicts, dishonesty, or betrayal?
- Have they ever violated your trust and then downplayed or dismissed your feelings about it?

- Do they seem to enjoy or show no concern about causing emotional distress to others?
- Are they often charming, persuasive, or overly flattering when they want something?
- Have they ever pressured you or others into decisions that felt wrong or uncomfortable?
- Does this person frequently act impulsively or recklessly without considering consequences?
- Do they lack empathy, struggle to understand, or care about how others feel?
- Have you seen them use people as tools to achieve their goals without genuine regard for their well-being?
- Do they struggle to accept responsibility for their mistakes, often deflecting or blaming others?
- Are they overly focused on their own needs, desires, or achievements, dismissing the concerns of others?
- Have they ever isolated you or tried to control your social connections with friends or family?
- Do they seem to have a "double life," acting charming in public but controlling or cruel in private?
- Have you noticed they frequently criticize, belittle, or undermine others to feel superior?
- Does this person rarely follow through on promises or commitments, often leaving others disappointed?
- Do you feel consistently drained, anxious, or confused after interactions with this person?

If you answered "**Yes**" to **3 or more** statements, It is safe to assume that this person may exhibit traits of antisocial personality disorder (ASPD) or mild sociopathy.

Compare with the **Checklist for Psychopathy:**

- Does this person exhibit superficial charm, easily winning people over but lacking genuine warmth?
- Do they appear emotionally cold or detached, even in situations that typically evoke empathy?
- Have you noticed they show no remorse or guilt, even for actions that caused significant harm?
- Does this person manipulate others in calculated, premeditated ways to achieve long-term goals?
- Do they take excessive risks or engage in criminal behavior without regard for the consequences?
- Have they ever lied to you in a way that felt deliberate, strategic, and devoid of emotional investment?
- Do they maintain a calm, composed demeanor, even in high-stress or confrontational situations?
- Does this person exhibit superficial charm, easily winning people over but lacking genuine warmth?
- Do they appear emotionally cold or detached, even in situations that typically evoke empathy?
- Have you noticed they show no remorse or guilt, even for actions that caused significant harm?
- Does this person manipulate others in calculated, premeditated ways to achieve long-term goals?

- Do they take excessive risks or engage in criminal behavior without regard for the consequences?
- Have they ever lied to you in a way that felt deliberate, strategic, and devoid of emotional investment?
- Do they maintain a calm, composed demeanor, even in high-stress or confrontational situations?
- Does this person view relationships as transactional, treating others as tools for their own benefit?
- Have you noticed they seem unaffected by the feelings or struggles of others, even close friends or family?
- Do they exhibit a sense of grandiosity, believing they are superior to others and above societal rules?
- Does this person engage in manipulation that feels rehearsed or methodical rather than impulsive?
- Have they ever mirrored your emotions or values in a way that felt calculated to gain your trust?
- Do they seem to lack long-term emotional attachments, even with family or romantic partners?
- Does this person show a consistent pattern of lying or deceit, even when it seems unnecessary?
- Do they use their charm and wit to disarm or manipulate people in social situations?
- Have you noticed they rarely express genuine fear, anxiety, or vulnerability?
- Does this person consistently seek power or control over others, even in subtle ways?

- Do they rationalize or justify unethical or harmful behavior with ease?
- Have they ever sabotaged someone else's success or well-being for personal gain without remorse?
- Do you feel like this person operates on a completely different emotional wavelength, detached from normal human connection?

A person with **psychopathic traits** would show more calculated, emotionally detached behavior, with manipulation aimed at achieving long-term goals. They maintain a polished facade, blending into society while harboring a complete lack of empathy or remorse.

Fewer than three traits likely indicate a personality that does not align closely with psychopathy. If **7-10 traits** were checked off, this strongly suggests psychopathy.

If **4-6 traits** were checked off, the person may have some psychopathic tendencies but may not meet the clinical threshold.

However, it's essential to remember that only a trained professional can make a formal diagnosis.

APPENDIX B

Practical Dos and Don'ts for Partners of Psychopaths

Do:

- **Document Everything:** Keep a detailed record of interactions, especially if legal proceedings are involved. Psychopaths thrive on denial and distortion; hard evidence can counter their manipulation.

- **Establish Clear Boundaries:** Psychopaths will exploit any emotional or physical access they have to you. Limit communication to what is absolutely necessary, such as through legal representatives or supervised channels.

- **Focus on Self-Healing:** Therapy, support groups, and mindfulness practices can help rebuild your confidence and restore your sense of self-worth. Prioritize your mental health as the foundation of your recovery.

- **Educate Yourself:** Knowledge is power. Learn about psychopathy, gaslighting, and trauma recovery to understand what you've endured and how to protect yourself in the future.

- **Surround Yourself with Support:** Cultivate a strong network of trusted friends, family, or professionals who can provide emotional and practical support during this time.

Don't:

- **Don't Engage in Emotional Arguments**: Psychopaths feed off conflict and use your emotions against you. Keep your responses calm, concise, and factual.

- **Don't Expect Closure**: Psychopaths rarely admit wrongdoing or offer genuine apologies. Seeking closure from them will only prolong your pain.

- **Don't Isolate Yourself**: Shame and fear may tempt you to retreat, but isolation only makes you more vulnerable to their influence. Reach out to others who can help you regain perspective.

- **Don't Fall for Their Charm**: If they attempt to reconcile, remember that their charm is a tool for control, not a sign of change.

APPENDIX C

How Not to Be Prey

RED FLAGS

- **Too Much Too Soon:** Fairytale romance.
- **Inconsistencies:** Stories don't match.
- **Gaslighting:** Manipulate reality making you question yours.
- **Control Disguised as Caring:** "*I just want what's best for you,*" while they dismantle your independence.
- **Lack Genuine Emotion:** Hollow, performative like an actor reading from a script.

ACTION STEPS

- **Don't Justify Poor Behavior:** Stop making excuses. This prevents enabling and keeps your focused on the reality of their actions.
- **Gradually Disengage:** Limit contact, secure your digital footprint, change passwords, strengthen privacy settings, ad avoid sharing locations online. Inform a trusted ally of your plans and prepare financial and emotional resources.
- **Set Boundaries: Trust your intuition.** Your gut feelings are a powerful early warning system for potential danger.
- **Seek Professional Support:** Reach out to therapists, support groups, hotlines, allies.

- **Keep a detailed Journal:** Record dates, times and descriptions of incidents (eg. Abusive behaviors, manipulations, threats). This provides a clear, chronological account for litigation and law enforcement
- **Save All Communications:** Emails, texts, social media, voicemails, cards. This is direct evidence of patterns of abuse.
- **Photograph physical evidence:** Property damage, injuries, other tangible signs of abuse. This adds to your credibility and affirms your reality.
- **Witnesses:** Identify friends, neighbors, colleagues who have witnessed the abuse or its effects. Testimonials corroborate your account and strengthen your credibility.
- **Compile Financial Records:** Gather evidence of financial abuse, unauthorized transactions, withheld access, password changes, debts, sudden purchases. This reveals economic control/abuse.

KNOW YOUR RIGHTS

- **Choose Wisely:** An experienced lawyer in domestic violence and coercive control.
- **Be Transparent:** Share all relevant details even those you find embarrassing or minor. You are presenting patterns of abuse and the whole story for context.
- **Ask About Strategies:** Ask the attorney to explain your legal options, the pros and cons of restraining orders, financial reparations, custody rights.

- **Practice:** If you are headed to trial you will testify. Review questions and responses beforehand as this will build confidence, manage emotions and help you maintain composure.
- **Use Protection:** If in family court, request Our Family Wizard, DocuSafe, Safe at Home, obtain a post office box for important mail, a bank safe for important documents.

APPENDIX D

Practical Tips for Schools and Parents

For Schools:

ACTION	WHAT IT INVOLVES	WHY IT'S IMPORTANT
EARLY BEHAVIOR ASSESSMENTS	Implement structured tools like behavioral checklists to identify patterns of aggression, lying, or manipulation.	Helps distinguish normal misbehavior from traits requiring intervention.
TRAIN STAFF IN PSYCHOLOGICAL AWARENESS	Provide teachers and counselors with training to recognize and address early signs of psychopathy or severe conduct disorders.	Ensures early detection and appropriate handling of problematic behaviors.
INTERVENE WITH RESTORATIVE PRACTICES	Use programs that focus on accountability and empathy-building, such as restorative justice circles.	Encourages children to understand the impact of their actions and develop empathy.
FOSTER SOCIAL-EMOTIONAL LEARNING (SEL)	Incorporate SEL programs that teach emotional regulation, conflict resolution, and interpersonal skills.	Strengthens skills often deficient in children exhibiting psychopathic traits.
ENGAGE MENTAL HEALTH PROFESSIONALS	Refer children for evaluation by psychologists or therapists skilled in behavioral and emotional disorders.	Provides expert assessment and tailored intervention strategies.
CREATE ACCOUNTABILITY STRUCTURES	Enforce consistent, fair consequences for harmful behavior to prevent a sense of impunity.	Reinforces that actions have consequences, reducing manipulative tendencies.
COMMUNICATE WITH PARENTS REGULARLY	Set up frequent, detailed communications to share observations and collaborate on behavioral management plans.	Ensures consistency in approach between home and school environments.

ANTI-BULLYING PROGRAMS	Implement anti-bullying initiatives that address relational aggression and manipulation.	Helps mitigate the damage such children can inflict on peers while teaching prosocial behavior.

For Parents:

ACTION	WHAT IT INVOLVES	WHY IT'S IMPORTANT
RECOGNIZE WARNING SIGNS	Pay attention to cruelty to animals, deceit, lack of remorse, and repeated defiance of rules.	Early acknowledgment allows for timely intervention.
AVOID EXCUSING PROBLEMATIC BEHAVIOR	Resist the urge to dismiss harmful actions as "just a phase" or "harmless curiosity."	Prevents enabling and addresses concerning patterns head-on.
SEEK PROFESSIONAL GUIDANCE	Consult child psychologists or behavioral specialists to evaluate and guide interventions.	Provides insights into underlying causes and effective treatment plans.
MODEL EMPATHY AND ACCOUNTABILITY	Demonstrate empathy in your own interactions and hold your child accountable for their actions.	Fosters emotional awareness and ethical behavior.
ENCOURAGE EMOTIONAL LITERACY	Teach your child to identify and articulate their emotions through conversations, books, or therapy.	Builds emotional self-awareness and a foundation for empathy.
SET CLEAR, NON-NEGOTIABLE BOUNDARIES	Establish and enforce rules consistently, ensuring there are predictable consequences for violations.	Reinforces the importance of structure and limits manipulative or testing behaviors.
SUPERVISE PEER RELATIONSHIPS	Monitor how your child interacts with peers and intervene if bullying or manipulation occurs.	Prevents harm to others and provides opportunities to teach appropriate social behavior.
LIMIT EXPOSURE TO NEGATIVE INFLUENCES	Reduce access to violent media or unsupervised online activity that might reinforce harmful behavior.	Protects against the normalization of aggression or manipulation.

| PROVIDE STRUCTURED ACTIVITIES | Engage your child in team sports, volunteering, or group hobbies that require cooperation | Encourages teamwork, accountability, and positive social connections. |

How Schools and Parents Can Work Together

Collaborate: Hold regular meetings to align strategies and reinforce consistent consequences at school and home.

Share Insights: Teachers can share observed patterns, and parents can provide context from home life.

Create a Safety Net: Identify supportive mentors (e.g., coaches, counselors) to guide and model healthy relationships.

APPENDIX E:
Legal Strategies for Victims of Psychopaths

Recognizing Legal Manipulation Tactics

- **Frivolous Litigation:** Filing excessive lawsuits to exhaust the victim emotionally and financially.

- **Parental Alienation:** Using the family court system to manipulate children against the other parent.

- **False Allegations:** Accusing the victim of abuse, fraud, or mental instability to gain legal leverage.

- **Deliberate Delays & Obstruction:** Withholding financial records, missing court dates, or refusing mediation to prolong legal battles.

- **Threats & Coercion:** Using legal threats to silence the victim (e.g., defamation claims, non-disclosure agreements).

- **Red Flag:** If you feel trapped in a cycle of litigation or manipulation, seek a legal professional who specializes in high-conflict cases.

Gathering Evidence to Strengthen Your Case

When fighting a psychopath in court, **facts over feelings** are your strongest weapon. Judges and attorneys respond to documented evidence—not emotional testimony. Here's what you need to build a solid case:

Appendix: Questionaires, Forms, Samples

Key Documents & Evidence to Collect

- **Emails & Text Messages** – Screenshots of coercion, threats, or contradictory statements.
- **Financial Records** – Bank statements, contracts, and proof of fraud or financial abuse.
- **Court Filings & Police Reports** – Documentation of past legal actions, restraining orders, or complaints.
- **Witness Statements** – Friends, co-workers, or therapists who can confirm manipulative behavior.
- **Therapist & Medical Reports** – Diagnoses of PTSD, anxiety, or trauma resulting from the abuse.
- **Social Media Posts** – Any incriminating content posted by the abuser (discrediting false claims).
- **Voicemails & Recordings (if legal in your state)** – Capturing threats or gaslighting in real-time.
- **Pro Tip:** Keep all evidence in a secure location (cloud storage, USB, or with an attorney). Psychopaths are known for **deleting, altering, or stealing documents** to cover their tracks.

Protective & Restraining Orders

- **Temporary Restraining Order (TRO)** – Issued quickly if immediate danger is present.
- **Permanent Restraining Order** – Requires a hearing but offers long-term protection.

- **No-Contact Orders** – Prevents the abuser from reaching out directly or indirectly.
- **Workplace Protective Orders** – If harassment occurs at your job.

Key Factors for Approval:

- Clear documentation of harassment or threats.
- Evidence of previous legal complaints or law enforcement reports
- Witness statements (neighbors, co-workers, therapists).
- A well-prepared case with dates, events, and proof of harm.

Note: If the abuser violates a restraining order, immediately report it to law enforcement. Multiple violations increase the likelihood of criminal charges.

Winning a High-Conflict Custody Battle

If a psychopath is using children as pawns in court, you need a strategic legal approach.

- **Request a Guardian ad Litem (GAL)** – A court-appointed representative for the child's best interest.
- **Ask for Psychological Evaluations** – If the abuser's mental fitness is in question.
- **Refuse Direct Communication** – Use court-approved messaging apps (*Our Family Wizard, Talking Parents*) to keep records.

- **Document Alienation Tactics** – Log any efforts to turn the child against you.
- **Stay Composed in Court** – Do not react emotionally to provocations; psychopaths try to paint their victims as unstable.

Warning: Psychopaths thrive in family court due to their charm and manipulation skills. Judges unfamiliar with their tactics may not recognize the warning signs—which is why evidence, not emotion, is key.

Suing for Defamation or Fraud

If a psychopath is publicly spreading lies, falsely accusing you of crimes, or financially defrauding you, you may have grounds for a defamation lawsuit or fraud claim.

- **Defamation (Libel & Slander)** – If they publish false claims that damage your reputation.
- **Fraud & Financial Exploitation** – If they stole money, used false identities, or engaged in deceptive business practices.
- **Harassment & Cyberstalking Laws** – If they target you online.

Tip: Work with an attorney **who specializes in high-conflict cases**—not just family or civil law.

Psychological Defense Tactics: Outsmarting a Manipulator in Court

Psychopaths aim to **provoke emotional reactions** and create **chaos** in court. To win against them, you must master psychological **counter-tactics**.

Strategic Mindset for Legal Battles

- **Stay Emotionally Neutral** – Never show fear, anger, or distress.

- **Stick to Facts & Evidence** – Judges respond to proof, not emotional pleas.

- **Use Clear, Concise Language** – Do **not** engage in personal attacks.

- **Anticipate Their Lies** – Prepare counterevidence ahead of time.

- **Have a "Gray Rock" Presence** – Appear unshaken by provocations.

Pro Tip: Judges are more likely to side with the calm, prepared party rather than the one who appears reactive or aggressive.

Finding the Right Legal & Psychological Support

Hiring the Right Lawyer

- Choose an attorney experienced in high-conflict cases (psychopaths, narcissists, domestic litigation).

- Find someone who understands coercive control and psychological abuse.
- Ask if they are familiar with parallel parenting strategies (to reduce conflict).

Resource: The National Crime Victim Bar Association provides legal assistance for victims of psychological and financial abuse seeking justice through the civil court system.

Mental Health Support During Litigation

- **Therapists specializing in PTSD & legal trauma** (for support during court battles).
- **Certified forensic psychologists** (if expert testimony is needed).
- **Support groups for legal abuse victims** (*One Mom's Battle, National Domestic Violence Hotline*).

Pro Tip: High-conflict legal battles can last years. Prioritize your mental and financial resources accordingly.

Psychopaths thrive on confusion, fear, and control. Knowledge is your greatest weapon. With a strategic legal plan, documented evidence, and an emotionally detached approach, you can outmaneuver even the most manipulative adversary.

APPENDIX F

Recognizing and Documenting Psychological Abuse

Psychological abuse can be subtle, insidious, and difficult to prove—which is exactly why manipulators use it as a weapon. Victims often second-guess themselves, struggling to pinpoint when the abuse started or how it escalated. This appendix provides a structured worksheet to document incidents, a red flag checklist to identify manipulation in relationships, workplaces, and legal disputes, and journal prompts to track patterns of coercion over time.

Keeping a **written record** is crucial, whether for personal clarity, therapy, or legal proceedings. Documentation can serve as **proof in court** or simply as a tool to **recognize toxic patterns and break free** from the cycle of abuse.

Part 1

Incident Documentation Worksheet

Each time you experience a manipulative or abusive interaction, record the details below. Over time, patterns may emerge, making it easier to see how the abuse unfolds. This documentation can also help you remain grounded when gaslighting makes you question events.

Appendix: Questionaires, Forms, Samples

DATE & TIME	LOCATION	WHO WAS INVOLVED	WHAT HAPPENED (FACTS ONLY)	HOW DID IT MAKE YOU FEEL?	GASLIGHTING OR EXCUSES USED?	WITNESSES OR EVIDENCE?
Example: 02/05/2025 - 3:30 PM	At home	Partner	He yelled and called me 'crazy' for questioning missing money	Anxious, doubted myself	"You're just overreacting."	The voicemail message was saved.

Tips for Effective Documentation:

- Stick to facts, not emotions.
- Include direct quotes when possible.
- Note any physical evidence (emails, texts, recordings, financial records, medical reports).
- If applicable, record how your abuser "spins" the event later (gaslighting, blame-shifting).
- Save all documentation in a secure, private location.

Part 2

Red Flag Checklist for Psychological Abuse

- **Love-Bombing:** Over-the-top affection, followed by sudden withdrawal of love.
- **Gaslighting:** They make you doubt your memory, experiences, or emotions.
- **Isolation:** They discourage contact with friends, family, or support systems.
- **Control Over Finances:** Hiding money, restricting access to joint accounts, or sabotaging your job.

- **Guilt-Tripping & Emotional Blackmail:** Using shame, threats, or self-harm claims to manipulate you.
- **Constant Criticism:** Nothing you do is ever "good enough," no matter how hard you try.

Red Flags in Workplaces & Professional Settings

Manipulative Boss or Colleague: Spreading false rumors, undermining your credibility, taking credit for your work.

Unclear or Changing Expectations: You're constantly set up for failure because the rules shift.

Public Humiliation: Criticizing you in front of others to assert dominance.

Gaslighting at Work: Denying previous conversations and rewriting history to make you appear incompetent.

Retaliation for Speaking Up: Being punished, demoted, or ostracized after reporting mistreatment.

Red Flags in Legal Battles & Courtroom Manipulation:

- **Frivolous Lawsuits:** They use legal action as a weapon to drain you financially and emotionally.
- **Parental Alienation:** Manipulating children to turn against the other parent.
- **Fabricated Allegations:** False claims of abuse, fraud, or mental instability to gain leverage.

- **Courtroom Charm Offensive:** Abusers often appear polite and calm in court while painting the victim as "unstable."
- **Deliberate Delay Tactics:** Withholding evidence, missing deadlines, or refusing to cooperate to prolong litigation.

Part 3

Journal Prompts for Recognizing Manipulation & Abuse

These prompts are designed to help you process experiences, recognize toxic patterns, and rebuild your sense of reality.

Identifying Gaslighting & Manipulation

1. **Have I started doubting my own memory or sanity after certain interactions?**
    - Has someone repeatedly denied things they previously said or did?
    - Do I often feel like I need to "prove" my version of events?

2. **Emotional & Behavioral Changes**
    - How has my emotional state changed since this relationship/situation began?
    - Do I feel safe expressing my emotions, or do I fear retaliation?
    - Have I started downplaying my own pain to make peace with someone's behavior?

3. Boundaries & Self-Worth

- Have my personal boundaries been ignored, mocked, or violated?
- Do I feel drained, anxious, or "on edge" after spending time with a particular person?
- When was the last time I did something for my own well-being without guilt?

4. Control & Isolation Tactics

- Has someone discouraged me from talking to friends or family or seeking professional help?
- Have I been subtly or directly threatened when I tried to set boundaries?
- Do I feel like I'm constantly "walking on eggshells" around someone?

5. Healing & Moving Forward

- If my best friend described a relationship like mine, what advice would I give them?
- What are three things I can do today to regain control of my life?
- What small action can I take to begin separating myself from this toxic dynamic?

Tip: Writing is a form of reclaiming your reality. Keep a private journal or digital log to track changes in your emotional and mental state over time.

Final Thoughts: Why Documentation Matters

- **Awareness Leads to Action:** Recognizing manipulation is the first step toward breaking free.

- **Written Records Counteract Gaslighting:** If you ever doubt yourself, revisit your documented incidents.

- **Evidence Can Be Powerful in Court:** If legal action becomes necessary, detailed notes strengthen your case.

- **Healing Begins with Understanding:** Tracking patterns helps survivors recognize, process, and escape psychological abuse.

Further Reading & References

Understanding Psychopathy & Criminal Minds

Hare, Robert D. (1993). *Without Conscience: The Disturbing World of Psychopaths Among Us*. Pocket Books, Simon & Schuster.

- A foundational text on psychopathy, this book by Dr. Robert Hare—creator of the Psychopathy Checklist-Revised (PCL-R)—offers insight into how psychopaths operate in everyday life, their lack of empathy, and why they can be so dangerous yet difficult to detect.

Cleckley, Hervey. (1976). *The Mask of Sanity*. 5th ed., Mosby.

- One of the earliest and most influential works on psychopathy, Cleckley's book describes how high-functioning psychopaths often appear charming and normal while hiding their complete emotional detachment. A must-read for understanding the "mask" that psychopaths wear.

Dutton, Kevin. (2013). *The Wisdom of Psychopaths: What Saints, Spies, and Serial Killers Can Teach Us About Success*. Scientific American/Farrar, Straus and Giroux.

- Examines how certain psychopathic traits—fearlessness, manipulation, and charm—can be advantageous in professions like law enforcement, business, and intelligence.

Fallon, James. (2014). *The Psychopath Inside: A Neuroscientist's Personal Journey into the Dark Side of the Brain.* Portfolio.

- Neuroscientist James Fallon discovers his own brain scan resembles those of diagnosed psychopaths, leading to a deep dive into the neurological basis of psychopathy.

Raine, Adrian. (2013). *The Anatomy of Violence: The Biological Roots of Crime.* Vintage.

- Explores the neuroscientific and genetic factors contributing to violent criminal behavior and psychopathy.

Eagleman, David. (2012). *Incognito: The Secret Lives of the Brain.* Vintage.

- A deep dive into the unconscious mind, explaining how hidden brain functions shape behavior, emotions, and decision-making—a crucial concept in understanding the mind of a psychopath.

Hyde, Luke, et al. "*Developmental Origins of Psychopathy.*" Annual Review of Clinical Psychology, 2018.

- A scholarly article that examines how psychopathic traits emerge in childhood, discussing potential genetic and environmental influences.
- ABC Nightline documentary, "Secrets of Your Mind." The psychopath's brain.

Case Studies, Serial Killers & Mass Shooters

Michaud, Stephen G., and Hugh Aynesworth. (1989). *Ted Bundy: Conversations with a Killer*. New American Library.

- A chilling deep dive into Ted Bundy's psyche, based on firsthand interviews. This book showcases Bundy's manipulative tactics, his ability to deceive even those closest to him, and his complete lack of remorse for his crimes. Essential for understanding the criminally psychopathic mind.

The Jinx: The Life and Deaths of Robert Durst. Directed by Andrew Jarecki, HBO, 2015.

- This HBO documentary series follows the life of real estate heir Robert Durst, who is suspected of multiple murders. The final episode features his shocking off-camera confession: "What the hell did I do? Killed them all, of course." A gripping case study in how wealth, power, and psychopathy intersect.

Carlo, Philip. (2009). *The Ice Man: Confessions of a Mafia Contract Killer*. St. Martin's Paperbacks.

- A profile of Richard Kuklinski, a contract killer with psychopathic traits who led a double life as a loving family man.

Ramsland, Katherine. (2017). *Confession of a Serial Killer: The Untold Story of Dennis Rader, the BTK Killer*. ForeEdge.

- A psychological analysis of Dennis Rader, who lived a seemingly normal life while committing horrific murders.

Whitney, Brian, and Anna Yourkin. (2018). *My Son, The Killer: The Untold Story of Luka Magnotta and "1 Lunatic 1 Ice Pick."* WildBlue Press.

- Examines the media-driven narcissism of Luka Magnotta, a killer who craved attention.

Wuornos, Aileen. (2012). *Dear Dawn: Aileen Wuornos In Her Own Words.* Soft Skull.

- A collection of letters written by serial killer Aileen Wuornos, offering insight into her disturbed psyche.

Fenton, Lynne, and Kerrie Droban. (2022). *Aurora: The Psychiatrist Who Treated the Movie Theater Killer Tells Her Story.* Berkley.

- A unique perspective from the psychiatrist who treated James Holmes, the Aurora movie theater shooter, discussing warning signs and missed intervention opportunities.

Kass, Jeff. (2009). *Columbine: A True Crime Story.* Ghost Road Press.

- A detailed account of the Columbine High School shooting, shedding light on the killers' psychological profiles.

Seierstad, Åsne, and Sarah Death. (2015). *One of Us: The Story of Anders Breivik and the Massacre in Norway.* Farrar, Straus and Giroux.

- A powerful examination of Anders Breivik's 2011 mass killing in Norway, his radicalization, and the psychology of ideological violence.

Michael R. Canfield, *Theodore Roosevelt in the Field.*

Law Enforcement & Psychopathy in Criminal Behavior

United States Department of Justice, Federal Bureau of Investigation. (1992). *Killed in the Line of Duty: A Study of Selected Felonious Killings of Law Enforcement Officers*. Uniform Crime Reports Section.

- This FBI study analyzes patterns in violent attacks against law enforcement, identifying common traits in offenders—including traits associated with psychopathy, such as lack of empathy and impulsive aggression. A valuable resource for understanding how psychopaths interact with law enforcement.

Legal & Psychological Strategies for Handling Manipulators

Eddy, Bill, and Randi Kreger. (2021). Splitting: *Protecting Yourself While Divorcing Someone with Borderline or narcissistic personality disorder*. New Harbinger Publications.

- A must-read for those facing high-conflict divorces, this book provides legal and psychological strategies for dealing with partners who use manipulation, false allegations, and emotional abuse in family court.

Stark, Evan. (2007). *Coercive Control: How Men Entrap Women in Personal Life*. Oxford University Press.

- A landmark study on coercive control explains how psychological abuse—rather than physical violence—is often the real mechanism of control in abusive relationships.

Stern, Robin. (2018). *The Gaslight Effect: How to Spot and Survive the Hidden Manipulation Others Use to Control Your Life.* Harmony.

- A deep dive into gaslighting, the psychological tactic used by narcissists and psychopaths to distort reality and make their victims doubt themselves. Essential for anyone recovering from emotional manipulation.

The Dark Web & Cyber Predators

Cohen, Aaron. (2024). *The Cyber Predators: Dark Personality & Online Misconduct.* Cambridge University Press.

- Investigates how sociopaths exploit digital platforms for fraud, deception, and cyberstalking.

The Lie: The Murder of Grace Millane. Directed by Helena Coan, Brainstorm Media, 2024. A true-crime film examining psychological manipulation and coercive control in digital dating.

"*Dirty John.*" Netflix, created by- Alexandra Cunningham, 2018. Based on a true story, this series explores the manipulation and deception of a psychopathic con artist.

De Becker, Gavin. (1997). *The Gift of Fear: Survival Signals That Protect Us from Violence.* Dell Publishing.

- A must-read on intuition and recognizing early warning signs of danger, including psychopathic predators.

Media Portrayals of Psychopathy & Criminal Profiling

Dexter. Created by James Manos Jr., Netflix, 2006-2013.

- A fictional series exploring the mind of a high-functioning psychopath who channels his urges into vigilantism.

You. Created by Greg Berlanti and Sera Gamble, it is a psychological thriller television series based on the books by Caroline Kepnes.

- A psychological thriller exploring how a charming, yet dangerous stalker rationalizes his crimes through obsessive love.

We Need to Talk About Kevin. Directed by Lynne Ramsay, 2011.

- A chilling film questioning the nature vs. nurture debate in child psychopathy.

20/20 Special Episode: Escape from a House of Horror: A Diane Sawyer Special Event. ABC News, Nov. 2021.

- A documentary special covering the case of the Turpin children, who were held captive by their abusive parents. This real-life story highlights how coercive control and psychological abuse operate in extreme cases.

The Man Behind Mindhunter: Face to Face with Serial Killers, Dec. 8, 2020. BBC Documentary.

- A documentary exploring the early days of FBI profiling, featuring real interviews and insights into the study of serial killers and criminal psychology.

Inside the Criminal Mind. Netflix, 2017.

- A docuseries that examines the psychology behind criminal behavior, focusing on serial killers, fraudsters, and other offenders.

Inventing Anna. Created by Shonda Rhimes, Netflix, 2022.
- Based on real events, this series portrays a high-functioning female con artist with psychopathic tendencies.

The Dropout. Created by Elizabeth Meriwether, Hulu, 2022.
- The story of Elizabeth Holmes and Theranos showcases how corporate fraud can be linked to psychopathic traits.

Psychological Abuse & Trauma Recovery

Van der Kolk, Bessel. (2014). *The Body Keeps the Score: Brain, Mind, and Body in the Healing of Trauma*. Penguin Books
- A must-read on how psychological trauma affects the brain and body—crucial for survivors of abuse.

Alexander, Annely. (2020). *Trauma Bonding: How to Stop Feeling Stuck, Overcome Heartache, Anxiety and PTSD*. Independently published.
- A self-help guide for breaking free from toxic relationships with narcissists and psychopaths.

Clayton, Ingrid. (2021). "*What Is Trauma-Bonding?*" Psychology Today, 9 Sept.
- Read here. Examines how victims become psychologically trapped in abusive relationships.

Kreisman, Jerold, and Hal Straus. (2021). *I Hate You—Don't Leave Me: Understanding the Borderline Personality*. 3rd ed., Tarcher Perigee.

- This book explores borderline personality disorder (BPD) and its impact on relationships, offering insights into emotional dysregulation, fear of abandonment, and intense mood swings—traits often seen in high-conflict court cases.

Mason, Paul T.T., and Randi Kreger. (2020). *Stop Walking on Eggshells: Taking Your Life Back When Someone You Care About Has Borderline Personality Disorder.* 3rd ed., New Harbinger Publications.

- A self-help guide for those dealing with loved ones who have BPD, offering strategies for setting boundaries, managing emotional manipulation, and navigating legal or custody disputes.

Durvasula, Ramani. (2017). *Should I Stay or Should I Go: Surviving a Relationship with a Narcissist.* Reprint ed., Post Hill Press.

- This book helps victims of narcissistic abuse decide whether to leave or stay in a toxic relationship, offering insights into the psychological tactics of narcissists in court battles and custody disputes.

Self-Help & Recovery from Psychological Abuse

Mackenzie, Jackson. (2015). *Psychopath Free: Recovering from Emotionally Abusive Relationships with Narcissists, Sociopaths, and Other Toxic People.* Berkley.

- A step-by-step guide for survivors of toxic relationships with psychopaths and narcissists, covering trauma bonding, emotional healing, and breaking free from manipulation.

Northrup, Christiane. (2019). *Dodging Energy Vampires*. Hay House LLC.

- Explores how certain people, particularly narcissists and sociopaths, drain emotional and psychological energy and how to set boundaries to protect oneself.

Newberg, Andrew, and Mark Robert Waldman. (2013). *Words Can Change Your Brain*. Avery.

- A fascinating look into how language affects the brain, including how manipulative people use words to control and influence others.

McLeod, Saul. (2023). "Harry Harlow Theory & Rhesus Monkey Experiments in Psychology."

Simply Psychology. https://www.simplypsychology.org/harlow-monkey.html

- Covers early research on attachment and psychological manipulation, explaining the effects of isolation and abuse.

Clinical Studies on Psychopathy & Personality Disorders

American Psychiatric Association. (1994). *The DSM-IV Personality Disorders*. New York: Guilford.

- The Diagnostic and Statistical Manual of Mental Disorders (DSM-IV) is the foundational reference for psychiatric diagnoses. This edition details the classification and criteria for antisocial personality disorder (ASPD) and other Cluster B disorders, including borderline, narcissistic, and histrionic personality disorders.

Millon, Theodore. (2004). *Personality Disorders in Modern Life.* 2nd ed., John Wiley & Sons.

- Dr. Millon is one of the leading experts in personality psychology. This book provides an in-depth analysis of various personality disorders, including their causes, symptoms, and real-world implications in relationships, workplaces, and society.

Dobbert, Duane. (2007). *Understanding Personality Disorders: An Introduction.* 1st ed., Praeger.

- A beginner-friendly introduction to personality disorders, this book explains the psychological and behavioral traits of individuals with narcissistic, borderline, and psychopathic tendencies, offering insights for both clinicians and general readers.

McCord, William, and Joan McCord. (1964). *Psychopath: An Essay on the Criminal Mind.* 1st ed., D. Van Nostrand Company.

- One of the earliest books to analyze criminal psychopathy, this classic study examines the connection between psychopathy and violent crime, providing case studies of real-life offenders.

Dutton, Kevin. *The Wisdom of Psychopaths.* Arrow Books, Ltd.2013.

- A fascinating exploration of what psychopaths can teach us about fearlessness.

Books on Psychopathy, Sociopathy, & Manipulation

Stout, Martha. (2006). The Sociopath Next Door. 1st ed., Harmony.

- A highly accessible book explaining how sociopaths operate in everyday life, why they lack a conscience, and how to recognize their manipulative tactics before becoming their next victim.

Navarro, Joe, and Toni Poynter Sciarra. (2018). *Dangerous Personalities: An FBI Profiler Shows You How to Identify and Protect Yourself from Harmful People.* Reprint ed., Harmony/Rodale Books.

- Former FBI agent Joe Navarro breaks down different dangerous personality types, including narcissists, sociopaths, and psychopaths, offering practical tools to recognize and protect yourself from them.

Handler, Beate. (2023). Featured in *"The Art of Deception: How to Recognize a Sociopath."*

- This documentary-style work explores real-world sociopaths in business, relationships, and criminal activity, with expert commentary from Beate Handler on how they manipulate and deceive.

Simon, George. (2010). I*n Sheep's Clothing: Understanding and Dealing with Manipulative People.* Parkhurst Brothers Publishers Inc.

- A practical guide to spotting and defending against covert manipulators, including workplace narcissists, emotionally abusive partners, and psychopathic individuals.

Thomas, M.E. (2013). *Confessions of a Sociopath: A Life Spent Hiding in Plain Sight*. Crown.

- A first-person account written by a self-identified sociopath, offering rare insight into the thought processes and manipulative strategies of individuals with no emotional conscience.

Babiak, Paul, and Robert Hare. (2019). *Snakes in Suits: Understanding and Surviving the Psychopaths in Your Office*. Updated ed., Harper Business.

- This book explores how psychopaths thrive in corporate environments, using charm, deceit, and ruthlessness to manipulate workplaces for their advantage. Essential reading for identifying workplace psychopaths and protecting yourself.

Cult Psychology, Coercion, and Authoritarian Control

Hassan, Steven. (2015). *Combating Cult Mind Control*. Freedom of Mind Press.

- A practical guide for breaking free from cults and high-control groups, written by a former cult member turned deprogrammer. Examines manipulation tactics used by cult leaders, charismatic predators, and authoritarian figures.

Kramer, Joel, and Diana Alstad. (1993). *The Guru Papers: Masks of Authoritarian Power*. Frog Books.

- This book deconstructs the psychology of authoritarian control, explaining how charismatic leaders use deception, isolation, and mental conditioning to dominate their followers.

Lalich, Janja, and Madeleine Tobias. (2006). *Take Back Your Life: Recovering from Cults and Abusive Relationships*. Bay Tree Publishing.

- A step-by-step recovery guide for survivors of cults, coercive relationships, and mind-control environments. Provides strategies for escaping, healing, and regaining autonomy.

Netflix Documentary. (2024). *Dancing for the Devil: The 7M TikTok Cult*.

- A documentary exploring how social media was used as a tool for cult-like manipulation, featuring firsthand accounts from survivors of the controversial 7M TikTok influencer group.

Books on Emotional Intelligence, Crime, & Criminal Psychology

Goleman, Daniel. (2005). Emotional Intelligence: Why It Can Matter More Than IQ. Bantam.

- This book explains why emotional intelligence (EQ) is more important than intelligence quotient (IQ) in predicting success and interpersonal relationships. It also offers insight into how psychopaths lack emotional intelligence but can make it through learned behavior.

Miller, Michael H. (2015). *Edmund Kemper: The True Story of The Co-ed Killer*. CreateSpace Independent Publishing Platform.

- A case study of serial killer Edmund Kemper provides insight into his psychopathic tendencies, intelligence, and calculated manipulation.

Wiehl, Lis, and Lisa Pulitzer. (2021). *Hunting the Unabomber: The FBI, Ted Kaczynski, and the Capture of America's Most Notorious Domestic Terrorist*. Thomas Nelson.

- A true-crime investigation into Ted Kaczynski, the Unabomber, detailing his psychological profile and how law enforcement used forensic psychology to track him down.

Rodriguez, Brandon (2016). *"The Criminological Dissection of Pogo the Clown."*

- A criminological analysis of John Wayne Gacy, aka "Pogo the Clown," one of America's most infamous serial killers, explores his psychological and behavioral patterns.

Kahn, Jennifer. (2012). *"Can You Call a 9-Year-Old a Psychopath?"* The New York Times Magazine, 11 May.

- A controversial yet thought-provoking article discussing whether psychopathy can be diagnosed in children and the ethical implications of labeling young individuals with this disorder.

O'Neill, Eric. (2020). *Gray Day: My Undercover Mission to Expose America's First Cyber Spy*. Crown.

- A thrilling first-person account from an FBI agent who helped expose cyber espionage and sociopathic deception in high-stakes intelligence work.

The Ethics of Labeling & AI in Psychopathy Diagnosis

"Could you spot a psychopath by just looking at them? A new AI can." BBC Science Focus Magazine, 12 Aug., 2021.

https://www.sciencefocus.com/the-human-body/could-you-spot-a-psychopath A discussion on how artificial intelligence may one day diagnose psychopathy based on facial and body movements.

McEvoy, Fiona J. (2021). "Here's How AI Could Diagnose You With Psychopathy." You The Data, 12 Aug., 2021

https://youthedata.com/2021/08/12/heres-how-ai-could-diagnose-you-with-psychopathy/ Explores the potential and ethical dilemmas of AI-driven psychopathy diagnostics.

Additional Resources for Psychological & Legal Support

National Domestic Violence Hotline – www.thehotline.org 1-800-799-SAFE (7233)

Forensic Psychology Association – Provides expert witnesses for high-conflict legal cases.

Institute for the Study of Psychopathy – www.psychopathyis.org

ABOUT THE AUTHOR

Kerrie Droban is an award-winning true crime author, attorney, national speaker and expert consultant on criminal pathology and organized crime. She has appeared on 20/20, American Greed, A&E, Investigation ID, Netflix and many more. Her books have been optioned for film and made into a television series now streaming on Hulu.

www.ingramcontent.com/pod-product-compliance
Ingram Content Group UK Ltd.
Pitfield, Milton Keynes, MK11 3LW, UK
UKHW022238230426
12048UKWH00018BA/1330